reliGion in the
Japanese experience

sources and interpretations

The Religious Life of Man Series
FREDERICK J. STRENG, *Series Editor*

Texts

Understanding Religious Life, Third Edition
  Frederick J. Streng

The House of Islam, Second Edition
  Kenneth Cragg

Japanese Religion: Unity and Diversity, Third Edition
  H. Byron Earhart

Chinese Religion: An Introduction, Third Edition
  Laurence G. Thompson

The Christian Religious Tradition
  Stephen Reynolds

The Buddhist Religion: A Historical Introduction, Third Edition
  Richard H. Robinson and Willard L. Johnson

The Way of Torah: An Introduction to Judaism, Third Edition
  Jacob Neusner

The Hindu Religious Tradition
  Thomas J. Hopkins

Native American Religions: An Introduction
  Sam D. Gill

African Cosmos: An Introduction to Religion in Africa
  Noel Q. King

Anthologies

The Chinese Way in Religion
  Laurence G. Thompson

Religion in the Japanese Experience: Sources and Interpretations
  H. Byron Earhart

The Buddhist Experience: Sources and Interpretations
  Stephan Beyer

The Life of Torah: Readings in the Jewish Religious Experience
  Jacob Neusner

Islam from Within: Anthology of a Religion
  Kenneth Cragg and R. Marston Speight

Native American Traditions: Sources and Interpretations
  Sam D. Gill

RELIGION IN THE JAPANESE EXPERIENCE

SOURCES AND INTERPRETATIONS

H. Byron Earhart

Western Michigan University

Wadsworth Publishing Company
Belmont, California
A Division of Wadsworth, Inc.

BOOKS BY THE SAME AUTHOR

Japanese Religion: Unity and Diversity, 3rd edition (Wadsworth)

The New Religions of Japan: A Bibliography of Western-Language Materials, 2nd edition (Michigan Papers in Japanese Studies)

A Religious Study of the Mount Haguro Sect of Shugendo (Sophia University)

Translation from the Japanese: *Japanese Religion in the Modern Century*, Shigeyoshi Murakami (University of Tokyo Press)

Library of Congress Catalog Card Number: 73-81295

Printed in the United States of America

Printing (last digit): 9 8 7 6

ISBN 0-8221-0104-1

For
Kenneth, David, and Paul

contents

CONTENTS

fOREWORò

The power of religious life is often self-evident to the participant, but very difficult to communicate to the uncommitted observer. Therefore, in an attempt to allow students to understand the thoughts, feelings, and attitudes of participants in the major religious traditions, we present companion volumes of readings in the Religious Life of Man Series.

The aim of this series of readings is to introduce the literature of a tradition, and provide sympathetic interpretations and descriptions of important activities which expose the dynamics and some of the concrete variety in a religious tradition. Every book of readings is selective in the material it includes, and the focus here is on religious life, in the past and present, that defines the religious options available today. The selections seek to reveal the goals, experiences, activities, symbolic imagery, and community life of a religious tradition. Hopefully the reader can thereby imaginatively participate in some of the feelings and experiences which are exposed.

Each of the volumes is edited by a university or college teacher who is also a specialist in the major languages and cultures of a religion. Several volumes have new translations of material made especially for them, and each reading is introduced with a brief comment about its place in the tradition and its general religious significance. Further background is found in the companion textbook in the Religious Life of Man Series; at the same time, these books of readings might well be used in combination with other books and media.

Frederick J. Streng
Series Editor

preface

My interest in Japanese religion began in graduate school, deepened with several years of research in Japan, and has continued through a number of years teaching Japanese religion in American classrooms. This interest alone is sufficient motivation to complete the present book, but two more practical factors prompt this publication. First, my own experience in the classroom demonstrates the need for concrete materials to illustrate the variety and richness within Japanese religion. Second, the favorable acceptance of my text, *Japanese Religion: Unity and Diversity*, has made the present venture feasible.

The intention in compiling these materials is to help the reader see Japanese religion more concretely, as it is found within the history of the tradition and experience of the people. The selections vary considerably, from prehistoric to modern examples, from archaeological descriptions and mythological records to folk festivals and modern religious movements. And yet the overall purpose of the selections is to show what religion means in the Japanese experience.

I would be the first to admit the difficulty of trying to compress Japanese religion within a few hundred pages. One simply cannot exhaust the several thousand years and wide range of Japanese religion in such limited space. The selections are all too brief, but this brevity is necessary in order to cover the range of Japanese religion. For more complete information concerning specific aspects of the subject, the reader may turn either to the original from which the selection was taken, or to the additional readings listed at the end of each part.

In the difficult task of selecting and organizing material for this book I have profited from the combined wisdom of advice from friends: Professors Robert S. Ellwood, Wilbur M. Fridell, and Richard Pilgrim, fellow teachers in the field of Japanese religion, and Frederick J. Streng, general editor for this series. Acknowledgment of their help, of course, does not guarantee that the book fulfills all their suggestions or satisfies all their criticisms. I would like to thank Western Michigan University and Mrs. Pat Kei-Fun Wang for secretarial assistance in typing the manuscript.

H. Byron Earhart
Western Michigan University

pARt ONE

INTRODUCTION: the NATURE Of JAPANESE RELIGION

Japanese religion comprises an amazing panorama of a wide variety of practices and traditions through several thousand years; even a bird's-eye view of the history of Japanese religion reveals its richness and diversity. Archaeological evidence from prehistoric times points to religious activity regarding fertility and afterlife. In early historic times, influence from China helped stimulate the organization of Shinto out of the earliest tradition; at the same time, Chinese influence brought Buddhism, Confucianism, and Taoism to Japan. Through time, Shinto and Buddhism developed as elaborate organized religions, whereas Confucianism and Taoism penetrated the thought and life of the people. Folk religion existed outside of organized religion, and in the late medieval period and again in modern times, Christianity was introduced to Japan. To top off this already interesting religious scenario, in the past century many new religious movements (usually called New Religions) have arisen.

With such a broad spectrum of traditions to draw on, it is not surprising that the picture of Japanese religion is painted with every imaginable color. The story of prehistoric religion is told by the remains of stone circles, fertility figurines, phallic emblems, and burial sites. From the dim past, Shinto has preserved the mythological origin of Japan and liturgical prayers while continuing to build shrines and celebrate festivals. In Buddhist temples we find scriptures and statues as well as rituals and memorials for the dead. The Confucian tradition is less conspicuous, made known more through the factors of social hierarchy and sense of obligation. Taoism influenced such areas as the calendar, astrology, and beliefs about what is lucky and unlucky. Folk religion operates in the activities of many seasonal celebrations in the home, in unorganized shamanism, and even in folk tales. Christianity, although it has never attracted a large percentage of the population, has exerted an important stimulus for edu-

cational and social reform. The New Religions[1] in many ways reflect the earlier tradition: they incorporate practices from divination and faith healing to shamanism and seasonal festivals, and their beliefs range from unsystematic folk beliefs to scriptures and elaborate doctrines.

However, the hues of Japanese religion are not strictly confined to these traditions; they spill over into every aspect of the culture and life of its people. For example, the family is equally important, if not more important, as a traditional center of religious activity than the Shinto shrine and Buddhist temple. Artistic and religious themes intermix, and the Japanese view of nature is as much religious as it is aesthetic. Even filial piety and national patriotism are colored by religious devotion. In order to see the whole picture of Japanese religion, then, we must look into many aspects of Japanese culture.

Japanese religion is by no means static; instead, it forms a moving picture, one that proceeds by leaps and bounds rather than in a continuous, straight line. One tradition may dominate the scene while others lie dormant, then another tradition may make a new appearance. Each tradition has a transcendent ideal which is more or less realized within the ambiguities of life, but strange as it may first seem, periods of flourishing institutional strength do not always indicate times when religious ideals are most fully realized. For example, institutional Shinto flourished before and during World War II, but it did not always hold up the highest ideals of Shinto.

How can we understand this kaleidoscope of changing patterns? As with any foreign tradition, the first clue to understanding is the proper attitude. Often we who are associated with the European, or "Western," tradition tend to think that the "Eastern" tradition is one vast unity and that this mysterious or spiritual East is the direct opposite of the rational and materialistic West. However, no single entity can be called Eastern culture or "the East," because a great number of cultures exist between the Middle East and the Far East. In the same fashion, there is no distinctive set of characteristics within the cultures of this area that cannot be found also in Western culture. Hajime Nakamura, one of the foremost Japanese scholars of Buddhism, has stated this point well: *"There are no features of the ways of thinking exclusively shared by the East Asians as a whole,* unless they are universal traits of human nature in the East and West. Furthermore, if the ways of thinking differ according to the cultural history of each people, then we should expect the cultures formed by these nations to be heterogeneous."[2]

At the outset, we must realize that Japanese religion has a long history and that it possesses its own internal unity. The primary guide, then, is to place Japanese religion within its own historical context and to conceive

[1]Throughout this book the term *New Religions* with initial capitals is used to identify the distinctive Japanese new religious movements.
[2]Hajime Nakamura, *Ways of Thinking of Eastern Peoples*, p. 22. (Complete information is given in Selected Readings.)

it within its own basic assumptions. Above all, we must avoid using the basic assumptions of our own tradition to interpret Japanese religion. For example, in the United States and most Western countries, religion is usually understood as belief in One God and exclusive affiliation to one religious organization; ethical behavior is seen as obedience to God. In sharp contrast, in Japanese religion exclusive affiliation to one religious tradition is rare; the general rule is a plurality of religions, with the same person participating in several religions simultaneously. Some other important features of Japanese religion also contrast with Western religion, as pointed out by Hideo Kishimoto, a distinguished Japanese scholar of religious studies: "The peculiar nature of Japanese religions has brought forth two conspicuous cultural features. One is a distinct separation in the sphere of activities between the religious system and the ethical system. The other is the close relation between religious value and aesthetic value."[3] To apply Western assumptions about religion to Japanese religion, then, would be as confusing as mixing the pieces from two jigsaw puzzles.

In order to understand Japanese religion, we must comprehend it within its own context, in its own historical setting, and through its own activities. The materials in this book are selected and organized to aid this understanding and at the same time to cover as many aspects of Japanese religion as possible: the content of the various traditions, the basic characteristics of the religious heritage as a whole, the changes and ambiguities through the passage of time, and the relationship of religion to other cultural areas. Parts 2 through 7 examine the major Japanese traditions: Shinto, Buddhism, Confucianism, religious Taoism, folk religion, and Christianity. Part 8 focuses directly on the syncretism among these traditions. Parts 9 through 14 treat basic characteristics or persistent themes that constitute the cross section of Japanese religion: (1) the closeness of man, gods, and nature; (2) the religious significance of the family, living and dead; (3) the importance of purification, rituals, and charms; (4) the prominence of local festivals and individual cults; (5) the penetration of religion into everyday life; and (6) the natural bond between religion and state. Parts 15 and 17 treat the dilemma and future of Japanese religion, and Part 16 treats the New Religions. All the chapters suggest the historical changes that religion undergoes and discuss the other areas of life in which religion is active.

Each of the following selections may be likened to one of the patterns in the kaleidoscope of Japanese religion: the material in every selection has its own distinctive pattern, yet it shares many religious elements with the materials in other selections. For example, a selection in the part on Shinto not only describes the basic character of Shinto but also might reflect a persistent theme such as the closeness of gods, man, and nature; at the same time, it might depict the situation of early Japanese religion

[3]Hideo Kishimoto, "Some Japanese Cultural Traits and Religions," p. 115..

and also illustrate the relationship between rice agriculture and religious life. Therefore, each selection should be read not only for its own content but also for its interrelationship with other selections. In many cases the interconnections will be apparent, but cross-references within the introductions make it easier to trace related themes and materials. The patterns of a kaleidoscope are almost endless — that is one reason the instrument is so fascinating; similarly, the aspects of Japanese religion are almost without number. The purpose of these materials is not to exhaust the subject but to provide firsthand experience of some important configurations of Japanese religion.

SELECTED READINGS

Suggestions for further reading will be listed at the end of each chapter. The reader may also wish to consult the original materials from which the selections have been excerpted.

For general works on Japanese religion see:

Anesaki, Masharu. *History of Japanese Religion.* London: Kegan Paul, Trench, Trubner, 1930; reprinted, Rutland, Vt.: Charles E. Tuttle Co., 1963.

Bloom, Alfred. "Japan." In *Religion and Man,* edited by W. Richard Comstock, pp. 336-94. New York: Harper & Row, 1971.

Earhart, H. Byron. *Japanese Religion: Unity and Diversity,* 2nd ed. Belmont, Calif.: Dickenson Publishing Co., 1974.

Hori, Ichiro, ed. *Japanese Religion.* Translated by Yoshiya Abe and David Reid. Tokyo and Palo Alto: Kodansha International, 1972.

Japanese Association for Religious Studies, ed. *Religious Studies in Japan.* Tokyo: Maruzen, 1959.

Kishimoto, Hideo. "Some Japanese Cultural Traits and Religions." In *The Japanese Mind. Essentials of Japanese Philosophy and Culture,* edited by Charles A. Moore, pp. 110-21. Honolulu: East-West Center Press, 1967.

Kitagawa, Joseph M. *Religion in Japanese History.* New York: Columbia University Press, 1966.

Kitagawa, Joseph M. "Religions of Japan." In *The Great Asian Religions,* compiled by Wing-tsit Chan et al., pp. 231-305. London: Macmillan & Co., 1969.

Nakamura, Hajime. *Ways of Thinking of Eastern Peoples: India, China, Tibet, Japan.* Revised English translation edited by Philip P. Wiener. Honolulu: East-West Center Press, 1964.

Most of the above works contain bibliographies; for specialized bibliographies on Japanese religion see:

Bando, Shojun, et al. *A Bibliography on Japanese Buddhism.* Tokyo: Cultural Interchange Institute for Buddhist Press, 1958.

Earhart, H. Byron. *The New Religions of Japan: A Bibliography of Western-Language Materials*. Tokyo: Monumenta Nipponica, Sophia University, 1970.

Ikado, Fujio, and McGovern, James R., comps. *A Bibliography of Christianity in Japan: Protestantism in English Sources (1859-1959)*. Tokyo: Committee on Asian Cultural Studies, International Christian University, 1966.

Kato, Genchi, et al. *A Bibliography of Shinto in Western Languages from the Oldest Times till 1952*. Tokyo: Meiji Jingu Shamusho, 1953.

Kitagawa, Joseph M. "The Religions of Japan." In *A Reader's Guide to the Great Religions*, edited by Charles J. Adams, pp. 161-90. New York: Free Press, 1965.

pARt two

shinto

Shinto grew out of the earliest Japanese traditions and gradually took shape as an organized religion under the influence of Buddhism and Chinese culture. Several factors in the history of Shinto have led people to consider Shinto as the only indigenous or national religion of Japan: Shinto is the only organized religion to arise in Japan, Shinto preserves the most ancient Japanese heritage, and there has been close identification between Shinto, emperor, and state. However, it is well to remember that Shinto, like most religions, includes influences from several other traditions and therefore is not totally Japanese in origin. And Shinto is not the only national religion, because Buddhism also became identified with state purposes. In fact, some of the central features of Shinto, such as the idea of *kami* (defined in selection 2) and the veneration of nature, are not exclusive to Shinto but penetrate the whole of Japanese culture. (For example, see the selections in Part 9.)

Most important in the practice of Shinto are humble respect for the *kami* and voluntary participation in shrine ceremonies (rather than the Western pattern of rational proof for God and exclusive membership in one local institution). Children grew in the religious life of Shinto not through regular Sunday School services or training in catechism but through participation in local festivals and respect for the national tradition. In traditional Japan (especially before the past century of rapid modernization), the countryside was felt to be alive with *kami,* and the children paid their respects to the local *kami,* although they became increasingly aware of the national tradition chronicled in history and idealized in mythology.

During the past century, Shinto's fate has undergone two major changes. After the Meiji Restoration of 1868, Shinto shrines were used by the government as part of the official rationale for unifying the people in the new nation-state (see also selections 42 and 44). This placed Shinto's religious status in an ambiguous position, but at the end of World War II Shinto underwent another momentous change. In 1945 the Allied Occu-

pation forces entered Japan and initiated the disestablishment of shrine Shinto which placed it on an equal footing with all other religions in Japan. Shinto shrines had already felt the change from a rural agricultural nation to an urban industrial nation, and the defeat in World War II was a severe blow to Shinto, due to its close tie to the war effort. (For a description of attitudes toward Shinto in postwar Tokyo, see selection 45.) Shinto leaders are still trying to recover from the disestablishment order.

Although Shinto defines one long Japanese tradition, a number of different facets exist within this tradition. On the most informal level is folk, or popular, Shinto. Folk Shinto refers to the many traditional religious practices surrounding purification, blessing, agriculture, and the home which are not actually a part of institutional Shinto; in this book, such practices are generally treated as part of Japanese folk religion. The simplest form of Shinto organization is the local shrine in villages and smaller divisions of cities. Some major features of these local shrines are the relationship of the *kami* to the Japanese people, the agricultural blessing and protection of local areas by specific *kami,* the periodic celebration of contact with the *kami,* annual (especially seasonal) festivals, and religious observances for stages of life (for example, birth) and special crises (such as sickness).

From ancient times Shinto was also related to the state. In Japanese mythology the *kami* of Shinto heritage are responsible for the creation of the land and the people, and the emperor (as a descendant of the Sun Goddess) is a manifest *kami* who heads both government and worship. Although the emperor performed special rituals on behalf of the nation, and although some larger shrines were rather closely related to the state, this ideal of the unity of state and religion was never fully realized. The common people generally appreciated the legendary origin of Japan from the *kami* and venerated the emperor as a divine or semi-divine figure; but their most direct participation in Shinto was through the activities of the local shrine. However, from 1868 to 1945 Shinto was drawn into a much closer relationship to the newly formed nation-state. In contrast to the Tokugawa period (1600 - 1867), when Buddhism and Neo-Confucianism were more closely tied to government rationale and activities, starting with the Meiji Restoration of 1868 the government relied more on Shinto shrines and notions for supporting the state. The government appealed to the ancient ideal of the unity of state and religion, but had difficulty implementing this ideal within the emerging nation-state. After several experiments the government made a fundamental distinction between the ordinary local shrines, which it called shrine Shinto *(jinja Shinto),* and the sect movements within Shinto (that actively propagated their teachings), which it called sect Shinto *(kyoha Shinto).* Only shrine Shinto could call their buildings "shrines" *(jinja);* shrine Shinto was gradually brought into more formal administrative connection with the state, in terms of

such actions as financial aid and designation of shrine priests as government officials. Shrine Shinto was even declared "non-religious" and officially considered as part of the state, in contrast to sect Shinto, Buddhism, and Christianity, which were treated as religions. By this maneuver the state could provide a guarantee of religious freedom, while at the same time, it used "non-religious" Shinto notions in the schools and the administrative control of shrines to reinforce nationalism and unify the state.

Sect Shinto was required to use the term *kyokai* (church) for its buildings, since its activities were considered to be religious. Whereas shrine Shinto supposedly had originated out of the natural unity of state and religion, sect Shinto generally developed out of historical founders and independent teachings. Eventually thirteen movements were granted official recognition as members of sect Shinto. Some of the members of sect Shinto may also be considered as new religious movements in their own right; see Konko Kyo in selection 16 and Tenrikyo in selection 48. After 1945, the special status of shrine Shinto was abolished, placing it on the same level as other religious organizations; at this time the former groups within sect Shinto (as well as Buddhist and Christian groups) were able to organize freely. Meanwhile, the religious rhythm of local shrines, which depended on such factors as annual festivals and agricultural-seasonal celebrations, continued its own life, especially within the small village shrines.

1

the centrality of kami in shinto

One of the most important aspects of Shinto is belief in the power of the many *kami*. Because the *kami* include mythological divinities, powers of nature, revered human beings and even spirits of the dead, no one English term translates *kami*. In this selection, Holtom provides many examples of *kami* and advises that the best treatment of the word *kami* is to leave it untranslated, thinking of it in the general sense of "sacred."

Even the greatest Japanese scholars have had difficulty in defining the term *kami*, partly because its meaning is lost in antiquity, partly because Shinto has never emphasized rational proof for the existence of *kami* or "theology" as a systematic statement of the nature of *kami*. In

religious life, it has been sufficient to recognize the hoary sanctity of the *kami* in the traditional founding of Japan (as seen in selection 2) and humble veneration for the *kami* in one's own neighborhood.

The notion of *kami* is too important in Japanese culture to be confined to Shinto as an organized religion, for the belief in *kami* is directly related to the Japanese appreciation of nature, which is understood as a living, sacred force. This notion of *kami* even interacts with the Buddhist pantheon (as demonstrated in selection 7). The *kami* have always been present in Japan, even before there were shrines dedicated to them. Although Buddhist images were often housed in Shinto shrines, the *kami* were rarely depicted in concrete form. Rather, the shrine was usually considered the place of descent, which the *kami* temporarily visited during the ceremonies that invoked the *kami's* presence.

Reprinted by permission of the publisher from D. C. Holtom, *The National Faith of Japan: A Study in Modern Shinto* (New York: Paragon Book Reprint Corp., 1965).

The Meaning of Kami

In the preceding paragraphs occasion has already been found for introducing the important term, *kami*. It will be necessary to make constant use of it in the ensuing pages and, at this point, in connection with the elucidation of the main characteristics of Old Shinto, its primary significance should be carefully noted. No other word in the entire range of Japanese vocabulary has a richer or more varied content and no other has presented greater difficulties to the philologist.

The most comprehensive and penetrating account of the meaning of *kami* that has appeared in Japanese literature was given by the great eighteenth century scholar, Motoori Norinaga. Written long before the age of the modern study of folk psychology had dawned, his analysis, in spite of certain insufficiencies, yet may be taken to stand as a remarkable and almost classical definition of the now widely used term, mana.

He says,

"I do not yet understand the meaning of the term, *kami*. Speaking in general, however, it may be said that *kami* signifies, in the first place, the deities of heaven and earth that appear in the ancient records and also the spirits of the shrines where they are worshipped.

"It is hardly necessary to say that it includes human beings. It also includes such objects as birds, beasts, trees, plants, seas, mountains and so forth. In ancient usage, anything whatsoever which was outside the ordinary, which possessed superior power or which was awe-inspiring was called *kami*. Eminence here does

not refer merely to the superiority of nobility, goodness or meritous deeds. Evil and mysterious things, if they are extraordinary and dreadful, are called *kami*. It is needless to say that among human beings who are called *kami* the successive generations of sacred emperors are all included. The fact that emperors are called 'distant *kami*' is because, from the standpoint of common people, they are far-separated, majestic and worthy of reverence. In a lesser degree we find, in the present as well as in ancient times, human beings who are *kami*. Although they may not be accepted throughout the whole country, yet in each province, each village and each family there are human beings who are *kami*, each one according to his own proper position. The *kami* of the divine age were for the most part human beings of that time and, because the people of that time were all *kami*, it is called the Age of the Gods (*kami*).

"Furthermore, among things which are not human, the thunder is always called 'sounding-*kami*.' Such things as dragons, the echo, and foxes, inasmuch as they are conspicuous, wonderful and awe-inspiring, are also *kami*. In popular usage the echo is said to be *tengu*[1] and in Chinese writings it is referred to as a mountain goblin. . . .

"In the *Nihongi* and the *Manyoshu* the tiger and the wolf are also spoken of as *kami*. Again there are the cases in which peaches were given the name, August-Thing-Great-*Kamu*-Fruit, and a necklace was called August-Storehouse-shelf-*Kami*. There are further instances in which rocks, stumps of trees and leaves of plants spoke audibly. They were all *kami*. There are again numerous places in which seas and mountains are called *kami*. This does not have reference to the spirit of the mountain or the sea, but *kami* is used here directly of the particular mountain or sea. This is because they were exceedingly awe-inspiring."

Much similar material could be adduced from Japanese sources. . . . Summarized briefly, it may be said that *kami* is essentially an expression used by the early Japanese people to classify experiences that evoked sentiments of caution and mystery in the presence of the manifestation of the strange and marvelous. Like numerous other concepts discoverable among ancient or primitive people, *kami* is fundamentally a term that distinguishes between a world of superior beings and things which are thought of as filled with mysterious power and a world of common experiences that lie within the control of ordinary human technique. Often the best translation is simply by the word "sacred." In this sense it has an undifferentiated background of everything that is strange, fearful, mysterious, marvelous, uncontrolled, full of power, or beyond human comprehension. The conviction of the reality of the world that is registered was supported by the experience of extraordinary events, such as the frenzy of religious dances, or by outstanding objects that threw the attention into special activity, such as large, or old, or strangely formed trees, high mountains, thunder, lightning, storm and clouds, or by implements of magic, or by uncanny animals, such as foxes, badgers, and manifestations of albinism. These old attitudes exist in the present and strongly influence modern Shinto.

As this sacred, mysterious background became more and more articulated with the progress of experience and thought, descriptive elements were at-

[1]A long-nosed, red-faced, winged goblin.

tached to the word, *kami,* and the names of the great deities were evolved, as, for example, *Amaterasu-Omikami,* "Heaven-shining-Great-August-*Kami,*" for the Sun Goddess, or *Taka-Mimusubi-no-Kami,* "High-August-Producing-*Kami,*" the name given one of the creation deities or growth principles of the old cosmogonic myth.

In addition to the general sense of sacred as just outlined, the specific meanings of *kami* should be noted. They are: spirits and deities of nature; the spirits of ancestors (especially great ancestors, including emperors, heroes, wise men and saints) ; superior human beings in actual human society, such as living emperors, high government officials, feudal lords, *etc.;* the government itself; that which is above in space or superior in location or rank (declared, without warrant, by some Japanese scholars to be the primary meaning) ; "the upper times," *i.e.,* antiquity; God; the hair on the human scalp; paper.

Evidence which cannot be cited here goes to show that the classification of the hair on the human scalp under the *kami* concept had probable origin, not in the very apparent fact that the hair was on the top of the head and hence "superior," but in the association of the hair with a primitive supernaturalism or with the idea of mysterious superhuman force.

Kami in the sense of paper may be a totally unrelated word. It has been suggested, however, that it found its way into the sacred classification because of its unusual importance in the social life.

A phonetic variation of *kami* is *kamu* (or *kabu*), the latter being perhaps the older term. *Kamu* strikingly resembles in both word form and meaning the *tabu* (sometimes written *kabu* or *kapu*) of Polynesia, from which the term taboo is derived. The Ainu *kamui* is also worthy of comparative study in this connection.

Another term, *mi-koto,* is frequently affixed to the descriptive elements of divine names as a substitute for *kami.* This also will be encountered here and there in the pages that follow and its meaning should be explained at this point. The parts signify: *mi* (honorific) and *koto* ("thing" or "person") . The word was originally a title of reverence applied to exalted individuals in the ordinary social life. It is sometimes used of the gods and in such cases is perhaps best translated "deity," as, for example, Susa-no-Wo-no-Mikoto, "The-Impetuous-Male-Deity," the name commonly given the storm god.

Shinto gods and goddesses are sometimes referred to in the literature as the "deities of heaven and earth." As already mentioned, Shinto itself is sometimes called the Way of the Deities of Heaven and Earth. The terminology is an old one and appears in the early writings in the form of a distinction between the so-called *amatsu kami* ("deities of heaven") and the *kunitsu kami* ("deities of earth") . This has caused a bit of perplexity to the commentators. A favored, though problematical interpretation, takes "heavenly deities" in the sense of the original *kami* of the dominant Yamato tribe. They are the gods and goddesses of Takama-ga-Hara. The "earthly deities" are

understood to be those which were already being worshipped in the land
when the early representatives of the Yamato race entered it. Both terms are
interpreted, without good grounds, in a legitimate ancestral sense as ancient
chieftains.

In general outline the mythology of old Shinto is closely similar to what
is found almost universally among other peoples at like stages of culture. The
great deities are the unknown forces of nature formulated in terms of the
current social and political patterns. The justification of these statements will
be given in detail at a later point in the discussion. Yamato culture, in the
form which eventually became prominent, centered in the adoration of the
sun. Dynastic interests were quick to make the most of the uniqueness and
majesty deriving from claims for the descent of the Imperial Line from a solar
ancestry. By the sixth century of the Western era an imperial solar ancestral-
ism had become the paramount motive in the Yamato state worship. Its influence has widened with the passing centuries until today it constitutes the
predominant interest of all Shinto.

Study of the early rituals indicates that the primary interests expressed
in the public religious rites were to safeguard the food supply, to ward off
calamities of fire, wind, rain, drought, earthquake and pestilence, to obtain
numerous offspring and peaceful homes, to secure the prosperity and permanence of the imperial reign, and to effect purgation of ceremonial and moral
impurity.

The earliest worship of the *kami* was not necessarily at man-made shrines.
Mountains, groves, trees, rivers, springs, rocks, and other natural objects
served as primitive sanctuaries. The oldest shrines known to have been constructed by human hands were simple taboo areas formed by the dedication
of sacred trees and stones. We do not know when houses first began to be built
for the gods. The date is lost in the mist of antiquity. Man-made shrines,
copied from the dwellings of chiefs, must have appeared very early in the
historical development, however. The records of the oldest existing shrines
of the present, that of Omiwa in Yamato and that of the great shrine of Izumo,
state that these edifices were first built in the Age of the Gods. By the time of
the compilation of the *Engi Shiki* in the tenth century of the Western era the
shrines had become sufficiently numerous and diverse to be graded into so-
called upper, middle and lower classes. A census given in this document names
2,861 shrines. It is improbable that this figure exhausted the list for the entire
country.

2

the ancient mythology

The oldest recorded document of Japanese mythology is the *Kojiki*, which is written in an early form of Japanese. This written mythology does not constitute a sacred scripture like the Christian Bible, but it is important because it helps us recognize early Japanese religious notions that have had lasting influence. Although the *Kojiki* reflects some borrowing from China, it establishes the origin and distinctiveness of the Japanese tradition. The story depicts the creation of the world and the appearance of the mythological deities who created the Japanese islands and the Japanese people, but it contrasts sharply with the biblical account of creation. For example, creation is neither by the power of one divinity nor a sudden act but a process whereby the universe emerges amidst many *kami*. The male, Izanagi, and the female, Izanami, provide divine models for procreation and also introduce death into the world. A crowning point of the story is when Ninigi (piko-Po-Ninigi), heir of the Sun Goddess (Ama-Terasu), descends to rule the earth and thereby establishes imperial rule. These episodes constitute the traditional account of the divine origin of Japan and the imperial family.

This mythological tradition is known in outline by every Japanese person, but it is appreciated more as an idealized story of the origin and greatness of Japan than as a description of a historical event. (Compare the ancient poetry in selection 25 for similar sentiments.) Even modern Japanese people would have difficulty with all the specific names of the *kami*, and for the Western reader, too, the important thing is to note the presence of the many *kami* in the universe and their responsibility for simultaneously creating the world and founding the Japanese nation.

Reprinted by permission of the publisher from Donald L. Philippi, translator, *Kojiki* (Tokyo: University of Tokyo Press, 1968).

The Age of the Kami

Chapter 1: The Five Separate Heavenly Deities come into existence.

1   At the time of the beginning of heaven and earth, there came into existence in TAKAMA-NO-PARA a deity named AME-NO-MI-NAKA-NUSI-NO-KAMI; next, TAKA-MI-MUSUBI-NO-KAMI; next, KAMI-MUSUBI-NO-KAMI. These

three deities all came into existence as single deities, and their forms were not visible.

2   Next, when the land was young, resembling floating oil and drifting like a jellyfish, there sprouted forth something like reed-shoots. From these came into existence the deity UMASI-ASI-KABI-PIKO-DI-NO-KAMI; next, AME-NO-TOKO-TATI-NO-KAMI. These two deities also came into existence as single deities, and their forms were not visible.

3   The five deities in the above section are the Separate Heavenly Deities.

Chapter 2: The Seven Generations of the Age of the Gods come into existence.

1   Next there came into existence the deity KUNI-NO-TOKO-TATI-NO-KAMI; next, TOYO-KUMO-NO-NO-KAMI. These two deities also came into existence as single deities, and their forms were not visible.

2   Next there came into existence the deity named U-PIDI-NI-NO-KAMI; next, his spouse SU-PIDI-NI-NO-KAMI. Next, TUNO-GUPI-NO-KAMI; next, his spouse IKU-GUPI-NO-KAMI. Next, OPO-TO-NO-DI-NO-KAMI; next, his spouse OPO-TO-NO-BE-NO-KAMI. Next, OMO-DARU-NO-KAMI; next, his spouse AYA-KASIKO-NE-NO-KAMI. Next, IZANAGI-NO-KAMI; next, his spouse IZANAMI-NO-KAMI.

3   The deities in the above section, from KUNI-NO-TOKO-TATI-NO-KAMI through IZANAMI-NO-KAMI, are called collectively the Seven Generations of the Age of the Gods.

Chapter 3: Izanagi and Izanami are commanded to solidify the land. They create Onogoro island.

1   At this time the heavenly deities, all with one command, said to the two deities IZANAGI-NO-MIKOTO and IZANAMI-NO-MIKOTO:

"Complete and solidify this drifting land!"

2   Giving them the Heavenly Jeweled Spear, they entrusted the mission to them.

3   Thereupon, the two deities stood on the Heavenly Floating Bridge and, lowering the jeweled spear, stirred with it. They stirred the brine with a churning-churning sound, and when they lifted up [the spear] again, the brine dripping down from the tip of the spear piled up and became an island. This was the island ONOGORO.

Chapter 4: Izanagi and Izanami marry and bear their first offspring .

1   Descending from the heavens to this island, they erected a heavenly pillar and a spacious palace.

2   At this time [Izanagi-no-mikoto] asked his spouse IZANAMI-NO-MIKOTO, saying:

"How is your body formed?"

3   She replied, saying:
        "My body, formed though it be formed, has one place which is
formed insufficiently."

4   Then IZANAGI-NO-MIKOTO said:
        "My body, formed though it be formed, has one place which is formed
to excess. Therefore, I would like to take that place in my body which is
formed to excess and insert it into that place in your body which is formed
insufficiently, and [thus] give birth to the land. How would this be?"

5   IZANAMI-NO-MIKOTO replied, saying:
        "That will be good."

6   Then IZANAGI-NO-MIKOTO said:
        "Then let us, you and me, walk in a circle around this heavenly pillar
and meet and have conjugal intercourse."

7   After thus agreeing, [Izanagi-no-mikoto] then said:
        "You walk around from the right, and I will walk around from the
left and meet you."

8   After having agreed to this, they circled around; then IZANAMI-NO-
MIKOTO said first:
        "Ana-ni-yasi, how good a lad!"

9   Afterwards, IZANAGI-NO-MIKOTO said:
        "Ana-ni-yasi, how good a maiden!"

10   After each had finished speaking, [Izanagi-no-mikoto] said to his
spouse:
        "It is not proper that the woman speak first."

11   Nevertheless, they commenced procreation and gave birth to a leech-
child. They placed this child into a boat made of reeds and floated it away.

12   Next, they gave birth to the island of APA. This also is not reckoned
as one of their children.

Chapter 5: Izanagi and Izanami, learning the reason for their failure, repeat the marriage ritual.

1   Then the two deities consulted together and said:
        "The child which we have just borne is not good. It is best to report
[this matter] before the heavenly deities."

2   Then they ascended together and sought the will of the heavenly
deities. The heavenly deities thereupon performed a grand divination and
said:

3   "Because the woman spoke first, [the child] was not good. Descend
once more and say it again."

4   Then they descended again and walked once more in a circle around
the heavenly pillar as [they had done] before.

5   Then IZANAGI-NO-MIKOTO said first:
        "Ana-ni-yasi, how good a maiden!"

6   Afterwards, his spouse IZANAMI-NO-MIKOTO said:
        "Ana-ni-yasi, how good a lad!"

The story continues with the account of how Izanami died giving birth to fire and descended to the underworld. Her spouse, Izanagi, followed her to the impure underworld, unsuccessfully trying to bring her back to life; this episode is sometimes compared with the Greek story of Orpheus. When Izanagi escaped from the underworld he purified himself, thereby creating many deities, including Ama-Terasu.

Chapter 12: Izanagi entrusts their missions to the three noble children.

1   At this time IZANAGI-NO-MIKOTO, rejoicing greatly, said:
"I have borne child after child, and finally in the last bearing I have obtained three noble children."

2   Then he removed his necklace, shaking the beads on the string so that they jingled, and, giving it to AMA-TERASU-OPO-MI-KAMI, he entrusted her with her mission, saying:
"You shall rule TAKAMA-NO-PARA."

3   The name of this necklace is MI-KURA-TANA-NO-KAMI.

4   Next he said to TUKU-YOMI-NO-MIKOTO, entrusting him with his mission:
"You shall rule the realms of the night."

5   Next he said to TAKE-PAYA-SUSA-NO-WO-NO-MIKOTO, entrusting him with his mission:
"You shall rule the ocean." . . .

Chapter 38: Piko-po-no-ninigi-no-mikoto is commanded to descend from the heavens and rule the land. Saruta-biko meets him to serve as his guide.

1   Then AMA-TERASU-OPO-MI-KAMI and TAKA-KI-NO-KAMI commanded the heir apparent MASA-KATU-A-KATU-KATI-PAYA-PI-AME-NO-OSI-PO-MIMI-NO-MIKOTO, saying:

2   "Now it is reported that the pacification of the Central Land of the Reed Plains has been finished. Therefore, descend and rule it, as you have been entrusted with it."

3   Then the heir apparent MASA-KATU-A-KATU-KATI-PAYA-PI-AME-NO-PO-MIMI-NO-MIKOTO replied, saying:

4   "As I was preparing to descend, a child was born; his name is AME-NIGISI-KUNI-NIGISI-AMA-TU-PIKO-PIKO-PO-NO-NINIGI-NO-MIKOTO. This child should descend."

5   This child was born of his union with the daughter of TAKA-KI-NO-KAMI, YORODU-PATA-TOYO-AKI-TU-SI-PIME-NO-MIKOTO, who bore AME-NO-PO-AKARI-NO-MIKOTO; next, PIKO-PO-NO-NINIGI-NO-MIKOTO. (Two deities)

6   Whereupon, in accordance with his words, they imposed the command upon PIKO-PO-NO-NINIGI-NO-MIKOTO:

7   "Toyo-asi-para-no-midu-po-no-kuni has been entrusted to you as the land you are to rule. In accordance with the command, descend from the heavens!"

8   Then, as Piko-po-no-ninigi-no-mikoto was about to descend from the heavens, there appeared in the myriad heavenly crossroads a deity whose radiance shone above through Takama-no-para and below through the Central Land of the Reed Plains.

9   Then Ama-terasu-opo-mi-kami and Taka-ki-no-kami commanded Ame-no-uzume-no-kami, saying:

10   "Although you are a graceful maiden, you are [the type of] deity who can face and overwhelm [others]. Therefore go alone and inquire: 'Who is here on the path of my offspring descending from the heavens?'"

11   When she inquired, the reply was:

"I am an earthly deity named Saruta-biko-no-kami. I have come out because I have heard that the offspring of the heavenly deities is to descend from the heavens, and I have come forth to wait that I might serve as his guide."

Chapter 39: Piko-no-no-ninigi-no-mikoto descends from the heavens bearing the three items of the sacred regalia and accompanied by various deities. He establishes his palace at Taka-ti-po.

1   Then assigning [their respective] roles to Ame-no-ko-yane-no-mikoto, Puto-tama-no-mikoto, Ame-no-uzume-no-mikoto, Isi-kori-dome-no-mikoto, and Tama-no-ya-no-mikoto, altogether five clan heads, they had them descend from the heavens.
they had them descend from the heavens.

2   Hereupon, she imparted [unto him] the myriad maga-tama beads and the mirror which had been used to lure, as well as the Sword *Kusa-nagi*; and also [sent along] Toko-yo-no-omopi-kane-no-kami, Ta-dikara-wo-no-kami, and Ame-no-ipa-to-wake-no-kami, and said:

3   "This mirror — have [it with you] as my spirit, and worship it just as you would worship in my very presence. Next, let Omopi-kane-no-kami take the responsibility for the affairs of the presence and carry on the government."

4   These two deities are worshipped at the shrine of Isuzu of the bell-bracelets.

5   Next [was] Toyu-uke-no-kami; this is the deity who dwells in Watarapi, the Outer Shrine.

6   Next [was] Ame-no-ipa-to-wake-no-kami, also named Kusi-ipa-mado-no-kami, also named Toyo-ipa-mado-no-kami. This deity is the deity of the Gate.

7   Next, Ta-dikara-wo-no-kami dwells in Sananagata.

8   Ame-no-ko-yane-no-mikoto is the ancestor of the murazi of the Nakatomi.

9   Puto-tama-no-mikoto is the ancestor of the obito of the Imube.

10   AME-NO-UZUME-NO-MIKOTO is the ancestor of the KIMI of the SARUME.

11   ISI-KORI-DOME-NO-MIKOTO is the ancestor of the MURAZI of the KAGAMI-TUKURI.

12   TAMA-NO-YA-NO-MIKOTO is the ancestor of the MURAZI of the TAMA-NO-YA.

13   Then AMA-TU-PIKO-PO-NO-NINIGI-NO-MIKOTO was commanded to leave the Heavenly Rock-Seat. Pushing through the myriad layers of the heavens' trailing clouds, pushing his way with an awesome pushing, he stood on a flat floating island by the Heavenly Floating Bridge, and descended from the heavens to the peak KUZI-PURU-TAKE of Mount TAKA-TI-PO of PIMUKA in TUKUSI.

14   Then the two deities AME-NO-OSI-PI-NO-MIKOTO and AMA-TU-KUME-NO-MIKOTO took on their backs heavenly stone-quivers, wore at their sides mallet-headed swords, took up heavenly bows of PAZI wood, held heavenly deer[-slaying] arrows, and standing in front of him served him.

15   AME-NO-OSI-PI-NO-MIKOTO — this is the ancestor of the MURAZI of the OPO-TOMO.

16   AMA-TU-KUME-NO-MIKOTO — this is the ancestor of the ATAPE of the KUME.

17   At this time he said:

"This place is opposite the land of KARA; [it is a place to which one] comes directly through the Cape of KASASA, a land where the morning sun shines directly, a land where the rays of the evening sun are brilliant. This is a most excellent place."

18   Thus saying, he rooted his palace-posts firmly in the bedrock below, raised high the crossbeams unto TAKAMA-NO-PARA itself, and dwelt [there].

3

shinto shrines

Probably in the dim past, Shinto "shrines" were nothing more than natural objects such as trees and stones that were set apart with straw ropes as specially venerated—that is, sacred—objects. Some such shrines survive even today—for example, the Nachi Waterfall and Mount Miwa. (See the photograph of Nachi Waterfall, figure 1.) But typical of Shinto from early times is the wooden shrine and encompassing grove. The shrine

is quite different from a Christian church or Jewish synagogue, since its purpose is not congregational worship, and originally it differed from the Buddhist temple, since it did not house statues or representations of divinities. Rather, the Shinto shrine was where men recited ritual prayers

Figure 1. Nachi Waterfall (in Wakayama Prefecture). The *torii* (sacred archway) erected in front of the waterfall indicates its sacred character.

and made offerings to *kami,* who at such times descended temporarily. The so-called *kami*-body *(shintai),* or object of worship, which might be an old sword or mirror, was considered technically as the resting place of the *kami* during its temporary descent; however, this *kami*-body was seldom seen by the people and only rarely by the Shinto priesthood.

In the following selection, first published in 1938, Holtom refers especially to the pre-World War II situation. (It should be noted that his reference in the first paragraph to "contemporary Japanese law" refers to the 1930s; the legal situation of Shinto changed radically after World

War II, as can be seen in selection 5.) Nevertheless, Shinto is very conservative, and several shrines, such as those at Ise and Izumo, probably
preserve ancient building practices harking back to southern Pacific
origins, and the general religious character of the Shinto shrine remains
rather constant throughout the course of history. In general, the shrine
and its compound represent a sacred space set apart from ordinary space.
The *torii,* or sacred archway, marks the entrance into sacred space, and
the water basin is provided to purify the person who prepares himself
for closer communion with the *kami* when he offers a prayer at the shrine.
A person might visit the shrine for a personal petition, but more frequently
the visit is part of a village celebration.

Reprinted by permission of the publisher from D. C. Holtom, *The National
Faith of Japan: A Study of Modern Shinto* (New York: Paragon Book Reprint
Corp., 1965).

Shinto Places of Worship

We turn first to the consideration of the nature of the Shinto places of
worship. In contemporary [1938] Japanese law the institutions which are
called "shrines" are generally designated *jinja*, from *shin* or *jin*, meaning
"deity" *(kami* in pure Japanese) and *sha,* or *ja,* which in this connection is
best rendered "house" or "dwelling place." The shrine, or *jinja,* then, is a
house or dwelling place in which the deity or deities, worshipped in the local
rites, are supposed to live, or where they are believed to take up residence
when summoned by appropriate ceremonies. They are the holy places where
the *kami* may be found and communicated with. Japanese law permits the use
of the term *jinja* only in connection with the traditional institutions of original Shinto wherein the *kami* are enshrined. The institutions of Buddhism and
of the existing Shinto sects are denied the right to use the designation. We can
preserve the distinction if we speak of the local foundations of State Shinto
as shrines, of those of Buddhism as temples *(tera)* and of those of the Shinto
sects as churches or chapels *(kyokai).*

Jinja is thus a modern Sino-Japanese legal designation and does not
represent the earliest known usage. Older and more widely used terms employed in the literature to indicate the abodes of Shinto deities are *miya* or
omiya, yashiro or *miyashiro, hokora, hokura,* and *mimuro. Miya (mi,* honorific
prefix, *ya,* "house") and *omiya (o-mi,* double honorific) are the designations
most commonly met with. It is not necessary to venture on an extended explanation of this varied terminology here. Suffice it to say that all the terms

just listed may properly be taken to mean dwelling place or superior dwelling place in one form or another.

The Shinto shrine may be a small god-house of wood or stone casually met with by the wayside. It may be a Grand Imperial Shrine of Ise or a Great Meiji Shrine of Tokyo, including in its appointments extensive landed holdings and numerous costly buildings along with various objects of ceremony and art, with a total valuation of millions of yen.

The ordinary shrine includes a definite enclosure of land, usually rectangular in shape, surrounded by a sacred fence or wall, one or more buildings where the deities are enshrined and, generally, certain auxiliary structures where special ceremonies are conducted, business transacted, or properties stored. The immediate entrance to the shrine is generally guarded by two stone lions arranged one on either side of the approach. In the case of shrines to the grain-goddess, Inari, the lions give place to the images of foxes, animals to which popular belief attributes the functions of messengers to this deity. Encompassing the shrine proper or adjacent thereto may lie more or less extended areas devoted to landscape gardening and parkland or utilized as a source of revenue. Associated with the great Meiji Shrine of Tokyo is a magnificent equipment providing for all sorts of athletic sports. The shrines, in their diversity of history, of ceremony and of architectural style, present a complicated and almost endless field of study. The most archaic type of shrine is simply a replica of the primitive house of ancient times, consisting of a small structure of natural wood, thatched with reeds or straw, the principal rafters in front and rear projecting through the roof, the total building elevated on piles in a manner that suggests the Swiss lake-dwellings or some of the Indonesian types of house architecture built above water.

Access to the shrine is gained through an opening in the fence or wall at the front, placed exactly in the middle between the left and right extremities, sometimes through similar apertures on either side, rarely, also, at the rear. Openings are guarded by the distinctive Shinto gateway, called the *torii*, a word whose correct etymology is unknown. The literal interpretation of the ideograms with which the term is written, in the sense of "bird-dwelling," offers no help toward the understanding of the proper function of the device. The *torii*, in its most characteristic form, consists of a single, elongated cylinder of wood, ordinarily made from a solid tree trunk, mounted horizontally on two upright posts set one on either side of the approach. A cross-brace is generally attached between the heads of the uprights. *Torii* made of stone or metal, preferably bronze, are not uncommon. The use of curved lines in the design of the horizontal cap-piece, as well as other elaborations, shows a Buddhist influence which orthodox Shinto is attempting to eliminate.

In its original significance the *torii* was not merely a decorative gateway. It was a magical, protective device which guarded the opening in the shrine fence against the entrance of evil and contamination of all sorts. Sometimes the approach to the shrine is made through a first, or outer, *torii,* then through

a second, and finally a third. Occasionally one meets with an extended series of *torii* set so close together as to make a veritable tunnel.

On advancing through the *torii* one generally finds immediately before him in the center of the enclosure a building called the *haiden,* meaning the "worship-sanctuary." The name indicates its main use. Before it the people clap their hands and ring a suspended bell to attract the attention of the gods, bow their heads, and occasionally kneel, in brief reverence or prayer, and deposit their offerings in a money chest or on a cloth conveniently placed for the purpose. Within the *haiden* rituals are carried out on stated occasions by the priests in charge. These are for the most part official ceremonies on behalf of the local community or the state, but sometimes, also, purely private rites on behalf of individuals or small groups. Ordinary worshippers do not enter the shrines.

Just beyond the worship-sanctuary is usually placed an inner building called the *honden* or "chief-sanctuary." This is the holy of holies of the shrine where the deities dwell and to which the laity have no access. Two or more deities are sometimes enshrined in a single edifice; sometimes a special sanctum is provided for each deity. The principal function of the *honden* is to shelter a sacred object called the *shintai* or "god-body." This is sometimes also designated *mitama-shiro* ("spirit-substitute"). An older name is *kamusane,* or *kamuzane,* meaning "god-seed," or perhaps, better, "sacred kernel." The *shintai* is sometimes explained as a symbolic representation of the deity. It is more generally regarded by priests and people alike as the object in which the enshrined deity takes up residence. The *shintai,* which in and of itself is generally of small intrinsic value, is regarded with such awe and reverence that the members of the priesthood, themselves, are prohibited under law from viewing or handling it except by special permit. The popular attitude is well indicated in the numerous stories of local folklore which tell how those curious and profane people who have dared to steal a peep at the *shintai* have been struck dead or smitten with blindness for life. Japanese attitudes toward the *shintai* suggest the relic worship of the European middle ages.

In spite of its sacredness and all the sentiments of awe with which it is hedged about, it not infrequently happens that judicious questioning of priests and pilgrims will elucidate the nature of the god-body. Stones, sacred texts, old scrolls, ancient swords, phallic emblems, strips of consecrated paper cut in forms that possibly represent the sacred tree, locks of human hair, balls of crystal, jewels (*magatama*), pictures and numerous other like objects appear among the *shintai*. Under Buddhist influence images of men and deities have found their way into the holy of holies of Shinto. It has sometimes happened in the past that when loyal subjects have been deified, objects intimately associated with their lives, such as head-wear, batons, weapons, writing implements and clothing have been made into *shintai*. Occasionally an unhoused natural object is worshipped as the *shintai,* in which case concealment is im-

possible, of course. Living trees are most common in this connection. The *shintai* of the Omiwa shrine of Yamato is a mountain; that of the Yudono shrine on the slopes of Gassan in Yamagata Prefecture in the north-central part of the Hondo is a hot-spring....

Shrines which are recognized and counted by the government in its classification are divided into twelve groups. At the head stands the Ise Dai Jingu, or the Grand Imperial Shrine of Ise, listed in the official statistics as one great shrine, but really consisting of a group of sixteen shrines, large and small. Below these are arranged eleven grades which vary from the large government shrines (*kampeisha*) and national shrines (*kokuheisha*) and their sub-classes down through those of prefecture (*kensha*), district (*gosha*), and village (*sonsha*) to a large group of more than sixty-one thousand shrines which are designated as being without grade, the so-called *mukakusha,* or "unranked shrines." Outside of these again lie tens of thousands of little shrines that are not officially counted or recognized in any way. The total number of shrines in Shinto, large and small, is unknown. The number is legion. Shrines which are recognized and counted by the government, as given in the latest statistics available total 110,967. Attached to these are 15,606 priests. No statistics of adherents of the state shrines are kept by the national government, the assumption evidently being that all Japanese by virtue of nationality are naturally included within the sphere of shrine fealty.

4

pilGRimaGe and devotion at a shinto shrine

Worship and devotion in the context of Shinto are usually expressed informally in an experience of gratitude and reverent unity with the *kami*. This contrasts sharply with the Western tendency toward more precise forms: a critical moment of conversion, a statement of faith, and the recitation of creeds. The present document, taken from a fourteenth century pilgrimage diary, describes the unaffected sincerity and warmth of a pilgrim toward the *kami* when he reaches his goal of the Ise shrines. Saka, the pilgrim who wrote the diary, is a Buddhist priest, and he freely

draws on several traditions (including religious Taoism) in interpreting his pilgrimage. (An interesting comparison is the example of Buddhist devotion in selection 10.) Saka's devotion might not be typical for Shinto priests, but his tendency to blend several traditions with simple piety toward the *kami* is reflected in popular attitudes toward Shinto.

The Ise shrines, actually two large shrine complexes, form one of the holiest centers of Shinto. Their origin is associated with the enshrinement of the Sun Goddess here in ancient times. The holiness of the shrines is further attested by the traditional practice of having a princess of the imperial line serve as high priestess. These shrines were centers of Shinto scholarship and ritual and have been objects of popular pilgrimage since medieval times.

Remarkable in Saka's account is his increasing sense of awe and reverence as he approaches the shrines. He even experiences the sacredness of the landscape as he nears, and in order to preserve the Shinto purity of the site, he readily observes the rule that prohibits Buddhist priests from drawing too close. Nevertheless, as he approaches one shrine, he realizes the significance of pilgrimage to Ise: by becoming absolutely pure one is able "to become thus one with the Divine." With this realization, he "could not refrain from shedding tears of gratitude." This kind of simple appreciation of the presence of the *kami,* rather than a formal argument for the existence of God, has characterized the Shinto tradition. In contemporary Japan, the same kind of simple piety can be found wherever people pay their respects at Shinto shrines, although it is not as widespread now as it was in the fourteenth century.

Reprinted by permission of the publisher from A. L. Sadler, *The Ise Daijingu Sankeiki or Diary of a Pilgrim to Ise* (Tokyo: Zaidan Hojin Meiji Seitoku Kinen Gakkai [Meiji Japan Society], 1940).

A Pilgrimage to Ise

When on the way to these Shrines one does not feel like an ordinary person any longer but as though reborn in another world. How solemn is the unearthly shadow of the huge groves of ancient pines and chamaecyparis, and there is a delicate pathos in the few rare flowers that have withstood the winter frosts so gaily. The cross-beams of the Torii or Shinto gate way is without any curve, symbolizing by its straightness the sincerity of the direct beam of the Divine promise. The shrine-fence is not painted red nor is the shrine itself roofed with cedar shingles. The eaves, with their rough reed-hatch, recall memories of the ancient days when the roofs were not trimmed.

So did they spare expense out of compassion for the hardships of the people. Within the Shrine there are many buildings where the festival rites are performed, constructed just like those in the Imperial Palace. Buddhist monks may go only as far as the Sacred Tree known as the Cryptomeria of the Five Hundred Branches (Ioe-no-sugi) . They may not go to the Shrine. This, too, is a ceremonial rule of the Imperial Court. . . .

When I went to worship at the Shrine of the Moon-Deity Tsukiyomi the fallen leaves in the grove covered my traces and the winter powdered the foliage in the court. And the name of Tsukiyomi recalled so vividly the age of the deities that I was inspired to write:

> How many long years
> Has this ancient shrine-fence stood
> Wet with countless dews,
> And the Moon of the Gods' Age
> Is this selfsame autumn moon.

I fear that my clumsy pen can hardly do justice to the road from Yamada to the Inner Shrine. Sometimes the spray over the hills seems to reflect their reversed silhouettes, sometimes the way is shrouded in cloud so that the countless peaks of the hills are hidden. As we approach the village of Uji the name is welcome to us with its suggestion of nearness to the Capital, and as it lies under the hills at the south-west of the Outer Shrine it is a place where you might imagine people would make cottages to live in retirement. As we went on deep in the shade of the chamaecyparis groves there was not even the smoke of any habitation to be seen, and we felt as though we had suddenly transcended the bounds of this painful world, while the hills with their cloud-capped mystery transported us to the world of Taoist fairyland.

When I entered the second Torii or Shinto Gate Way to worship it was dark under the pines at the foot of the hill and the branches were so thick-matted that one could hardly discern "the Pine of one hundred branches." The cryptomerias within the Shrine precincts were so dense that even the oblique projecting roof-beams could hardly be made out. When I came to reflect on my condition my mind is full of the Ten Evils and I felt shame at so long forsaking the will of Buddha, yet as I wear one of the three monkish robes, I must feel some chagrin at my estrangement from the Way of the Deities.

And particularly is it the deeply-rooted custom of this Shrine that we should bring no Buddhist rosary or offering, or any special petition in our hearts and this is called "Inner Purity." Washing in sea water and keeping the body free from all defilement is called "Outer Purity." And when both these Purities are attained there is then no barrier between our mind and that of the Deity. And if we feel to become thus one with the Divine, what more do we need and what is there to pray for? When I heard that this was the true way of worshipping at the Shrine, I could not refrain from shedding tears of gratitude.

5

the disestablishment of shinto and the emperor's "renunciation of divinity"

In medieval times, Shinto was dominated by Buddhism, but in late medieval times, Shinto attempted to restrengthen her own tradition. The major political changes of 1868 favored Shinto, and from that time until 1945, Shinto was increasingly treated as a state religion, which Holtom calls State Shinto. During this period most Shinto shrines and Shinto priests came to be considered state institutions and state officials. Attendance at shrines amounted to more than a simple religious act; because it was a patriotic obligation, it was considered to be the duty of every Japanese as a citizen of the state. Schools taught an ethical system based on the mythological origin of the Japanese people and absolute loyalty to the state as embodied in the person of the emperor. It should be remembered that Shinto was only one of several elements which were used to support this all-embracing nationalism. (For greater detail, see Part 14, especially selection 42.) On one hand, for many people, Shinto meant the annual festivals, seasonal celebrations, observances in the home, and veneration of the *kami*—living within a world blessed by the *kami*. On the other hand, especially as an institution and a social force, "State Shinto" was used to support ultranationalism and militarism before and during World War II.

At the end of World War II, the Allied military leaders and many Japanese intellectuals felt that Shinto had become a tool of the ultra-nationalists and the military rather than a religion of the people. Therefore, the Allied occupation forces in Japan required the disestablishment of Shinto and stated this requirement in a document. Shinto (including sect Shinto) would be allowed to exist as a religion on the same legal basis as other religious organizations in Japan. The general restrictions were spelled out more in terms of the state—to prevent the state from giving special privileges to any religious group.

Since 1945, various problems have arisen regarding the interpretation and implementation of this document. Shinto authorities claim that the directive was a foreign intervention into the Japanese tradition, creating an artificial division of state and religion which had never existed in Japan. Controversy arises particularly around such concrete issues as the religious status of the emperor and whether his annual ritual ceremonies are only a private matter or (according to Shinto authorities) are actually state ceremonies; whether the national shrine for war dead (Yasukuni

Shrine in Tokyo) is only a religious institution or (according to Shinto authorities) is also a national monument; whether rites at the Ise Shrine and the periodic rebuilding are only religious ceremonies or (according to Shrine authorities) also involve state concern. Within the present Japanese constitution, all three issues are treated as private religious concerns rather than as state matters.

The second part of this selection is, in effect, the emperor's answer to the directive on disestablishment. Although the status of the emperor is at stake, he begins with a reference to the highly revered Emperor Meiji, who was seen as the architect of modern Japan. This is the beginning of an appeal for the people to band together in the love of their country to overcome defeat and rebuild the nation. This speech, broadcast over the radio, brought the emperor into closer contact with his subjects than ever before; the placing of the emperor on the same level of humanity with his subjects in "mutual trust and affection" is also quite new. The denial of a mythical support for the emperor and his status as a manifest god, although a departure from prewar indoctrination and a surprise for the lesser educated, was an unvoiced understanding among educated people. However, the postwar decline of popular interest in Shinto was not solely due to the disestablishment order or the emperor's radio speech but was partly the result of Shinto's involvement in the war machine, followed by the sudden defeat in 1945. (See also selection 45 for attitudes toward Shinto in postwar Japan.)

Reprinted by permission of the publisher from D. C. Holtom, *Modern Japan and Shinto Nationalism: A Study of Present-Day Trends in Japanese Religions* (New York: Paragon Book Reprint Corp., 1963).

Directive for the Disestablishment of State Shinto

Orders from the Supreme Commander for the Allied Powers to the Japanese Government

15 December 1945

MEMORANDUM FOR: IMPERIAL JAPANESE GOVERNMENT
THROUGH   : Central Liaison Office, Tokyo
SUBJECT   : Abolition of Governmental Sponsorship, Support, Perpetuation, Control, and Dissemination of State Shinto *(Kokka Shinto, Jinja Shinto)*

1. In order to free the Japanese people from direct or indirect compulsion to believe or profess to believe in a religion or cult officially designated by the state, and

In order to lift from the Japanese people the burden of compulsory financial support of an ideology which has contributed to their war guilt, defeat, suffering, privation, and present deplorable condition, and

In order to prevent recurrence of the perversion of Shinto theory and beliefs into militaristic and ultra-nationalistic propaganda designed to delude the Japanese people and lead them into wars of aggression, and

In order to assist the Japanese people in a rededication of their national life to building a new Japan based upon ideals of perpetual peace and democracy,

It is hereby directed that:

a. The sponsorship, support, perpetuation, control, and dissemination of Shinto by the Japanese national, prefectual, and local governments, or by public officials, subordinates, and employees acting in their official capacity are prohibited and will cease immediately.

b. All financial support from public funds and all official affiliation with Shinto and Shinto shrines are prohibited and will cease immediately.

  (1) While no financial support from public funds will be extended to shrines located on public reservations or parks, this prohibition will not be construed to preclude the Japanese Government from continuing to support the areas on which such shrines are located.

  (2) Private financial support of all Shinto shrines which have been previously supported in whole or in part by public funds will be permitted, provided such private support is entirely voluntary and is in no way derived from forced or involuntary contributions.

c. All propagation and dissemination of militaristic and ultra-nationistic ideology in Shinto doctrines, practices, rites, ceremonies, or observances, as well as in the doctrines, practices, rites, ceremonies and observances of any other religion, faith, sect, creed, or philosophy, are prohibited and will cease immediately.

d. The Religious Functions Order relating to the Grand Shrine of Ise and the Religious Functions Order relating to State and other Shrines will be annulled.

e. The Shrine Board (*Jingi-in*) of the Ministry of Home Affairs will be abolished, and its present functions, duties, and administrative obligations will not be assumed by any other governmental or tax-supported agency.

f. All public educational institutions whose primary function is either the investigation and dissemination of Shinto or the training of a Shinto priesthood will be abolished and their physical properties diverted to other uses. Their present functions, duties, and administrative obligations will not be assumed by any other governmental or tax-supported agency.

g. Private educational institutions for the investigation and dissemination of Shinto and for the training of priesthood for Shinto will be per-

mitted and will operate with the same privileges and be subject to the same controls and restrictions as any other private educational institution having no affiliation with the government; in no case, however, will they receive support from public funds, and in no case will they propagate and disseminate militaristic and ultra-nationalistic ideology.

    h. The dissemination of Shinto doctrines in any form and by any means in any educational institution supported wholly or in part by public funds is prohibited and will cease immediately.

        (1) All teachers' manuals and text-books now in use in any educational institution supported wholly or in part by public funds will be censored, and all Shinto doctrine will be deleted. No teachers' manual or text-book which is published in the future for use in such institutions will contain any Shinto doctrine.

        (2) No visits to Shinto shrines and no rites, practices, or ceremonies associated with Shinto will be conducted or sponsored by any educational institution supported wholly or in part by public funds.

    i. Circulation by the government of "The Fundamental Principles of the National Structure" (*Kokutai no Hongi*), "The Way of the Subject" (*Shinmin no Michi*), and all similar official volumes, commentaries, interpretations, or instructions on Shinto is prohibited.

    j. The use in official writings of the terms "Greater East Asia War" (*Dai Toa Senso*), "The Whole World under One Roof" (*Hakko Ichi-u*), and all other terms whose connotation in Japanese is inextricably connected with State Shinto, militarism, and ultra-nationalism is prohibited and will cease immediately.

    k. God-shelves (*kamidana*) and all other physical symbols of State Shinto in any office, school institution, organization, or structure supported wholly or in part by public funds are prohibited and will be removed immediately.

    l. No official, subordinate, employee, student, citizen, or resident of Japan will be discriminated against because of his failure to profess and believe in or participate in any practice, rite, ceremony, or observance of State Shinto or of any other religion.

    m. No official of the national, prefectural, or local government, acting in his public capacity, will visit any shrine to report his assumption of office, to report on conditions of government, or to participate as a representative of government in any ceremony or observance.

    2. *a.* The purpose of this directive is to separate religion from the state, to prevent misuse of religion for political ends, and to put all religions, faiths, and creeds upon exactly the same legal basis, entitled to precisely the same opportunities and protection. It forbids affiliation with the government and the propagation and dissemination of militaristic and ultra-nationalistic

ideology not only to Shinto but to the followers of all religions, faiths, sects, creeds, or philosophies.

b. The provisions of this directive will apply with equal force to all rites, practices, ceremonies, observances, beliefs, teachings, mythology, legends, philosophy, shrines, and physical symbols associated with Shinto.

c. The term State Shinto within the meaning of this directive will refer to that branch of Shinto (*Kokka Shinto* or *Jinja Shinto*) which by official acts of the Japanese Government has been differentiated from the religion of Sect Shinto (*Shuha Shinto* or *Kyoha Shinto*) and has been classified as a non-religious national cult commonly known as State Shinto, National Shinto, or Shrine Shinto.

d. The term Sect Shinto (*Shuha Shinto* or *Kyoha Shinto*) will refer to that branch of Shinto (composed of 13 recognized sects) which by popular belief, legal commentary, and the official acts of the Japanese Government has been recognized to be a religion.

e. Pursuant to the terms of Article I of the Basic Directive on "Removal of Restrictions on Political, Civil, and Religious Liberties" issued on 4 October 1945 by the Supreme Commander for the Allied Powers in which the Japanese people were assured complete religious freedom,

(1) Sect Shinto will enjoy the same protection as any other religion.

(2) Shrine Shinto, after having been divorced from the state and divested of its militaristic and ultra-nationalistic elements, will be recognized as a religion if its adherents so desire and will be granted the same protection as any other religion in so far as it may in fact be the philosophy or religion of Japanese individuals.

f. Militaristic and ultra-nationalistic ideology, as used in this directive, embraces those teachings, beliefs, and theories, which advocate or justify a mission on the part of Japan to extend its rule over other nations and peoples by reason of:

(1) The doctrine that the Emperor of Japan is superior to the heads of other states because of ancestry, descent, or special origin.

(2) The doctrine that the people of Japan are superior to the people of other lands because of ancestry, descent, or special origin.

(3) The doctrine that the islands of Japan are superior to other lands because of divine or special origin.

(4) Any other doctrine which tends to delude the Japanese people into embarking upon wars of aggression or to glorify the use of force as an instrument for the settlement of disputes with other people.

3. The Imperial Japanese Government will submit a comprehensive report to this Headquarters not later than 15 March 1946 describing in detail all action taken to comply with all provisions of this directive.

4. All officials, subordinates, and employees of the Japanese national, prefectural, and local governments, all teachers and education officials, and all citizens and residents of Japan will be held personally accountable for compliance with the spirit as well as the letter of all provisions of this directive.

For the Supreme Commander:

[*Signed*]   H. W. ALLEN,
Colonel, A.G.D.,
Asst. Adjutant General.

[NOTE.—The above is a transcription of an original received from the Civil Affairs Division of the War Department, Washington, D. C. I am responsible for the title that appears at the heading of this order — "Directive for the Disestablishment of State Shinto." Everything else is the official text. — D. C. H.]

Imperial Rescript on the Reconstruction of New Japan

[NOTE BY THE TRANSLATOR. —The following rescript was promulgated on January 1, 1946. It is chiefly noteworthy for the fact that it contains the passage in which the Japanese emperor makes renunciation of divinity. The translation is made from the *Tokyo Asahi Shimbun* for January 1, 1946.— D. C. H.]

Imperial Edict

Facing now a new year, we recall how, at the beginning of the Meiji Era, Emperor Meiji deigned to hand down the Charter Oath in Five Articles as the policy of the state.
He declared:
1. Conference shall be inaugurated widely, and all things shall be settled by public discussion.
2. Upper and lower classes shall be of one mind, and governmental administration shall be carried out vigorously.
3. Each and every person, in one and the same manner, beginning with the civil and military authorities and extending to all the masses, shall have opportunity to realize his aspirations, that the human spirit be not frustrated.
4. The evil practices of former times shall be broken down, and everything shall be founded on the just and equitable principles of nature.

    5. Knowledge shall be sought throughout the world, that the foundations of imperial rule may be strengthened.

His majesty's wishes were impartial and just. What can we add to them? We herewith renew the oath and resolve on the promotion of the welfare of the nation. At all costs we must pattern our actions according to the spirit of the Charter Oath, we must leave behind the evil practices of former years, we must foster the will of the people, raise up government and people, and carry through in the spirit of peace, we must enrich education and strengthen the foundations of culture, and thus undertake the advancement of the life of the people and the establishment of a new Japan.

Cities and towns, large and small, that have sustained the ravages of war, the sufferings of an afflicted people, the stagnation of industry, the lack of food, the growing trend of unemployment — all this wounds the heart. Yet we doubt not that if our countrymen [waga kokumin], by squarely facing the ordeals of the present and by firmly resolving to seek civilization through peace, bring this resolution to good issue, then not only for our country but also for all mankind a bright future will open up.

Moreover, we know that the spirit of love of home and the spirit of love of country are especially strong in our nation. Now in truth is the time for expanding this and for putting forth sacrificial efforts for the consummation of the love of mankind. When we reflect on the results of the long-continued war which has ended in our defeat [haiboku], we fear that there is danger that our people find the situation hard to bear and that they sink to the depths of discouragement. As the winds of adversity gradually heighten, there is peril in the weakening of moral principles and the marked confusion of thought that they bring.

We stand together with you our countrymen. Our gains and losses have ever been one. We desire that our woe and weal should be shared. The bonds between us and our countrymen have been tied together from first to last by mutual trust and affection. They do not originate in mere myth and legend. They do not have their basis in the fictitious ideas that the emperor is manifest god [akitsu mikami] and that the Japanese people are a race superior to other races and therefore destined to rule the world.

In order to alleviate the trials and sufferings of the people, my government will exhaust all means for devising every kind of plan and program. At the same time, it is our wish that our countrymen should trample disaster underfoot and rise above it, and that they should go forward bravely in making good the suffering of the present and in building up industry and civilization. In the development of the characteristics of tolerance and mutual forgiveness, in mutual dependence and assistance, in the unity of the civil life of our country — in these things there is well revealed the true worth of our supreme tradition, for which we are not ashamed. We doubt not that herein is the reason why in truth our countrymen can make a tremendous contribution to the happiness and progress of mankind.

Plans for the year are made at the beginning of the year. We earnestly desire that our countrymen, on whom we rely, may have the same purpose as ourselves, that we personally take warning and that we personally take heart in order that we may bring to fulfilment this great task.

[*Imperial Sign Manual, Imperial Seal*]   January 1, 1946
[*Countersigned by*

The Prime Minister
Other Cabinet Ministers]

SELECTED READINGS

For works on various aspects of Shinto, see first the citations for each selection; some additional works are:

Aston, W. G., trans. *Nihongi: Chronicles of Japan from the Earliest Times to A.D. 697.* Originally published in *Transactions of the Japan Society,* Supplement I. London, 1896; reprinted, two volumes in one with original pagination. London: George Allen & Unwin, 1956.

Bownas, G. "Shinto." In *The Concise Encyclopedia of Living Faiths,* edited by R. C. Zaehner, pp. 348-64. Boston: Beacon Press, 1967.

Creemers, Wilhelmus H. M. *Shrine Shinto after World War II.* Leiden: E. J. Brill, 1968.

Institute for Japanese Culture and Classics, *Proceedings of the Second International Conference for Shinto Studies: Continuity and Change.* Tokyo: Kokugakuin University, 1968.

Kato, Genchi, et al. *A Bibliography of Shinto in Western Languages from the Oldest Times till 1952.* Tokyo: Meiji Jingu Shamusho, 1953.

Kato, Genchi, and Hoshino, Hikoshiro, trans. *Kogoshui: Gleanings from Ancient Stories.* 2d ed., rev. Tokyo: Meiji Japan Society, 1925.

Muraoka, Tsunetsugu. *Studies in Shinto Thought.* Translated by Delmer M. Brown and James T. Araki. Tokyo: Ministry of Education, Japan, 1964.

Ono, Sokyo. *Shinto: The Kami Way.* Rutland, Vt.: Charles E. Tuttle Co., 1962.

Phillipi, Donald L., trans. *Norito: A New Translation of the Ancient Japanese Ritual Prayers.* Tokyo: Institute for Japanese Culture and Classics, Kokugakuin University, 1959.

Ponsonby-Fane, R. A. B. *Studies in Shinto and Shrines.* Rev. ed. Kamikamo, Kyoto: Ponsonby Memorial Society, 1953. (See also the other works of Ponsonby-Fane.)

part three

Buddhism

Buddhism arose in India and was transmitted through China and Korea to Japan. On one hand, Buddhism in Japan still displays Indian religious concepts and artistic images, and it is expressed in Chinese forms, such as the scriptures in Chinese translation; on the other hand, Buddhism became thoroughly nationalized in Japan, and it shares the persistent themes of the Japanese religious tradition.

Buddhism came to Japan as a foreign religion, but it tended to blend with the native tradition rather than to try to oust the tradition and "convert" the people. The Buddhist divinities of India and China and the *kami* of Japan were more often seen as complementing one another than as competing with each other. In fact, Buddhist art and ritual were so impressive that they were borrowed and used in Shinto shrines too.

Buddhism as a philosophical and metaphysical system is a match to any other heritage, but Buddhism usually enters the religious life of the people through more direct means, such as memorial rites. A cardinal teaching of Buddhism is the need for all men to overcome the illusion that life can be lived by the senses; to realize the impermanence of life is to awaken to a higher awareness of life and compassion for all forms of life. This insight is a clue to the power of Buddhism, which is able to drive out adversity and lead the person to a full life. The awakening can be sought through individual meditation, as in Zen; more often, however, the quest for this power is pursued through regular devotions such as are described in selection 10.

Buddhism entered Japan as a highly organized religion, and many of the doctrinal and ecclesiastical forms of Japanese Buddhism are direct descendants of Chinese and Indian forms of Buddhism. The many religious and philosophical writings of Buddhism, usually Indian materials in Chinese translation, found their way to Japan; usually a specific branch of Buddhism was organized around the study of several related texts and accompanying practices. As time passed and Buddhism became increasingly naturalized in its Japanese setting, new Buddhist branches

arose both through the introduction of Chinese patterns and through the development of more distinctively Japanese patterns (such as Nichiren Buddhism).

Buddhism has made extensive contributions to Japanese culture in many areas, such as providing a rationale for the nation and enriching artistic life. Buddhism features both a deep, diverse philosophical tradition and a number of impressive rituals. Once Buddhism became widely accepted on a popular level, its most important religious function has been the celebration of funeral and memorial masses. In fact, in the Tokugawa period (1600 - 1867), when Buddhism practically became an arm of the government, families were required to belong to a parish Buddhist temple and to have their parish temple perform rites for the dead. To this day, a small Buddhist altar for memorializing family ancestors is a prominent feature in many homes, even in homes in which there is no Shinto altar *(kamidana)* (see selection 45). Buddhist funerals are no longer required by law, but they still are the general rule. However, the continuation of this custom is not necessarily evidence of respect for Buddhism; rather, it reflects strong family tradition. The kind of Buddhist temple most familiar to the average Japanese person is this local parish temple. There are also the rather large headquarters of every denomination, and some temples are important for the granting of special petitions.

Japanese Buddhism was very much a part of feudal structures until the Meiji Restoration of 1868, when Buddhism was rejected as an arm of the government and government patronage turned toward Shinto. Nevertheless, Buddhist temples have not outlived their feudal past, and Buddhism also faces a dilemma today because it was close behind Shinto in nationalistic support of the war effort. In addition, Buddhism has been criticized in the past century as a carryover from feudal times whose main concern is for the souls of the dead. A number of Buddhist priests and scholars are aware of the validity of these criticisms and are attempting to restore Buddhism to its original ideals. Also, some of the New Religions are really lay movements of Buddhism which attempt to overcome the formalism of Buddhist temples and priests.

6

the entry of Buddhism into Japan

This selection from an eighth century national chronicle, *Nihongi*, records an important court event of the middle of the sixth century. The ruler of a Korean territory, Pekche, offered tribute to the Japanese court to gain a political ally. For our purposes, the most significant aspect is the tribute itself—Buddhism.

In this case, Buddhism means especially images, ritual decorations, and scriptures. This tradition is praised as hailing from distant India and as having the endorsement of China, a classical culture for both Korea and Japan. The power and wisdom of this great tradition are infinite.

The Japanese emperor's delight at this tribute is better understood by contrasting it with the native tradition, which lacked both statuary and scriptures. Also, the emperor approached Buddhism as a possible means of attaining religious power. At first, the Japanese court was unable to appreciate the profound philosophy of Buddhism; in fact, even the nobility could not read these scriptures (which were Chinese translations of Indian texts). After a brief setback, it became clear that Buddhism was not a threat to the harmony of the native *kami* but was an effective complement to the *kami*. This treatment of Buddhism as a source of power is the manner in which Buddhism often found its place in the religious life of the people.

Reprinted by permission of the publisher from W. G. Aston, translator, *Nihongi: Chronicles of Japan from the Earliest Times to A.D. 697* (London: George Allen & Unwin Ltd., 1956).

Buddhism: Tribute from Korea

Winter, 10th month. King Syong-myong of Pekche (also called King Syong) sent Kwi-si of the Western Division, and the Tal-sol, Nu-ri Sa-chhi-hye, with a present to the Emperor of an image of Shaka Butsu in gold and copper, several flags and umbrellas, and a number of volumes of "Sutras." Separately he presented a memorial in which he lauded the merit of diffusing abroad religious worship, saying:—"This doctrine is amongst all doctrines the most excellent. But it is hard to explain, and hard to comprehend. Even the Duke of Chow and Confucius had not attained to a knowledge of it. This

doctrine can create religious merit and retribution without measure and without bounds, and so lead on to a full appreciation of the highest wisdom. Imagine a man in possession of treasures to his heart's content, so that he might satisfy all his wishes in proportion as he used them. Thus it is with the treasure of this wonderful doctrine. Every prayer is fulfilled and naught is wanting. Moreover, from distant India it has extended hither to the three Han, where there are none who do not receive it with reverence as it is preached to them.

Thy servant, therefore, Myong, King of Pekche, has humbly despatched his retainer, Nu-ri Sa-chhi, to transmit it to the Imperial Country, and to diffuse it abroad throughout the home provinces, so as to fulfil the recorded saying of Buddha: 'My law shall spread to the East.' "

This day the Emperor, having heard to the end, leaped for joy, and gave command to the Envoys, saying:—"Never from former days until now have we had the opportunity of listening to so wonderful a doctrine. We are unable, however, to decide of ourselves." Accordingly he inquired of his Ministers one after another, saying:—"The countenance of this Buddha which has been presented by the Western frontier State is of a severe dignity, such as we have never at all seen before. Ought it to be worshipped or not?" Soga no Oho-omi, Iname no Sukune, addressed the Emperor, saying:— "All the Western frontier lands without exception do it worship. Shall Akitsu Yamato alone refuse to do so?" Okoshi, Mononobe no Oho-muraji, and Kamako, Nakatomi no Muraji, addressed the Emperor jointly, saying:— "Those who have ruled the Empire in this our State have always made it their care to worship in Spring, Summer, Autumn and Winter the 180 Gods of Heaven and Earth, and the Gods of the Land and of Grain. If just at this time we were to worship in their stead foreign Deities, it may be feared that we should incur the wrath of our National Gods."

The Emperor said:—"Let it be given to Iname no Sukune, who has shown his willingness to take it, and, as an experiment, make him worship it."

The Oho-omi knelt down and received it with joy. He enthroned it in his house at Oharida, where he diligently carried out the rites of retirement from the world, and on that score purified his house at Muku-hara and made it a Temple. After this a pestilence was rife in the Land, from which the people died prematurely. As time went on it became worse and worse, and there was no remedy. Okoshi, Mononobe no Ohomuraji, and Kamako, Nakatomi no Muraji, addressed the Emperor jointly, saying:—"It was because thy servants' advice on a former day was not approved that the people are dying thus of disease. If thou dost now retrace thy steps before matters have gone too far, joy will surely be the result! It will be well promptly to fling it away, and diligently to seek happiness in the future."

The Emperor said:—"Let it be done as you advise." Accordingly officials took the image of Buddha and abandoned it to the current of the Canal of Naniha. They also set fire to the Temple, and burnt it so that nothing was

left. Hereupon, there being in the Heavens neither clouds nor wind, a sudden conflagration consumed the Great Hall (of the Palace) .

This year Pekche abandoned Han-syong and Phyong-yang. Silla took advantage of this to make an entrance and to settle in Han-syong. These are the present Silla towns of U-to-pang and Ni-mi-pang [these names of places are unclear].

14th year, Spring, 1st month, 12th day. Pekche sent Kwa-ya Chha-chyu, Tok-sol of the Higher Division, the Han-sol, Nye-se-ton, and others to ask for troops.

15th day. The Pekche Envoys, Mok-hyop-keum-ton, Tok-sol of the Middle Division, and Kahachi Be no Asapita took their departure.

Summer, 5th month, 7th day. The following report was received from the province of Kahachi:—"From within the sea at Chinu, in the district of Idzumi, there is heard a voice of Buddhist chants, which re-echoes like the sound of thunder, and a glory shines like the radiance of the sun." In his heart the Emperor wondered at this, and sent Unate no Atahe [here we have only Atahe, and the personal name is not given, probably owing to the error of some copyist] to go upon the sea and investigate the matter.

This month Unate no Atahe went upon the sea, and the result was that he discovered a log of camphor-wood shining brightly as it floated on the surface. At length he took it, and presented it to the Emperor, who gave orders to an artist to make of it two images of Buddha. These are the radiant camphor-wood images now in the Temple of Yoshino.

7

harmony between the buddhist pantheon and shinto kami

As seen in the previous selection, the entry of Buddhism into Japan was marked by a brief conflict between Buddhas and *kami*, but this gave way to a general sense of harmony between the two groups of divinities. This harmony came to be expressed in terms of the Buddhist notion of incarnation (or reincarnation): the members of the Buddhist pantheon were the concrete manifestation of the hidden *kami*. This theory was very effective in both Shinto shrines and Buddhist temples for reconciling the unseen *kami* with the Buddhist statues. In the experience of the people, there is practically an identity between such Buddhas and *kami*.

One of the chief characteristics of Japanese Buddhism is this close blending with native tradition.

One good example of the Buddhist idea of reincarnation is the case of Prince Shotoku, often regarded as the founding father of Buddhism in Japan. (See the support of Buddhism in the "Constitution" attributed to him, selection 40.) Here Prince Shotoku is treated as the reincarnation of either a Chinese Buddhist priest or of a *bodhisattva* (a kind of Buddhist saint). Although Prince Shotoku is not a *kami* in the official mythology, in Japan a great person is often treated as a *kami* (see selection 31). As time passed, most *kami* were treated as hidden counterparts of Buddhist divinities in the form of statues, and the mutual influence between Shinto and Buddhism was considerable.

Reprinted by permission of the publisher from Alicia Matsunaga, *The Buddhist Philosophy of Assimilation* (Tokyo: Monumenta Nipponica, Sophia University, 1969).

Buddha and Kami

For centuries the Japanese have preserved and protected the priceless treasures they received from the continent at the dawn of their civilization. As early as the eighth century special treasure houses were constructed to house these precious objects and there they have remained intact until the present day. This concern was not merely limited to dead artifacts, but encompassed living skills and arts as well. For instance, the court music of T'ang China once adapted to Japanese tastes, has survived up to modern times while it has been long forgotten on the continent. In such a way Japan became a storehouse of the past, a place where treasures long obliterated in their native lands can be viewed and appreciated.

If we were to select one general classification for the majority of Japan's inherited treasures, it would be Buddhism, since in Japan, as in many other lands, Buddhism served as the vehicle of higher civilization. Buddhist philosophy, technology and art forms found their way from India, Central Asia, China and Korea to Japan where they were not only preserved but also added their influence to the course of Japanese thought.

What is known today as 'Japanese Buddhism' is the unique living product of these diverse origins and their combination with native elements. Any study that attempts to ignore these historical antecedents or explain the essence of Japanese Buddhist thought without giving them due consideration is in effect an attempt to study the branches of a tree while ignoring its life-giving trunk. Many existing works have created considerable confusion about

the nature and historical continuity of Japanese Buddhism with the result that its basic tenets are still very much misunderstood, particularly in the West.

If we were to select a single representative area where the mixed origins of Japanese Buddhism are most obviously evident, then the Buddhist pantheon would provide the best example. Here we can find deities of Indian, Chinese and Central Asian origin venerated beside the indigenous divinities who inhabited Japan prior to the introduction of Buddhism. In examining this phenomenon certain questions naturally arise such as: How was this process of assimilation carried out? Does it have a counterpart in other lands influenced by Buddhism? Is there a *Buddhist* philosophy of assimilation? And finally, does the Japanese form of assimilation markedly differ from that found in other lands?

In Japanese Buddhism we can find two important related terms specifically dealing with the problem of assimilation: the first is *shimbutsu-shugo* (unification of gods and Buddhas) and the second is the *honji-suijaku* (true nature — trace manifestation) theory. The former is a broad term encompassing all efforts to unite the indigenous faith with Buddhism, a process beginning with the inception of Buddhism in Japan and generally dealing with exterior phenomena brought together without systematization. On the other hand, the *honji-suijaku* theory is the culminating philosophy arising out of this initial exterior unificaton and although it can also be classified under the general category of *shimbutsu-shugo,* it represents a systematic Buddhist philosophy of assimilation.

In popular parlance, the *honji-suijaku* theory is described as the philosophy by which the native Japanese gods are believed to be manifestations of Buddhas or bodhisattvas in order to save sentient beings and lead them to Enlightenment. Since the terminology is Japanese and the deities involved appear to be native to Japan, modern Japanese have no hesitation in believing the theory originated in their land. . . .

It is our purpose here to demonstrate how the Japanese theory of *honji-suijaku* is merely an expression of the ancient Buddhist philosophy of assimilation that commenced with the first dawning of Buddhist thought to serve as an essential handmaiden of Buddhist doctrine in every new land the religion entered. In Japan with the rich heritage of Indian and Chinese thought, the philosophy of assimilation was systematized and given practical application, yet the components for this systematization and application were already present in Chinese Buddhism. Finally, even in the applied Japanese theory, which was not so systematical, we find that Indian deities appear both as the *honji* (true nature) as well as the *suijaku* (trace manifestation) of various Buddhas and bodhisattvas. These facts alone make it apparent that the *honji-suijaku* theory is not an isolated phenomenon that can be studied within the framework of Japanese thought or folk beliefs alone.

The practice of absorbing native gods and various other rites into Buddhism began in India. The popularity of the practice is attested by the fact

that many of these Indian elements were exported all the way to China, Korea and Japan. In order to study the Japanese theory of assimilation we must first of all discover what is the *Buddhist* philosophy of assimilation. To do this, we must begin with the tenets of Early Buddhism or the Buddhism practiced in India during the life of the historical Buddha and by his disciples directly after his death. It was in the framework of this early philosophy that the Buddhist theory of assimilation had its origin. . . .

The Elevation of Japanese Buddhist Saints

The earliest forms of what we might term *honji-suijaku* application did not apply to the relationship between the Japanese gods and Buddhist but rather to the relationship between Buddhas proper and the Buddhas or bodhisattvas. We can find the first evidence of such application appearing in the late Nara and early Heian period in regard to Shotoku Taishi.

Immediately after the death of Prince Shotoku in 622 he began to be regarded as a deified legendary figure in popular thought. In view of his own active belief and support of Buddhism, it was natural that a Buddhist effort would be made to elevate him to the position of a saint, and this was best accomplished by considering him to be some form of a Buddha or bodhisattva. Since Prince Shotoku had never belonged to any particular sect of Buddhism, he was in a sense the common property of all. He also was considered as a national heritage, since he had played such an important role in introducing Chinese culture and civilization to Japan.

It is uncertain exactly when Shotoku Taishi first became regarded as the manifestation of a bodhisattva, although we can estimate that it probably occurred at the end of the Nara period. The earliest account of such an incident can be found in the *To-daimajo-toseiden*, which relates the following story that supposedly took place in China:

> The Buddhist monk Ei-ei went to the Daimyoji Temple and saluted the Great Elder [Ganjin], telling him the reason for his visit. He said 'Buddhism came from the East to arrive in Japan and although there was Buddhism, there was no person to teach it Formerly in Japan, Shotoku Taishi lived and said: "After two hundred years the Buddhist doctrine will arise in Japan." Now may you [Ganjin] follow this tradition and go to the East to instruct the people.' So the Great Elder answered, 'I have heard before that after Nangaku Zenji died he would be born as a prince of Japan to make Buddhism flourish and enlighten sentient beings.'

This is one of the earliest correlations between Shotoku Taishi and Nangaku Zenji, second patriarch of the Chinese T'ien T'ai sect. In Ninchu's biography of Saicho, the *Eizandaishiden*, a similar story is related:

> In the Sui Dynasty there lived Shi (Szu) Zenji on Mt. Nangaku. This monk always hoped and said 'after my death I will certainly be born in the East—Japan, to introduce Buddhism.' Later Prince Shotoku was born in Japan . . . All the contemporary people say that Prince Shotoku is the *goshin* of Shi Zenji.

Here Prince Shotoku clearly appears as the 'after-body' (*goshin*) of Nangaku. This theory was set forth by Saicho, founder of the Japanese Tendai sect, and his support of the belief that Shotoku was an after-body of Eshi made the Prince into one of the Tendai saints during the Heian period. After the death of Saicho, his disciples Kojo, Ennin, and Chisho further propagated the belief. This opinion was not merely confined to the Tendai sect, however, for we can find that even Kukai believed it.

From the middle Heian period throughout the Kamakura, the belief in Shotoku Taishi so increased that he was transformed from merely the 'after-body' or manifestation to a *honji*. In this case, his own manifestations became such personages as Emperor Shomu, Kukai, and Rigen Daishi. On the other hand, the *honji* of Shotoku also developed, becoming not only Eshi in China, but also figures such as Dainichi Nyorai (Vairocana) and Kannon (Avalokitesvara). Such belief was further popularized with the compilation of the *Taishi-wasan* and *Taishi-koshiki* of later periods.

This belief in Shotoku Taishi can be considered as one of the first practical applications of the *honji-suijaku* theory in Japan; however, since it was not characteristic of the application of the theory in its early stages to the Japanese gods, it appears that the incident represented predominant Chinese influence. We have already mentioned a similar occurrence in the life of En no Gyoja, so the thought was not uncommon.

The Elevation of the Indigenous Gods

As we have seen in previous chapters, the first endeavors to create harmony between the native cult and Buddhism occurred almost immediately after the inception of the new religion and progressed with its growing popularity. This movement of harmonization falls into the general classification of *shimbutsu-shugo*, a trend representing practical accomplishments rather than any form of purposeful philosophy or systematization. Besides the previously mentioned reasons for the success and development of *shimbutsu-shugo* we can summarize some of the obvious factors as the following:

1 The Japanese indigenous faith as the religion of the Japanese race served the social and regional interests of the people, while Buddhism met the needs of the individual seeking personal spiritual salvation. Thus each belief had different characteristics.

2 Both religions had an interest in magical or mystical ritual.

3 Both were supported by the upper classes. (A factor that at times also became a source of friction when it became a matter of institutionalized vested interests.)

4 The early Shinto prosperity rituals were simple in content, while the Buddhists had an elaborate liturgy which appealed to the aesthetic tastes of the Japanese people. As the indigenous cult developed under the influence of Chinese culture, it was possible to incorporate forms of Buddhist liturgy into the Shinto rituals, particularly those advocating the protection of the nation and the needs of the individuals.

All of these reasons which augmented the growth and development of *shimbutsu-shugo* were sources of motivation leading to the gradual development of the *honji-suijaku* theory, as well as reasons for the Buddhists to take a favorable view of the native deities.

8

a Buôôhist scripture: the lotus sutra

The Christian Bible is small enough to be held in one hand, but the complete Buddhist canon consists of hundreds of volumes containing thousands of separate writings. Some of the Buddhist scriptures are sayings attributed to the historical Buddha, while others arose in China and Japan as commentaries on earlier writings. (Even in contemporary Japan, Buddhist scriptures are preserved mainly in Chinese translations.) Perhaps the single most important Buddhist scripture in the spread of Buddhism from northern India across China to Japan is the Lotus Sutra. Although the man in the street does not read the Chinese version of this scripture, he is probably familiar with its basic teachings.

The Lotus Sutra expresses several basic themes of Mahayana, the form of Buddhism which found greatest acceptance in China and Japan. Mahayana (the Great Vehicle) criticized earlier Buddhism as being too exclusive in limiting *nirvana* (enlightenment or salvation) to monks; Mahayana therefore used the disparaging term Hinayana (Small Vehicle) to describe an inferior form of Buddhism. Mahayana Buddhism emphasizes that everyone can attain enlightenment or "become Buddhas"; the Lotus Sutra teaches laymen the simple techniques which guarantee salvation.

According to tradition, after the historical Buddha had died, he once more appeared on earth to reveal the true meaning of his teaching. Here the Buddha is referred to as the Lord or Tathagata. From the top of a mountain he taught Shariputra (or Sariputra) and other disciples the message of Mahayana, which is also called the Supreme Way and One-Vehicle. The gist of this message is that even the lowliest person, by virtue of even the humblest act of devotion, is eventually able to achieve salvation and rank with the Buddhas themselves. The Buddha says that to follow his teaching (or "Law"), acts of devotion such as offering incense

and flowers are more important than intellectual reasoning. This enfolding compassion for the common person helped make the Lotus Sutra a religious classic for all people. Anyone could draw on the power of this scripture simply by reciting a phrase of praise to the title of the scripture (Namu Myoho Rengekyo). The Lotus Sutra is the chief scripture for the Tendai and Nichiren sects (including the modern Soka Gakkai), but it has been revered by most Japanese people, whether or not they were affiliated with these sects.

Reprinted by permission of the publisher from H. Kern, translator, *Saddharma-Pundarika or The Lotus of the True Law* (Oxford: Clarendon Press, 1884).

Enlightenment Is Possible for All People

Thereupon the Lord addressed the venerable Sariputra: . . .

It is but now and then, Sariputra, that the Tathagata preaches such a discourse on the law as this. Just as but now and then is seen the blossom of the glomerous fig-tree, Sariputra, so does the Tathagata but now and then preach such a discourse on the law. Believe me, Sariputra; I speak what is real, I speak what is truthful, I speak what is right. It is difficult to understand the exposition of the mystery of the Tathagata, Sariputra; for in elucidating the law, Sariputra, I use hundred thousands of various skilful means, such as different interpretations, indications, explanations, illustrations. It is not by reasoning, Sariputra, that the law is to be found: it is beyond the pale of reasoning, and must be learnt from the Tathagata. For, Sariputra, it is for a sole object, a sole aim, verily a lofty object, a lofty aim that the Buddha, the Tathagata, &c., appears in the world. And what is that sole object, that sole aim, that lofty object, that lofty aim of the Buddha, the Tathagata, &c., appearing in the world? To show all creatures the sight of Tathagata-knowledge does the Buddha, the Tathagata, &c., appear in the world; to open the eyes of creatures for the sight of Tathagata-knowledge does the Buddha, the Tathagata, &c., appear in the world. This, O Sariputra, is the sole object, the sole aim, the sole purpose of his appearance in the world. . . . By means of one sole vehicle, to wit, the Buddha-vehicle, Sariputra, do I teach creatures the law; there is no second vehicle, nor a third. This is the nature of the law, Sariputra, universally in the world, in all directions. For, Sariputra, all the Tathagatas, &c., who in times past existed in countless, innumerable spheres in all directions for the weal of many, the happiness of many, out of pity to the world, for the benefit, weal, and happiness of the great body of creatures, and who preached the law to gods and men with able means,

such as several directions and indications, various arguments, reasons, illustrations, fundamental ideas, interpretations, paying regard to the dispositions of creatures whose inclinations and temperaments are so manifold, all those Buddhas and Lords, Sariputra, have preached the law to creatures by means of only one vehicle, the Buddha-vehicle, which finally leads to omniscience; it is identical with showing all creatures the sight of Tathagata-knowledge . . . .

The Lord proceeded: Well, Bhaishagyaraga, all those Bodhisattvas Mahasattvas who in this assembly have heard, were it but a single stanza, a single verse (or word), or who even by a single rising thought have joyfully accepted this Sutra, to all of them, Bhaishagyaraga, among the four classes of my audience I predict their destiny to supreme and perfect enlightenment. And all whosoever, Bhaishagyaraga, who, after the complete extinction of the Tathagata, shall hear this Dharmaparyaya[1] and after hearing, were it but a single stanza, joyfully accept it, even with single rising thought, to those also, Bhaishagyaraga, be they young men or young ladies of good family, I predict their destiny to supreme and perfect enlightenment. . . .

Should some man or woman, Bhaishagyaraga, happen to ask: How now have those creatures to be who in future are to become Tathagatas, Arhats, &c.? then that man or woman should be referred to the example of that young man or young lady of good family. 'Whoever is able to keep, recite, or teach, were it but a single stanza of four lines, and whoever shows respect for this Dharmaparyaya, that young man or young lady of good family shall in future become a Tathagata, &c.; be persuaded of it.' For, Bhaishagyaraga, such a young man or young lady of good family must be considered to be a Tathagata, and by the whole world, including the gods, honour should be done to such a Tathagata who keeps were it but a single stanza of this Dharmaparyaya, and far more, of course, to one who grasps, keeps, comprehends, makes known, copies, and after copying always retains in his memory this Dharmaparyaya entirely and completely, and who honours that book with flowers, incense, perfumed garlands, ointment, powder, clothes, umbrellas, flags, banners, music, joined hands, reverential bows and salutations. Such a young man or young lady of good family, Bhaishagyaraga, must be held to be accomplished in supreme and perfect enlightenment . . . .

Again, Bhaishagyaraga, on any spot of the earth where this Dharmaparyaya is expounded, preached, written, studied, or recited in chorus, on that spot, Bhaishagyaraga, one should build a Tathagata-shrine, magnificent, consisting of precious substances, high, and spacious; but it is not necessary to depose in it relics of the Tathagata. For the body of the Tathagata is, so to say, collectively deposited there. Any spot of the earth where this Dharmaparyaya is expounded or taught or recited or rehearsed in chorus or written or kept in a volume, must be honoured, respected, revered, worshipped as if it were a Stupa, with all sorts of flowers, incense, perfumes, garlands, oint-

[1]Dharmaparyaya, the teachings of the Buddha. [ed.]

ment, powder, clothes, umbrellas, flags, banners, triumphal streamers, with all kinds of song, music, dancing, musical instruments, castanets, and shouts in chorus. And those, Bhaishagyaraga, who approach a Tathagata-shrine to salute or see it, must be held to be near supreme and perfect enlightenment. For, Bhaishagyaraga, there are many laymen as well as priests who observe the course of a Bodhisattva without, however, coming so far as to see, hear, write or worship this Dharmaparyaya. So long as they do not hear this Dharmaparyaya, they are not yet proficient in the course of a Bodhisattva. But those who hear this Dharmaparyaya and thereupon accept, penetrate, understand, comprehend it, are at the time near supreme, perfect enlightenment, so to say, immediately near it.

9

the Glory of Buddhist art

As seen in selection 6, the official entrance of Buddhism into Japan was marked in part by the tribute of statues of the Buddha. Indeed, art was one of the first attractions which this foreign religion held for the Japanese people, and it has proved to be one of the lasting contributions to Japanese culture. The entrance of Buddhism, along with the refinements of Chinese culture, meant not only priests to read Buddhist scriptures (in Chinese) but also artists to produce religious art and artisans to build and furnish temples. To understand the impact of Buddhist art on Japan, we must remember that at the time Buddhism entered Japan, there were no real statues and very little religious art in Japan.

The treasury of Buddhist art in Japan is so rich and its symbolism so complex that a brief treatment can only begin to tell the story. The present selection describes several examples of architecture and statues from the seventh century temple grounds known as Horyu-ji (such large Buddhist establishments usually included a number of different buildings). The pagoda features abundant symbolism, with each structural part contributing to the meaning of a representation of the universe.

Both the architecture and statues of Japanese Buddhism were influenced by other traditions, particularly Indian and Chinese. Buddhist statues in Japan range in style from the grotesquely menacing (the same as found in Tibet) to the calm tranquility more usually associated with the Buddha. The present selection describes a very early set of three statues, the Buddha in the middle flanked by two *bodhisattvas,* all of

which emphasize serenity and compassion. It is important for the scholar to recognize the various historical influences and specific symbolism in the statues, but even the Japanese layman and the sympathetic Westerner can appreciate the artistic grace and religious peace in these statues.

Reprinted from *The Arts of Japan: An Illustrated History,* by Hugo Munsterberg, with permission of the publisher, Charles E. Tuttle Co., Inc.

Buddhist Temples and Statues

Next to the Kondo the most characteristic structure of the temple complex is the pagoda, which the Japanese call *gojunoto,* or five-storied tower (figure 2). This typical Buddhist structure, whose purpose was to contain a sacred relic of a Buddhist saint, was originally derived from the Indian stupa, or relic mount. However, since in China it was modified by the form of the ancient Chinese watchtower, it bears little resemblance today to the Indian monument which inspired it. The Horyu-ji pagoda has five stories, which is a common number in Japan, although three-story pagodas like that at nearby Hokki-ji, the other authentic Asuka building, also occur, as well as seven-story pagodas and in later periods even thirteen-story pagodas. The most authentic are no doubt the seven-story ones, since the pagoda represents the magic Mt. Meru, which itself has seven stories. In Japan, however, five was considered a more auspicious number because it represents the five directions, that is, the four conventional ones plus the center. Another interpretation given in Japan is that the five stories symbolize the five elements, earth, water, fire, wind, and sky. The pagoda has no real function — in fact there is usually no room inside nor are the balconies on the various floors meant to be used. It is looked upon as a symbolical representation of the universe, with the square platform on which it rests symbolizing the earth and the central pillar which runs through the entire structure symbolizing the world axis which unites heaven and earth. It is crowned by a square shape with an inverted bowl on top representing the palace of the gods and by nine umbrellas, one set above the other, symbolizing the kingship of the Buddhas as the ruler of the universe. It terminates in a finial in the shape of a flaming jewel symbolizing the precious jewel of the Buddhist truth, which shines above everything. The original meaning of the flames has been lost; in Japan, where they are called *suien,* or spray, it is believed that they protect the building against fire. The pagoda as a whole symbolizes the supremacy of the Buddha and the Buddhist law which towers above the earth and its inhabitants, so it might be said that its function is similar to that of the spire in the Christian church. . . .

Buddhist images reached Japan with the very first missionaries who came from Korea, for they played a central part in the religious rites of the Buddhist church. At first the Buddhist community had to rely upon foreign importations, and even those statues actually made in Japan were largely the work of Chinese and Korean craftsmen. The earliest dated native Buddhist image is the great Buddha of Asuka. . . . Far better preserved is the Yakushi Buddha image at Horyu-ji, which is dated 607 and according to its inscription was made by order of Shotoku Taishi following the wishes of his father. Originally it served as the main icon of this famous temple. It is believed to be the work of the Tori school, since it is very close in style to the famous "Shaka Trinity," which is now the central image on the altar of the Kondo. Since it has an inscription indicating that it was made in 623 and is the work of Tori Bushi, the grandson of a Chinese immigrant,

Figure 2. The *gojunoto* (five-storied tower) or pagoda within the temple complex of Horyu-ji, near Nara. Reprinted from *The Arts of Japan: An Illustrated History*, by Hugo Munsterberg, with permission of the publisher, Charles E. Tuttle Co., Inc.

it is of particular interest both from a historical as well as an artistic point of view (figure 3). This celebrated image, although made in Japan, shows how close the Japanese sculpture of this period was to its Korean and Chinese prototypes, for both in iconography and style it reflects the sculpture of China of the Six Dynasties. In the center is the figure of the seated Buddha Shaka, the savior of Buddhism, and at his sides are two standing *bosatsu*, or Buddhist saints. Behind him is a large flaming *mandorla* with a halo in the form of a lotus and small images of the seven Buddhas of the Past who preceded the historical Buddha. The representation of Shaka is characteristic of the type found in China about a century earlier. It shows the Buddha seated with crossed legs (the yogi position associated with meditation), and wearing a monk's garment, a symbol of the fact that Gautama renounced the world and became a monk. His face is serene, mirroring his inner harmony, and a smile plays over his lips, showing the spiritual joy of one who, having achieved enlightenment, is no longer troubled by the cares and sorrows of this world. On his forehead is a dot called *urna*, a third eye indicating that the Blessed One sees all, just as his large ears indicate that he hears all, and the *ushnisha*, or raised protuberance on his head, indicates that he knows all. His hair is short, for when he became a monk he cut off his flowing locks which he had worn as a royal prince. He raises one hand in the *abhaya* mudra, a gesture telling the faithful that they should have no fear, while the other hand is held with palm up, the so-called *vara* mudra, or gesture of charity. He is seated upon a lotus, which in ancient Indian cosmology was a symbol of the earth, the center of which represents the Himalayas, while the petals stand for the four great countries of Asia, namely India, China, Central Asia, and Iran. Thus the lotus throne symbolizes the fact that the Buddha is regarded as the ruler of the entire world. The halo behind him and the flaming *mandorla* are ancient solar symbols probably indicating that originally the Buddha was a solar deity, but later merely a sign of sanctity like the halo in the Christian art of the West. The smaller Buddhas of the Past indicate that Shaka is only one in the long line of Buddhas which have preceded him and which follow him at some future date. His two attendants are represented in a smaller size, showing their lesser importance, just as their standing position indicates their lower status. In contrast to the central figure, they are not Buddhas, that is, beings who have achieved enlightenment, but bodhisattvas, or *bosatsu*, saintly figures who have renounced their chance at Buddhahood so that they might help save suffering mankind. In keeping with this they are shown in the garments of an Indian prince with crown, jewels, and elaborate scarfs, since Buddha, prior to his enlightenment, was an Indian prince who supposedly dressed in this manner. In their hands they hold precious jewels symbolizing the jewel of the lotus, or the spiritual riches which Buddhism gives to the faithful, the same symbol which is also found on the upper part of the central halo. The faces of the *bosatsu* have the same serenity as the Buddha, a look which reflects their inner peace. They stand on lotus pedestals, which are a sign of purity, for as the lotus grows in the mud

Figure 3. The Shaka Trinity (or Tori Bushi Trinity) in the Kondo, within the temple complex of Horyu-ji, near Nara. Reprinted from *The Arts of Japan: An Illustrated History*, by Hugo Munsterberg, with permission of the publisher, Charles E. Tuttle Co., Inc.

at the bottom of the lake but remains pure and beautiful, so the Buddha walked through the corruption and filth of this world but remained pure and holy. It may be seen from these brief comments how every detail of the iconography is deeply meaningful in terms of Buddhist faith, and is not the whim of the particular artist who happened to make the image. In fact the artist at this time was considered little more than a humble craftsman working for the glory of the Buddha and his church rather than as a creative person in his own right.

In keeping with the transcendental and spiritual nature of the image, the style is very abstract, for it would not seem proper to represent these other-worldly beings in a naturalistic manner suited only for creatures of this world. In order to achieve this effect the artist has flattened out the figure, placing more emphasis upon the abstract design than the plastic form, and he has created a feeling of tension by stressing the linear movement within the composition. Wherever the eye turns, be it to the hanging drapery in the center, the scarfs of the attendants, the lotus designs, or the flames of the *mandorla*, there are dynamic, moving lines, which bring out a wonderful feeling of inner tension balanced by the serenity of the facial expressions. Here again, as in the treatment of the iconography, the artist simply reflects the style of the Chinese models which inspired him and, although no such large bronze Buddhist images of this date have been discovered in China, there can be no doubt that they existed and that it was this type of image which was brought to Japan during the middle of the sixth century.

10

the Buddhist temple as a center of devotion

Buddhist temples differ from the American church or synagogue, which serves as the meeting place for a congregation at weekly services. Local parish temples usually house the ashes of family ancestors and provide funeral and memorial services for parish families. The parish as a whole will participate in several annual festivals, the precise character of which varies with the denomination and the Buddhist divinity enshrined in the local temple.

The present selection describes a more individual function of the Buddhist temple—as a center of devotion. The account is fictional, taken

from the novel *The Buddha Tree* (the author Niwa was himself a priest before taking up literature). This novel treats the problem of love and desire within the confines of a Buddhist temple (Butsuoji) of a Pure Land sect. Soshu is the chief priest of the temple, devout in his religion and suffering from the remorse of an immoral relationship with his mother-in-law, Mineyo, who is less conscientious than he is. The excerpts portray three episodes from the novel.

The first extract depicts an interesting contrast between Soshu and Mineyo in their simultaneous performance of morning prayers in the temple's main altar and in the family altar. Soshu is even more convicted of his sin by the penetrating presence of Saint Shinran (founder of a Pure Land Sect) and Amida (the major focus of worship and faith in Pure Land Buddhism), whereas Mineyo naively feels self-righteous in her punctual repetitions—without realizing the meaning of the words—of the prayer for repentance. (Shoju is an older priest assisting Soshu.)

The second extract is an evening conversation in the temple between Soshu and Tachi, a parish member who is also a union leader and staunch communist. Soshu does not try to counter Tachi's arguments for materialism; this is not necessary because Tachi finally explains how the pursuit of materialism led to his conversion once more to Buddhist faith. Soshu is impressed with Tachi's rational argument, and Tachi is equally impressed with Soshu's honesty about his uncertainty concerning salvation.

The third extract finds Soshu once more in the evening prayers, but this time in preparation for an evening service in which Soshu vows to confess his sins to his own parish. In this crisis of courage, Soshu recites the *nenbutsu* (or *nembutsu*), the prayer of sinners seeking compassionate help from Amida. This prayer might be simply mechanical repetition, but with Soshu it is a complete emptying of the heart and an earnest petition for the aid of Amida. All three of these episodes are fictional, but the content of devotion is not. In fact, the artistic context renders dramatically the dynamics of Buddhist devotion.

Reprinted by permission of the publisher from *The Buddha Tree*, by Fumio Niwa, published by Peter Owen, London.

Devotion to Amida and Repentance

Up to this point in the novel we have learned of Soshu's affair with his mother-in-law, and his increasingly heightened sense of repentance, which he expresses in his daily temple devotions to Shinran and Amida. On the other hand, Mineyo feels no repentance about her immoral affair and therefore performs her devotions mechanically. It was the custom

for the temple priest to recite the daily prayers before the temple altar
at the same time that the senior woman of the priestly family (Mineyo
in the absense of Soshu's wife) recited prayers before the smaller family
altar in the residential section of the temple. In this episode the setting
for Soshu is the temple altar, for Mineyo, the family altar; the time is
the same for both settings.

The gilded pillars flickered with the reflected light of row after row of
candles. From behind a thin line of incense-smoke St. Shinran looked Soshu
calmly in the face; from above, the bronze Kamakura-style Amida, blackened
by the smoke of incense, gazed down at him with its glittering, all-seeing eyes,
demanding insistently to know what had made his wife desert him and abandon their child. . . . From those eyes there was no escape; their light pierced
into the obscurest regions of Soshu's heart. Shoju was aware this morning of
an intense sincerity in his superior's prayers, a heart-felt quality which they
usually lacked. The sutra readings which Soshu and Shoju used at these brief
morning and evening services were simple and straightforward; they did not
include any gathas, for instance. These gathas, which appear in the Chinese
translations of the sutras, are rhymed songs or poems, with from four to seven
words in each line. Their function is to tell a congregation which sutra it is
that is being read. At Butsuoji, it was the custom to use only the Amida Sutra.
The old priest struck the great gong before him as Soshu intoned the ancient
text.

In the house, as the two men were beginning morning prayers in the
temple, Mineyo took their place at the family shrine. The dark, twelve-mat
room containing the shrine was sometimes called the 'altar-room'; the altar
itself, normally hidden behind the doors of the closet where it was kept, was
about six feet wide, a perfect replica on a smaller scale of the great altar in
the temple. Mineyo arranged the rice offerings on their little tables — which
looked like a child's toy meal set — lit the hanging oil-lamp with a candle, and
burnt some incense.

Sitting on the floor in front of the altar, Mineyo began to read the Shoshinge. The book was torn and curled at the corners from long years of use.
Mineyo read fast. It had never occurred to her to ask what the words on the
page meant, nor did she know that the Shoshin-nenbutsu-ge scripture, to give
it its full name, had been written by Shinran himself as the conclusion of the
section on 'Conduct' in his book, *Doctrine, Works, Faith and Attainment*.
For Mineyo, the morning and evening offerings and scripture reading were
merely a duty that had to be fulfilled as part of the inevitable routine of life
in a temple. After thirty years of daily reading, she practically knew the
Shoshinge by heart.

Let the sinner with his burden call upon Amida: it is all that is needful.
For He will save me, even me, with His loving mercy; though my eyes are dark-

ened by lust so that I can no more behold Him, yet with love unwearying He will lighten my way for ever.

The words were to be intoned: Mineyo did not understand what they meant. In thirty years she had never dreamt of trying to apply them to herself. It was enough if she could finish each morning's duty in good time. The fact that she had never once missed a morning seemed to her proof of the depth of her faith; and being convinced of her own saintliness, she convinced others of it too. . . .

As the story unfolds Soshu is driven almost to despair in his attempt to withdraw from the passionate entanglement with his mother-in-law. For the first time he really questions whether faith in Amida will deliver man from his selfish desires and ambitions. At this point enters Tachi, a professed communist, who comes to the Buddhist priest Soshu for assurance that salvation is available to men through Amida. But as the discussion continues, it is Soshu who asks Tachi if salvation is possible.

The *Doctrine, Works, Faith and Attainment* contains the whole of Shinran's thought. Tachi had borrowed an annotated edition of the volumes on Doctrine and Works; no doubt he wanted to go on now to the volume dealing with Paradise and Incarnation. A priest or specialist in religion would read the books as a matter of course, but for a layman it was another matter, and Tachi's interest in the work was the measure of how different he was from the ordinary Buddhist. Soshu had long felt inferior to Tachi, and never more so than now; he had begun to be afraid of him. In a mind so convinced of materialism as Tachi's, how could there be any room for spiritual ideas like those of Buddhism? Shinran had never depended on the abstract ideas of Buddhist philosophy. All through his life he believed man was made to call on Buddha and awaken to Him. By this single act of awakening to Buddha, a man would know the meaning of his life, and where and when he would die. Soshu remembered a verse from the Shozomatsu-wasan: 'Even those who cannot read may have true faith; but every word of him who boasts of his learning is vain.' Shinran had not offered an intellectual explanation of human destiny; instead, he had penetrated to the ultimate source of life itself, and had been overwhelmed with awe at the majesty of what he found there. That the Buddha-Vow should dwell in men who were yet in bondage to the flesh — he wept in gratitude for such boundless mercy, so far beyond all human understanding. Knowing himself to be no saint but an ordinary sinful man, he had experienced in his own person the saving compassion of Amida, and with deep thankfulness had accepted the Vow, sinner as he was. This was a natural stage in all our lives, he believed. 'When a man feels in his heart a desire to call upon the name of Buddha,' this is the first motion in him of the divine mercy. All men have within them both a Buddha-nature, and

that which is its enemy — the arrogant human intellect. When in times of danger we call on the name of Buddha, what makes us utter that involuntary cry, Shinran believed, is none other than the grace of Amida working within us. At such a time we have only to repeat that call, in simple faith; all questioning, all reasoning is vain.

Soshu wanted to find out how much of this teaching Tachi could understand and accept. In the meantime, he could not rid himself of the feeling that Tachi and himself were on opposite sides....

... Tachi began to fill a pipe. 'I was brought up in a religious atmosphere all right. Both my parents were very pious and strict. I had to learn by heart the *Monrui*, the *Shoshinge* and the Pure Land hymns; but it was only parroting what they taught me — there was never any question of thinking for myself about what the scriptures meant, or applying them to my own life. I was copying what mother and father did, that's all. I always had a vague feeling of awe, though, in front of the shrine at home, ever since I was small. Then when I grew up and had to go to work in the porcelain factory because we were so poor, I forgot all about Buddhism and didn't give a thought to it for years. A passion for social science took hold of me then.'

Soshu merely nodded, not wanting to interrupt.

'You know what I mean by "social science", no doubt.' Tachi had spent several short periods in prison, Soshu remembered.

'Marxism still rejects religion, you see, even if churches have now been recognised in the Soviet Union. When I was in prison, though — it's the way these things happen, I suppose — I found myself beginning to believe that there really might be such a thing as religious truth. I never told my wife about this; but when I came out she soon noticed how interested I was in the shrine all of a sudden. She certainly was surprised, and then relieved, I think, to see me so religious for a change.' The faint ironic smile with which he spoke these last words gave way suddenly to a look of intense concentration. He turned his face away from Soshu. 'Marx says in his critique of Hegel, "Religious misery is in one mouth the expression of real misery, and in another is a protest against real misery. Religion is the moan of the oppressed creature, the sentiment of a heartless world, as it is the spirit of spiritless conditions. It is the opium of the people. The abolition of religion, as the illusory happiness of the people, is the demand for their real happiness. The demand to abandon the illusions about their condition is a demand to abandon a condition which requires illusions. The criticism of religion therefore contains potentially the criticism of the Vale of Tears whose aureole is religion." There was a time when I believed every word of it.'...

'Gods, Buddha-spirits, and what have you — they're all the same, products of human consciousness.' Such directness shocked Soshu, but he let Tachi continue. 'Man made the gods in his own image. That's why they look like men and have so many human qualities,' he went on, looking almost angry. 'All that about God creating the world and everything in it — it's mythical

nonsense, as far as I'm concerned, and I don't believe a word of it.'

Soshu managed a smile.

'That's an elementary question. I know — not the sort of thing I should trouble you with, Father. But we shan't get anywhere if I don't make my position clear at the start.' Tachi smiled slightly, too — though the subject was hardly anything to smile about, nor did he consciously intend any irony. 'Man made the gods in his own image — not the other way about,' he repeated.

'It's natural, I suppose, for a Communist to want to reject anything that smacks of the irrational, or "mystical nonsense," as you call it.'

'I'm a hundred per cent materialist still — I believe emotion and consciousness and spirit are products of matter, and matter alone.'

'But what about the "religious truth" you were talking of a moment ago?'

'It's the product of consciousness,' Tachi said with finality, as if he were knocking religion down like a ninepin, 'and consciousness is simply the functioning of matter in the form of the human body.'

'And what's the connection between this religious truth and the social doctrines you believe in?'

'None — none whatever.'

'Then what about "Man shall not live by bread alone" and the high ideal of man that that implies?'

'When I talk of religious truth, what's happening is that I'm being conscious of my consciousness — making my mind take a look at itself, if you like. Forget about Shinran for a moment — it's all very well for people who already have faith to start right away on him and his teaching, but for unbelievers, if you don't begin by getting clear what religious truth is all about, none of his doctrines will mean a thing, no matter how profound and wonderful they may be.'

'I quite agree — go on.'

Tachi paused for a moment to order the thoughts that kept flooding into his mind. He had stopped smoking.

'There's no telling how far human knowledge is going. We've got the hydrogen bomb, and even space travel is within reach now. All this is just consciousness developed to a very high level. As science has advanced, so knowledge has covered more fields and got more and more exact; which means that we are in a position to deal more and more effectively with our environment — with the whole external world, that is. But religious truth has nothing to do with this outer world — so it isn't of the slightest use.'

Soshu listened intently.

'Religious truth is concerned only with our consciousness, not with our knowledge of the external world. A being capable of consciousness is conscious of himself — consciousness becoming self-conscious, you might call it — and that's where religious truth begins to operate.'

'If religious truth has to do with the self-consciousness of consciousness, as I think it does, it obviously depends on consciousness working in a very

special way, and can't be measured by the ordinary workings of the mind, because it's outside them altogether. That's the most fundamental thing about it. When we start thinking about prayer to God or Buddha with our ordinary mental processes, we get tied up in doubts and inconsistencies. Even talk about doing away with idols and images is absurd when you come to think of it — images make it possible for consciousness to operate *inwardly* in the way I spoke of, and to use the processes of ordinary consciousness to condemn them or do away with them is to destroy the basis of religion. . . . I don't have any use for these "new religions," and the material benefits some of them make such a noise about. They don't know what religion is. Religious truth and scientific truth are quite different — they deal with different worlds, religion with the inner world and science with the outer. People say, what about psychology then, but psychology treats the mind as science treats an object — the method is the same. The mind it talks about is not the mind alive, any more than the reflection of an eye in a mirror is the real eye itself. It's a mind objectified, solidified — dead.'

'Shinran says in the Ichimaikishomon, "A man shall cast aside learning, and all show of wisdom, and become as the nuns that have entered the Way," ' recited Soshu, half to himself. 'And again in the Yuishinsho, "He who longs for the Pure Land must no longer strive to seem wise or virtuous; let him harbour no secret thoughts, and make no show of pity." He was saying the same thing as you, I think — that religious experience can't even begin to be assessed by ordinary mental processes.'

'I don't think he meant that a man with a brilliant intellect couldn't be saved. He was simply warning us not to think of spiritual things in physical terms. The first thing is to realise that as far as insight into religious truth is concerned, ordinary knowledge and ordinary intellectual processes are not of the slightest use.'

'Ordinary knowledge' meant the reflection of external phenomena in the mind, phenomena being the object and mind the subject; relativity as between subject and object was an inevitable condition of such knowledge. Religious knowledge could only be reached by the mind contemplating itself, a form of activity transcending the subject-object opposition. Tachi held religious truth arrived at in this way to be absolute and unconditional. . . .

Soshu remembered a verse from the Jinen Honi: 'It is not the will or choice of the seeker, but the holy power of Amida, that causes us to have faith in the prayer with which we call upon His Name, and seeks to turn us to Himself. This working of His mercy, I have learned, is called Jinen. The meaning of the Vow is that Amida has promised to lead us to supreme Bud-dhahood. This final Buddha-hood or Nirvana is Being with form; and that is why it is called Jinen. When we describe it as having form, then it is no longer the supreme state that we are speaking of. It was Amida, I have heard, who first taught us that Nirvana is without form. . . .'

Paradise is described in the vaguest terms, such as 'the land which is real and yet not real,' which 'exists and yet does not exist,' and so on. What was

important is not whether or not it existed, thought Soshu, but whether one could or could not reach it. Where true faith was, there was Paradise already; where faith was lacking, Paradise could never be. The question was, did one believe in Paradise or not? Paradise, it was said, was in the peace that comes from faith in Buddha and in the calling on his name. It was invisible to the eye of reason, but could be known, the preachers said, by an instinct that lay hidden behind man's faculty of reasoning. If one asked who first became consciously aware of this instinct, the answer the preachers gave was — Amida; and it was through his Original Vow that all men learn of its presence in themselves. Such was the teaching; but nowadays people responded more readily to a rational explanation such as Tachi's.

'This is really where my problem begins,' said Tachi with a smile, relaxed again now. 'I've worked for the Union all these years, and can't remember ever having done anything I'd want to apologize for, as far as the Union's concerned anyway. When it comes to really personal problems, though, what you might call the spiritual side of me, I suppose — it's another story, and not a pleasant one. I've never liked to play second fiddle — always wanted to be at the top; and if I'm Chairman of the Union, it's not just pure disinterested zeal, but conceit, too. I'm twice as conceited as the next man, and more. I managed to hide it from other people, somehow, but a man can't fool himself. There was a time when I talked a lot about a life of unselfish service. It was only talk — self-deception, as I soon found out. Prison taught me something, and I'm grateful.'

'By "something," do you mean spiritual peace, or salvation?'

'Yes. At first I thought I'd go mad when they locked me up, from the loneliness. The *nenbutsu* was almost part of me, of course, I'd been so used to hearing and repeating it since I was a baby; but I never had any real faith. Then it happened, in prison. Suddenly, without thinking, I found myself repeating 'Namu Amida Butsu' . . . In that moment I knew I had a Buddha-nature. It was Mind becoming conscious of itself—'

'Tell me, do you think salvation is really possible?'

'I wanted to ask *you* that question, Father.'

'But I don't know . . . I don't know . . .' As he spoke the words, Soshu seemed to hear a drumming in his ears, as of lust and greed and all sin transmuted into sound — the cry of a wounded beast on a moor. . . . He would hear it forever . . . now it was the dull roaring of the sea, a sea of evil in which he was condemned to drown, beyond all forgiveness.

'What assurance can there be of salvation . . .' His voice was sad.

Tachi's expression showed that he was moved. 'You are honest, Father . . .' he said.

'I know all we have to do is to forget self and trust Him for everything — but I — I've a long way to go yet before I get that far . . . I haven't thought deeply enough about Shinran's teaching.'

Mineyo and the maid must have gone to bed while they were talking. Silence filled the house. . . .

The novel reaches a climax as Soshu's repentance forces him to consider confessing his immoral love affair before his assembled parish. Mineyo threatens him not to take this radical step, and Soshu is sustained only by his faith in Amida. The prayer 'Namu Amida Butsu' is the watchword of Pure Land Buddhism, whereby the believer acknowledges his helplessness and places absolute trust in the mercy of Amida. In this brief excerpt Soshu is once more before the temple altar, steeling himself for his meeting with the parishioners. The outcome of this personal dilemma is not divulged here, so as not to spoil the novel for those who wish to read it themselves.

Candles were already burning in the sanctuary. After pausing in the recess to bow before the portraits of the Seven Patriarchs of the Pure Land Sect, Soshu passed on to the sanctuary, where the old priest was already sitting, his head bent low over the sutra-table. According to custom, he first lit a stick of incense and stood with clasped hands in front of the statue of Amida, then turned to repeat the same act of reverence before the portrait of Shinran. Memories of his long priesthood at Butsuoji came crowding in heavily upon his mind, jostling the unspoken prayers.

Finally he sat down facing the statue, clasped his hands once more, and began to murmur the *nenbutsu*. The old priest joined in, but in a louder, more urgent tone, as though with the words he were expelling some tangible inner impurity. . . .

Then he stopped. Shoju followed suit instantly, so that their two voices died away in unison on the last syllable of the prayer. 'Namu Amida Butsu-u- u . . .' The old priest struck the sutra-bell as Soshu raised the book of scripture to his forehead in the gesture of devotion to the Holy Law — and caught his breath, for Soshu was still murmuring *nenbutsu* . . . oblivious of the sutra-book in his hand, of the bell, of the service he was there to conduct, he was repeating still the prayer of St. Honen and St. Shinran. 'Namu Amida Butsu. . . Namu Amida Butsu. . . Namu Amida Butsu. . .' The old priest was sitting at right angles to Soshu, not two yards away. In the younger man's face he could read the desperate intensity of his absorption in the words of the prayer; and was filled with a feverish, constricting sorrow, for he had glimpsed the conflict within. Knowing nothing of what was in Soshu's mind, sensing only the agony the struggle was costing him, he wondered what he could be going to propose to the meeting that night. During the day there had been no sign of anything unusual. But now the old man shivered; without looking, he knew that Soshu was weeping, no longer aware of his presence. Father Soshu weeping . . . he remembered how strained his face had looked recently. . . .

There had been other things: the hurried settling of odds and ends of temple business, the handing over to Shoju of the parishioner's death register.

And he was murmuring *nenbutsu* still, his head bent over clasped hands. . . . The old man wished he could have slipped away from the sanctuary and left him to his solitude.

Behind his praying lips Mineyo's words were echoing in Soshu's mind, taunting him with his weakness: 'if you did confess, I'd leave you, I promise — you'd have gone too far away from me then. *But it won't happen — you know it won't. . .'* Abruptly, the stream of murmured *nenbutsu* stopped. It was time, then, for the service? Soshu turned to look at the old priest; he was sitting with bowed head and closed eyes, no longer praying, but quietly waiting for Soshu to begin.

11

Buddhist Ritual: the Funeral Ceremony

Buddhism includes many rituals, but none is so crucial to the religious life of the people as the funeral and memorial rites, which constitute the single most important religious function of Buddhist priests and temples. The present selection relates briefly the historical circumstances by which every family was linked to a parish Buddhist temple and then describes the events surrounding a traditional funeral ceremony. Many of the traditional customs associated with funerals have changed since this description was published in 1891.

Practical matters were taken care of by the *kogumi,* a voluntary association for mutual aid. Religious beliefs concerning death enter from several traditions, such as folk religion and religious Taoism, but the funeral ceremony itself is Buddhist. The purpose of the ceremony is to enable the dead person to pass from the defiled state of death to a purified state in paradise. Philosophically and doctrinally, salvation is seen in terms of *nirvana,* but in ordinary religious experience the dead person is seen as entering paradise. In fact, a common term for a dead person is *hotoke,* the Japanese word for "a Buddha."

Means for attaining these ends are acted out by the Buddhist priest: granting a Buddhist name to the deceased, inscribing an *ihai* (memorial tablet) with this name, reciting sutras for the benefit of the deceased, and also cremating the body. The symbolism of cremation is a destruction of the material, with purification and elevation of the spiritual in the flame and smoke of the fire. Regular memorial services help pacify the spirit

of the dead and help it attain the ideal state of paradise. The *ihai* is placed in the family's Buddhist altar and is venerated by the family; memorial services by the priest may be conducted in either the home or in the parish temple. If only a few or no memorials were performed for a dead person, he was thought to be excluded from paradise; such spirits were feared because they haunted the living. This belief has provided the theme for many works of literature. (Compare the story of The Revengeful Spirit of Masakado in selection 19.) Shinto ceremonies for the dead are rarer than Buddhist rites for the dead, but it is worth noting that religious concern for the dead is a persistent theme throughout Japanese history. (For example, see Part 10 and also selections 36 and 45.)

Reprinted from Arthur Hyde Lay, "Japanese Funeral Rites," *Transactions, Asiatic Society of Japan*, 1st Series, Vol. 19, by permission of the Asiatic Society of Japan.

A Buddhist Funeral in Traditional Japan

In the time of the early Tokugawa Shoguns the country was divided for religious purposes into parochial districts over each of which a *dannadera,* or parish Buddhist temple, presided. The priests had power in spiritual matters over their *danke*, or parishioners, and were entrusted with the funeral ceremonies in their respective charges. When a death occurred the fact was notified to the priest of the parish Church. On receipt of the tidings he, accompanied by one or two acolytes, repaired to the bereaved house and completed the necessary arrangements for the religious services. He also saw that the *ihai* was properly made, and decided what inscription should be written upon it.

The arrangements of a secular nature were carried out by the *Kogumi* of the place. This *Kogumi* was a Corporation, formed by the householders of a town or village, for mutual help. When any member of the Corporation, or the tenant of a house owned by a member of the Corporation, died, his family were required to inform the Society at once. On receipt of the intelligence, an officer was forthwith sent to the spot to examine the body, and report upon its condition. Kaempfer tells us that when Christianity had become an object of the deepest hatred to those who for the time being held the chief power, the officers appointed "sat on the body and viewed it narrowly to see whether there were any external signs of violence or marks of the Christian religion." The *Kogumi* after satisfying themselves that death had resulted from natural causes, issued a certificate to that effect, and forwarded it to the Mayor of the place.

Twenty-four hours after death the body was washed with warm water

and the head shaved. The corpse was then either dressed in a white cloth or wrapped in a paper shroud covered with Pali characters. This done, it was introduced into the coffin, a heavy chest of white wood, either square or round in shape, and placed in a sitting posture, the head between the knees. Such a position may be traced to the habit, practised by devout believers, of sitting rapt in religious meditation, — the object of the erect posture and shaven head thus being to impart a saintly appearance. The sides of the receptacle were lined with bags containing vermilion: poor people substituted tea for the more costly article. Over the top was spread a linen cloth, and the lid fastened down. A good deal of superstition prevailed as to lucky or unlucky days for cremation and interment, and geomancers were often employed to choose a propitious time. The day having been satisfactorily fixed, the coffin was conveyed to the best room in the house, where the relatives, friends, and priests were assembled. The officiating priest began the services by turning to the box enclosing the dead and proceeding to read portions of the Buddhistic sacred scriptures. After that he burnt incense, and the relatives in turn advanced to the side of the casket, burnt a small quantity of incense, made a low bow, and retired. Thus ended the service in the house. The procession was then formed and winded its way slowly to the temple or crematorium, (in some cases a special service was gone through in a temple, at other times the remains were taken direct to the crematorium). In the front were attendants, in double file, bearing the floral offerings of friends. More attendants, some of whom carried lanterns, others flags of paper or silk, followed. Upon one of the flags was inscribed the posthumous title, upon another verses from the writings held most in esteem by the sect to which deceased belonged; the remaining flags were the gifts of friends and, differing as to their inscriptions, formed, as it were, a catalogue of the dead man's virtues. The car which supported the coffin was shaded by an ornamental canopy, called the *tengai*, and took its place after the flagbearers. Directly behind the hearse walked the *moshu*, or chief mourner, apparelled in rough hempen garments, in his hand a bamboo staff meant to support him, as he was supposed to be so crushed by affliction as to be unable to walk without assistance. On his feet were straw sandals covered with white cloth. Near by was an attendant bearing the *ihai* (memorial tablet). Four or five priests, each with an attendant, along with the relatives and friends followed. Last of all came servants bringing *dango*, dumplings, impaled on spits, and cakes, which were afterwards distributed among the bystanders. Arrived at the cremation ground, the coffin with its contents were handed over to the official in charge, and a receipt taken, which had to be presented on the next day at the same time that the ashes were asked for. The guests and some of the priests returned to the house, where the latter again read selections from their sacred writings. The following morning they all proceeded once more to the crematorium, and having received the urn in which lay the ashes, betook themselves to the neighboring cemetery, where, after the sacred scriptures had again been recited, dust was returned to dust.

The *ihai* was carried back to the house and placed in the *butsudan* (Buddhist altar) and flowers, &c., were presented in the morning and evening for some time after the death, and on anniversary days. The days specially set apart for offerings to the dead, and for the repetition of mass for their souls, began with the seventh day after death, and afterwards occurred at regular intervals of ten days, up till the seventy-seventh day. Further commemoration services were held on the hundredth day. The first anniversary of the death was a time for special services. Beyond that the third, seventh, thirteenth, seventeenth, twenty-third, twenty-seventh, thirty-third, thirty-seventh, and fiftieth anniversaries were selected upon which to call the departed to remembrance by offerings and prayers.

SELECTED READINGS

For works on various aspects of Japanese Buddhism, see first the citations for each selection; some additional works are:

Anesaki, Masaharu. *Buddhist Art in Its Relation to Buddhist Ideals: With Special Reference to Buddhism in Japan.* Boston: Houghton Mifflin Co., 1915.

Bando, Shojun, et al. *A Bibliography of Japanese Buddhism.* Tokyo: Cultural Interchange Institute for Buddhist Press, 1958.

Eliot, Sir Charles. *Japanese Buddhism.* London: Edward Arnold, 1935; reprinted, London: Routledge & Kegan Paul, 1959.

Kitagawa, Joseph M. "The Buddhist Transformation in Japan." *History of Religions* 4 (1965): 319-36.

Kiyota, Minoru. "Buddhism in Postwar Japan: A Critical Survey." *Monumenta Nipponica* 24, Nos. 1-2 (1969): 113-36. (See also his forthcoming book on Japanese Buddhism.)

Saunders, E. Dale. *Buddhism in Japan: With an Outline of Its Origins in India.* Philadelphia: University of Pennsylvania Press, 1964.

Tsukamoto, Zenryu. "Japanese and Chinese Buddhism." In *Religions and the Promise of the Twentieth Century,* edited by Guy S. Metraux and François Crouzet, pp. 229-44. New York: New American Library, 1965.

Visser, Marinus Willem de. *Ancient Buddhism in Japan: Sutras and Ceremonies in Use in the Seventh and Eighth Centuries A.D. and Their History in Later Times.* 2 vols. Leiden: E. J. Brill, 1935.

Watanabe, Shoko. *Japanese Buddhism: A Critical Appraisal.* Tokyo: Kokusai Bunka Shinkokai (The Society for International Cultural Relations), 1964.

pARt fOUR

confucianism

Shinto and Buddhism are the major organized religions in Japan; the influence of Confucianism and religious Taoism have been more subtle and diffuse. Neither Confucianism nor Taoism has ever constituted a full religious organization with priests, scriptures, regular worship services, and other ecclesiastical aspects. In general, Confucianism entered the stream of social ethics and government rationale, while Taoism pervaded the realm of everyday religious observances such as astrology and fortune telling. Some Japanese scholars and popular lecturers advocated Confucianism as a system of thought and code of ethics, sometimes in conjunction with other teachings. (For example, see selection 24.) However, most Japanese people implicitly felt the Confucian rationale in their social conduct and in their support of the government.

Confucianism entered Japan on the tidal wave of Chinese culture and soon became a main pillar of governmental order, as seen in Confucianism's support of the emperor. (See selection 40.) As time passed, Confucianism changed not only in terms of the transformation of neo-Confucianism in China but also in terms of its relationship to Japanese circumstances. It is ironic that in modern Japan Confucianism became a strong bulwark of Japanese nationalism and even an ideological tool for controlling colonial possessions of Japan.

12

neo-confucianism in later japan

Confucianism was present in the government and social rationale of early Japan, but it made its greatest impact on the life of the country in the form of Neo-Confucianism during the Tokugawa period (1600 - 1867). The commentaries of Neo-Confucianism were used to support the feudal government of the Tokugawa and also to reinvigorate Shinto studies.

The theories of Confucianism were important mainly for the Confucian scholars *(jusha);* the warrior class *(samurai)* depended on the practical ethical code of Confucian teaching along with other religious preferences. This tendency is typical of Confucianism, which remained a philosophical and ethical teaching but never grew into a full-fledged religion. It is also typical of the way in which religious traditions blended one with another and were embraced simultaneously by the same person. This interpretation of Confucianism offers a number of illustrations of Confucianism's blending with other traditions, some temporary and some more lasting. For example, Confucianism contributed the rationalization for the political order, or *kokutai,* but Shinto, as a more indigenous rationale, provided its own notion of *kokutai.* In such cases, there was mutual give-and-take between Confucianism and the Japanese tradition.

One of J. W. Hall's main points is that "the contribution of Neo-Confucianism to Tokugawa political theory was that it provided a universal rationale for the new order." Indeed, as we see in selection 23, a Tokugawa ruler argued for the unity and identity of the three traditions of Shinto, Confucianism, and Buddhism against the introduction of the foreign religion of Christianity.

Reprinted from "The Confucian Teacher in Tokugawa Japan," by John Whitney Hall, from *Confucianism in Action,* edited by David S. Nivison and Arthur F. Wright, with the permission of the publishers, Stanford University Press. © 1959 by the Board of Trustees of the Leland Stanford Junior University.

The Samurai Attitude Toward Confucianism

In the final analysis, the samurai attitude toward Confucianism and Buddhism as religions depended greatly on individual preference and conscience. The role of Confucianism as a religion was limited, and only an oc-

casional fanatical daimyo[1] attempted to assert its precedence over Buddhism as a religion for his domain. On the other hand, most Japanese of the time were not disturbed by the antagonism between Neo-Confucianism and Buddhism. Very often those very rulers who had done the most to encourage Confucianism became ardent Buddhists as they approached the ends of their lives. Tokugawa Tsunayoshi, for example, became almost fanatically Buddhist before his death, and Date Tsunamura, daimyo of Sendai, who had introduced Confucian ceremonies within his domain, turned to the patronage of Buddhism before his death.

It has been observed that in the struggle with Buddhism, the jusha, among them Hayashi Razan, looked to Shinto for an ally. Confucianists were able to turn Shintoism to their own use, working out various amalgams of it and Confucian thought. In view of the limitations of Confucianism as a religion, some pro-Confucian daimyo (such as Mitsumasa of Bizen) sought to combine Shinto with Confucianism as the officially supported religion of their domains. This alliance with Shinto was eventually to work against the Confucianists, however, for Shinto emancipated itself from Confucian control to become yet another competitive religious and intellectual system. The danger of this was not fully evident until after the middle of the Tokugawa period. But thereafter, under the impetus of the Kokugaku[2] scholars (scholars of "national learning"), Shinto as the basis of a nationalistically oriented world view became increasingly influential in the higher circles of the ruling class. And just as Confucianism had provided a rationalization of the political order (*koku-tai*), Shinto now became the basis of still another, and more indigenous, *kokutai* concept.

The role of Shinto is frequently not considered important until its appearance as a rational system of thought in the works of the Kokugaku scholars. Actually as an institutional vehicle for the expression of deeply felt attitudes toward the homeland and the traditional social and political relationships, Shinto played a vital role from the beginning of the Tokugawa period. We refer here to Shinto in its political sense: a set of practices involving attitudes of reverence toward the national deities (*kami*) and respect for the hereditary relationships between aristocratic families, a source of ritual justification of the aristocratic concept of *kokutai*, giving order and meaning to the relationship between emperor, the noble families, and their deified ancestors.

The contribution of Neo-Confucianism to Tokugawa political theory was that it provided a *universal* rationale for the new order. But Confucian ideals and the actual political order in Tokugawa Japan were never in perfect accord. In particular, there were difficulties with the Japanese practice of dual sovereignty. If Confucian theory could hold that "the Shogun receives author-

[1]*Daimyo*, feudal lord. [ed.]
[2]*Kokugaku*, a school of thought which arose in the Tokugawa period (1600-1867), emphasizing the intrinsic value of Japanese literature and culture. [ed.]

ity over the people of Japan as a trust from Heaven," it could also (as did the Mito school) support the traditional (and Shintoist) legal fiction that the authority came as a trust from the emperor. At any rate, the actual institutional and ceremonial relationship between emperor and shogun continued, in fact, to be ritualized in the practices of Shinto and in the familiar ceremonies of the Kyoto court. The rehabilitation of the imperial ancestral shrine at Ise and the elaborate ceremonial respect paid the imperial court by the Shogunate was clearly a recognition of the Japanese form of *kokutai* as a political order based not on supposedly universal values but on Japanese traditions and on reverence to the national deities.

The shogun also utilized a variety of religious practices to give sanction to his position within the country. The great shrine to Ieyasu at Nikko, though established under the guidance of Buddhist priests, was basically Shintoist in its conception. The periodic progress to Nikko carried out by successive shogun, and participated in by the daimyo and Tokugawa housemen, was an act of religious veneration toward the founder of the Tokugawa house. It implied a dedication to the political order which Ieyasu had created. Eventually miniature versions of the shrine were erected in the castle towns of the daimyo so that each locality could celebrate the Festival of Ieyasu. In Bizen the celebration of the Festival occurred on the 17th day of the fourth and ninth months. These were events of great pomp, participated in by large numbers of the daimyo's retainers.

Like the shogun, the daimyo too enshrined their founding ancestors and held yearly services to exalt the prestige of their families. Although these services were conducted by Buddhist priests, this sort of veneration for a "first ancestor" was an element of Shinto. In most domains also, as we discover in Bizen, there was an annual New Year's procession to the foremost local shrine, an important means of ritualizing the identification of political authority with the spirits of the local territory.

For the samurai, these ceremonies were infused with much more immediate political significance than the Confucian rituals honoring the Sages. In Tokugawa times, matters of lineage and ancestral status were of deep and pressing concern. Emperor, shogun, daimyo, family — these were all part of the immediate structure, the immediate *kokutai*, in which the samurai lived. And while Confucianism might provide a rational explanation of the social order, it was the traditional feudal and Shinto-based ceremonies and beliefs which gave emotional unity and meaning to it.

The typical Tokugawa samurai saw some value in each of the three world views that competed for his allegiance. Buddhism and Shinto provided for his religious needs; Confucianism gave him a rational cosmology and a social ethic; Confucianism and Shinto both contributed to his conceptions of the political order. To be sure, the professional advocates of these systems were constantly at odds, but the Tokugawa samurai found compatibility

among them an easy matter. His attitude is nicely revealed in the words of Ikeda Mitsumasa:

> According to the view of Lord Gongen [Ieyasu], Shinto, Confucianism, and Buddhism should all three be used. Shinto is the way of inner truth and of inner purity. Confucianism is the way of sincerity, love, and benevolence. Buddhism emphasizes selflessness and desirelessness, teaching forbearance and compassion.

If we can identify any primary commitment in the samurai's approach to these world views, it would be to what we should call immediate political realities, to a sense of his class importance, a sense of his tradition, a sense of national pride. Out of this commitment a unique amalgam of Confucian values and a Shinto-based sense of national destiny emerged to become the samurai's inspiration.

13

confucianism and nationalism in modern japan

Confucianism is a great achievement of Chinese culture and a positive contribution to the countries which received Chinese influence. But like other great philosophical and religious systems, it has also come to be used as an ideological tool to reinforce questionable programs. In modern Japan, Confucianism was one of several means used to support nationalism and militarism.

The Confucian notions of social harmony and respect for one's superiors were translated to mean that the Japanese people should unite in unquestioning loyalty to the political state and its aims. Following the ideal of social harmony would eliminate problems between management and labor, problems thought to be caused by the poisoning influence of Western individualism. In early Japan, Confucianism had reinforced the status of the emperor, and in modern times, the Confucian notion of loyalty was used to stimulate absolute loyalty to the state through the symbol of the emperor. As can be seen in selection 41, this ideal was promoted through the educational system.

The present selection describes how Confucianism became a popular rationale for fanatical support of nationalism, militarism, and patriotism.

Some people became convinced by this brand of Confucianism that Japan's problems were due to the introduction of Western culture, which had weakened Japan's distinctive heritage. The solution was to reject Western culture and to reaffirm Oriental culture—meaning Confucianism and absolute loyalty to the state. As a system of social philosophy, Confucianism usually emphasized filial piety to one's parents and continuing the family line. In this context, both the monastic life of Buddhism and loss of life in military service were contrary to Confucian philosophy because they disrupted family order. But in the nationalistic context, the soldier's sacrifice of his life during combat was seen as the supreme expression of Confucianism, since absolute loyalty was now interpreted as owed to the state, rather than to the family.

It is one of the curious ironies of history that Confucianism was invoked to bolster fanatical militarism and patriotism against China, the birthplace of Confucius and Confucianism, a fact which should remind us that Confucianism was not responsible for Japanese nationalism, in the sense that it created something that was not already there. At the same time, we can see why Confucianism in modern Japan tended to support the status quo, even when that status quo was questionable. Confucianism entered the religious life of the people, providing a sturdy bridge between the hazy areas of national identity and religious commitment, and although it is easy for us to see the inherent weakness of this bridge, the same problem of how to build nationalism faces every modern country. (Compare also Part 14.)

Reprinted by permission of the author and publisher from Warren W. Smith, Jr., *Confucianism in Modern Japan: A Study of Conservatism in Japanese Intellectual History* (Tokyo: The Hokuseido Press, 1959).

The Nationalisation of Confucianism in Japan

After 1933, the trends apparent in the development of Confucianism in Japan from 1918 to 1933 became accelerated, but the most prominent of these was the growing identification of Confucianism with the Japanese spirit, the Imperial way, and the Japanese *kokutai* (national polity). The term "Japanese spirit" in particular became a favorite after 1933 for speakers who wished to contrast Japanese civilization and ideals with those of the rest of the world. Often this was done in order to justify the motives of Japanese expansion, for it was claimed that Japan had a mission to perform in protecting and developing spiritual civilization in Asia which was threatened by the egoistical and materialistic culture of the West.

Ever since the Imperial Restoration in 1868, individual Confucianists and Confucian organizations had insisted on the dichotomy between the spiritual civilization of the East and the material civilization of the West. The latter was invariably felt to be inferior, and this point of view followed logically from the premises of Confucian philosophy in which man was considered to have a fundamental moral nature whose development constituted the primary aim of civilization.

Similar in this respect to Catholic philosophy in the West, Confucianism claimed that when preoccupation with material life led man to forget his moral nature, he was no longer fulfilling the purpose of his existence.[1] Closely related to this was the Confucian attitude towards Marxism as basically a product of the materialistic emphasis in the West. . . .

. . . From the isolated statements on Confucianism found in popular literature and educational books during the period from 1934 to 1945, it is clear that Confucianism came to have a valuable appeal in the ideological program of Japanese nationalists.

The rise of one new and apparently influential Confucian organization during this period needs to be mentioned, for statements by its members and interested individuals indicate how Confucian attitudes towards spiritual culture could serve to bolster the Japanese spirit.

The founding ceremonies of the Nippon Jukyo Senyokai (Japanese Society for the Promotion of Confucianism) were held in Tokyo on January 27, 1934 at the Tokyo Kaikan. About seven hundred people participated, including the Prime Minister, Saito Makoto, the Home Affairs Minister, Yamamoto Tatsuo, the Minister of Education (Hatoyama Ichiro, the head of the House of Peers, Prince Konoe Fumimaro, and the head of the Lower House, Akita Kiyoshi.

These men all made congratulatory statements in which they spoke of the value of Confucianism for stabilizing the people's thoughts and restoring traditional morality from the excess of Western materialism. But most significant of all was the address by Kato Masanosuke (b. 1854).

Kato, an influential politician and member of the House of Peers, was head of the Daito Bunka Gakuin (Academy of Oriental Culture). This was a cultural and educational institution formed in 1923 as a part of the Daito Bunka Kyokai (Society of Oriental Culture) for the purpose of combating dangerous thoughts and strengthening Japanese civilization. The

---

[1]Among the many passages in the Confucian classics which display this is one by Mencius:

The Minister of Agriculture taught the people to sow and reap, cultivating the five grains. When the five grains were brought to maturity, the people all obtained a subsistence. But men possess a moral nature; and if they are well-fed, warmly clad, and comfortably lodged, without being taught at the same time, they become almost like the beasts. This was a subject of anxious solicitude to the sage Shun, and he appointed Hsieh to be the minister of Instruction to teach the relations of humanity. James Legge, *The Confucian Classics*, second edition, revised (Oxford: Clarendon Press, 1895) , II, 251.

Daito Bunka Gakuin had for over ten years supported Confucianism as part of its own program of reviving the Japanese spirit. Kato and others had finally felt that in view of the times, it was necessary actively to spread Confucian ideas in society, and therefore they had organized the Nippon Jukyo Senyokai.

With this as a background, Kato's opening address takes on importance as representing the aims and attitudes of the new organization. He spoke in a particularly disparaging way of the materialistic civilization of the West and blamed it for many of Japan's ills.

> In the short space of forty or fifty years, threatened by the people of Europe and America, we realized great [material] progress which, needless to say, was felicitous for the nation. But what I feel is most deplorable is that together with the advance of material culture, every type of evil that should have been avoided was introduced. This was so-called individualism and utilitarianism. The result of revering individualism was that our traditional national principles were relegated to a secondary place; and the result of being infatuated with utilitarianism was that fame and profit occupied the foremost position, while justice and humanity were discarded. Without reflection, we have amplified the mad condition in which we have nothing but fame and profit in mind.
>
> Capitalists exploiting the flesh and blood of laborers while laborers unite and strike in opposition; landlords and tenants each wishing their own harvest to be large, with tenant disputes arising constantly; politicians taking advantage of their positions and yearning for unfair profits; the problem of the sale of doctor's degrees at the Nagasaki Medical College; the problem of the buying and selling of Tokyo school principalships; and the problem of Communist influence at Kyoto University and Nagano elementary school; all these are the poison of following material culture.

Kato then asked his audience to consider how the Emperor Meiji had dealt with a similar situation when materialism was sweeping Japan in 1886. He had published the *Seiyuki,* and ordered the creation of a special course in Japanese and Chinese studies at Tokyo Imperial University. Kato felt that the Nippon Jukyo Senyokai in 1934 could play a similar role in strengthening the spiritual culture of Japan, and copies of the *Seiyuki* were distributed to everyone in the audience. The address ended with Kato asserting that any help given to advance the aims of the Nippon Jukyo Senyokai would be felicitous for Japan.

Many letters of congratulation and encouragement poured into the offices of the Nippon Jukyo Senyokai, and typical of the kind of messages sent was one by Major General Horiuchi Bunjiro entitled "Confucianism and Chinese studies, a great critical problem."

General Horiuchi said that Confucianism was the basis of Oriental spiritual culture, which had no equivalent in Western material culture. At the present time, however, Confucianism existed primarily only in Japan, where it was most prominently displayed in the virtues of loyalty and filial piety. The examples of bravery by war heroes such as Commander Hirose

Takeo (1868-1905) in the Russo-Japanese war and the Bakudan Sanyushi[2] in the fighting around Shanghai in 1932 were the result of loyalty and filial piety. (See figure 4.)

To appreciate Confucianism, though, one had to master *kangaku* (Chinese studies) which had been used to express the Japanese spirit. Therefore *kangaku* was really a Japanese thing, and General Horiuchi felt it might more accurately be termed *Nihongaku* (Japanese studies). In any case, a study of Confucianism was especially needed in Japan in order to help her

Figure 4. The Bakudan Sanyushi (School children paying homage to the spirits of the Bakudan Sanyushi before a bronze likeness of these war heroes at the Seisho temple, Shiba, Tokyo, in February 1936). Reprinted by permission of the author and publisher from Warren W. Smith, Jr., *Confucianism in Modern Japan: A Study of Conservatism in Japanese Intellectual History* (Tokyo: The Hokuseido Press, 1959).

[2]The Bakudan Sanyushi were three Japanese soldiers who acted as human torpedoes in storming a Chinese position during the fighting between the Chinese and Japanese at Shanghai in February, 1932. They carried a torpedo into a Chinese barbed-wire entanglement and blew themselves up in accomplishing their mission. This heroic deed had a great effect on Japanese public opinion. For a description of the incident and its repercussions in Japan, see A. Morgan Young, *Imperial Japan, 1926-38,* (London: George Allen and Unwin Ltd., 1938), 141-142.

carry out her mission of cooperating with and guiding China and Manchuria. Japan had the great task of making a peaceful Orient, and the strength of Confucianism and Chinese studies could be re-exported to China for this purpose. This of course meant that in general, English would be unnecessary, and General Horiuchi hoped the Prime Minister and educational authorities would consider this basic problem.

SELECTED READINGS

For works on various aspects of Confucianism in Japan, see first the citations for each selection; some additional works are:

Armstrong, R. C. *Light from the East: Studies in Japanese Confucianism.* Toronto: University of Toronto Press, 1914.

Fisher, Galen M. "Kumazawa Banzan: His Life and Ideas." *Transactions of the Asiatic Society of Japan,* Second Series 16 (1938): 221-58.

Lloyd, A. "Historical Development of the Shushi (Chu Hsi) Philosophy in Japan." *Transactions of the Asiatic Society in Japan* 34, Pt. 4 (1906): 5-80.

Spae, Joseph John. *Ito Jinsai: A Philosopher, Educator, and Sinologist of the Tokugawa Period.* Monograph 12, *Monumenta Serica: Journal of Oriental Studies of the Catholic University of Peiping,* 1948. Reprinted, New York: Paragon Reprint Corp., 1967.

part five

Religious taoism

Taoism, like Confucianism, never enjoyed the status of an organized religion in Japan. In fact, Taoism's influence is even more difficult to trace in Japan than that of Confucianism. Confucianism had a clear identity in the Confucian *Analects* and socioethical systems; Taoism, by contrast, lived on in Japan primarily in the fragments of its tradition that found their way into organized religion, especially into folk religion.

Taoism's influence in Japan does include philosophy, since the text of philosophical Taoism, the *Tao Te Ching,* arrived in Japan at an early date. But the major influence of Taoism in Japan comes from the area known as religious Taoism, including a wide range of cosmological and calendrical beliefs and practices. The Chinese calendar, itself a watershed of cosmological calculations, was adopted in early Japan and soon was taken for granted in planning festivals and regulating personal life. (For example, see the astrological advice of a medieval writer in selection 22.) The average person experienced religious Taoism chiefly through this calendar, through the popular world view of lucky and unlucky beliefs, and through popular practitioners such as fortune tellers.

The Koshin cult, discussed below, is one of the rare examples of clear Taoistic influence, but still the people view it more as part of their own tradition than as a Chinese importation. The case of the New Religion Konko Kyo is also a rare case of explicit Taoistic influence, but Konko Kyo tends to transform rather than simply to transmit this influence.

14

ReLiGious taoism in a Japanese cult

By the sixth century A.D., when Taoist influence entered Japan with other Chinese culture, Taoism meant not simply Taoist literature but also the welter of beliefs and practices known generally as religious Taoism. This ambiguous term includes much of the popular religious life of ancient China, from astrological and calendrical systems to cultic practices and even unsystematized beliefs. One of the most clearly identifiable Taoist customs to make a lasting impression on the Japanese scene was the Koshin cult described in this selection.

The Koshin cult arose in China under the influence of ancient indigenous religious practices mixed with Buddhist and mainly Taoist elements. This selection is an interesting interpretation because the author analyzes both the theoretical and the practical aspects of the cult and then shows how it became such an integral part of Japanese life that its foreign origin was largely forgotten. The notion that mythological "worms" dwell within the body provides the rationale for holding regular meetings to honor these messengers to the gods. These meetings are characterized by nocturnal vigils and abstinence from sexual relations.

This document illustrates several important features of Japanese religion. It points up not only the contribution of religious Taoism but also the highly syncretistic character of Japanese religion. It shows how once aristocratic importations filtered down to the level of popular life. And it shows how cults of the *ko* type formed an important aspect of annual and devotional religious customs. (The word *ko* means religious association or pilgrim association and is not related to the word *Koshin;* although this *ko* happens to focus on a Taoist divinity, there were many *ko* organized around other religious traditions, and some *ko* were secular in nature.)

Reprinted by permission of the publisher from E. Dale Saunders, "Koshin: An Example of Taoist Ideas in Japan," in *Proceedings of the IXth International Congress for the History of Religions, 1958* (Tokyo: Maruzen Company Ltd., 1960). Also by permission of the Science Council of Japan.

Koshin; An Example of Taoist Ideas in Japan

In many ways Japan is a kind of storehouse. In the domain of the arts, the Shosoin[1] at Nara contains objects from various parts of the continent,

---

[1]*Shosoin,* an imperial storehouse dating from the eighth century. [ed.]

representing the cosmopolitan character of VIII century aristocratic taste. In the field of religion as well, Japanese beliefs bear the imprint of foreign influences, conserving sometimes concepts which have long since disappeared in the country of their origin. Such is the case of the belief connected with the koshin, or monkey day, the subject of this paper. The present aim, therefore, is to set forth, first, a résumé of the underlying koshin concept as it appeared in Chinese Taoist thought and, second, its transference to Japan and its evolution in that country from an historical and cultural standpoint.

The Chinese idea which seems to be the basis of the koshin practice is this. There exist in man's body three Worms, called the *san chu* (or *san shi*). The first, known as the old Blue (Ch. *ch'ung-ko*), lives in the head and causes blindness, deafness, baldness, loss of teeth, stuffy nose and bad breath. The second, the white Maid (Ch. *po-lo*), lives in the breast and is the cause of heart palpitations, asthma, and melancholia. Last of all, the bloody Corpse (Ch. hiue-shih?), dwells in the loins and causes intestinal cramps, drying of the bones, fading of the skin, rheumatism in the legs, aching of the wrists, weakening of the mind and will. Because of him, one is hungry but cannot eat, lacks vitality and is confused. One text adds that this worm is especially addicted to sexual intercourse.

These three parasitical worms are vindictive creatures, disposed to spy on the men in whose bodies they dwell, but which they look upon as a prison. They may gain their freedom only at the death of their host. On the koshin day, which occurs six times each year, they report to Heaven concerning the transgressions of their man, and his life is accordingly shortened by the director of destiny—300 days for the greater transgressions, three for the lesser. Moreover, it was specifically believed that on the koshin night, the Worms took advantage of man's slumber to make good their escape to Heaven and it was hence thought undesirable indeed to sleep either during the koshin day or on that night.

Interestingly enough these basic ideas present in Japan a contamination with a variety of concepts. Already in China, Buddhism had adopted to a certain extent koshin celebrations, and two non-Taoist divinities were associated with the observance of the monkey day. . . .

There is a further association between the koshin god in Japan and the Shinto divinity Sarutahiko no kami. Sarutahiko is known as the god of the crossways, and for this reason koshin stones (*koshin-to*) are often found even today by the wayside and are there worshipped as a protective divinity of travellers. This identification between koshin and Sarutahiko is difficult to explain conclusively. Perhaps it was due to the homophonous koshin, meaning both "monkey day" and "god of happiness," this latter denomination being synonymous with Sarutahiko. Or perhaps the existence of *"saru,"* meaning monkey, as a part of the god's name was sufficient to establish a connexion. Actually the koshin image is often shown accompanied by three monkeys covering their eyes, ears and mouth. These three acts are symbolic of the Japanese words 'not seeing,' 'not hearing,' 'not speaking' in

which the homonym *saru* occurs meaning monkey and at the same time being a negative verbal suffix. The use of these monkeys as images would seem to come from the fact that monkey (*shin*) is one of the elements of the koshin compound. . . .

A third association may be seen by the relation of the koshin divinity with the bodhisattva Myoken. Myoken controls longevity and *karma* and supposedly reports to the powers of the lower world. . . .

As a result of these associations, koshin, at least as it exists in Japan, may best be thought of as an example of what Professor Kubo . . . calls "acculturation arising from the introduction of Taoism into Japan."

The early introduction of Taoist concepts like the koshin—and the practice of *kata-tagae* (directional taboos) —is doubtless to be laid to the count of the masters of Yin and Yang (*ommyo-ji*). In the Heian period, the study of the Way of Yin and Yang (*ommyo-do*) assumed considerable importance. There was even a government bureau called the *ommyo-ryo,* which was one of the departments of state. *Ommyo-ji* were appointed in the capital as well as in the provincial centers and they became, in fact, official soothsayers. It is probably largely through them that Taoist concepts were introduced to Japan.

Although tradition has it that the koshin was early celebrated under Mommu at the Shitennoji (701), there is some doubt that such was really the case. However, it is certain that the koshin was celebrated by the beginning of the IX century at least. Ennin, in his diary under 838 (11 month, 26 day) refers indirectly to this observance when he says of the Chinese practice: "In the evening the people do not sleep—just like the koshin of the first month in Japan." In 834 and 836 the *Shoku-Nihongi* mentions that banquets were held on the koshin day but no note is made of the sleepless night that was later to become so characteristic of this day. It may consequently be assumed that koshin practices of some kind existed by the end of the VIII century, and by the beginning of the ninth there were doubtless people who observed the koshin day by staying up all night. Just who these people were is not known, but very probably they were mostly nobles and priests, for koshin observances during the Heian period appear to have been essentially aristocratic. Koshin celebrations at this time, it is known, took place in the palace where attendants arranged special mats and screens for the occasion. Cakes and wine were served and poems were composed during the night. As dawn approached it was the custom for the Emperor to give presents to the participating nobles, who in turn offered their best wishes to him. Sometimes *koto* and *biwa* were played for entertainment; games like dice and *go* were the order of the day. It appears that the time for the beginning of these past times was not set; perhaps they commenced around ten-thirty in the evening and continued until near dawn. . . .

The celebration of the koshin throughout the Heian and Kamakura periods remained an aristocratic cult and, like Buddhism, it was not until the end of the Muromachi period that it became a popular practice. Of this im-

portant period, there are few detailed texts, and it is actually the Edo period which not only furnishes abundant documentation on the subject of koshin but which forms as well the immediate basis of the modern cult. . . .

Unlike the aristocratic pursuits of the Heian nobles, modern koshin (i.e., from the end of the Muromachi period on) is characterized by much more simple patterns. In villages, gatherings were held, commonly in the home of the village head: at this time a purificatory bath was taken, offerings made to the gods, and sometimes sutras were recited. After a banquet stories were told to pass the hours until dawn, although the length of time spent in these past times differs from place to place.

This gathering of people (*ko*) is one of the characteristics of modern koshin. The *ko* may be organized on the basis of people from the same land or of the same family, or even of a mixture of the two. Moreover, they may be composed of men, of women, of men and women, or even of children. The celebration of this *ko* is often largely Buddhist in nature in view of the above mentioned relation with such divinities as Taishaku-ten and Shomen Kongo. But from the Edo period on there may be noticed a kind of Shinto koshin in association with Sarutahiko no kami. Here, instead of the recitation of sutras, *norito* are read and a meal of fish is prepared. Of course, in the Buddhist koshin (Shomen Kongo) no animal food is eaten. . . .

Actually the koshin divinity is thought of in a variety of ways. He is the protector of the harvest, children, horses, roads, he is a long life divinity, and many others. Even in the same locality people may think of the koshin deity differently. Of course, in agricultural areas he is largely a god of the harvest. In such communities there is a saying "the more one eats the better the harvest" and as a consequence abundant banquets are given on that day. In this connection, Koshin-san is also thought of as the "busy" god and, particularly in the form of the many-armed Shomen Kongo, he can help with the harvest.

Curiously enough in the Edo period, the belief sprang up that children born (sometimes conceived) on the koshin night were predestined to become thieves. This is traditionally explained by the fact that the famous thief Ishikawa Goemon was thought to have been conceived and/or born on a koshin day. His life was made the theme of a *joruri*,[2] and echos of this belief occur again and again in popular Tokugawa literature. For example, [the character] Kozo says: "Alas, evil as it may be, I am born a thief. And it is useless to let my conscience bother me. I may resist my desire to steal (with one hand) but the other hand gives in. When I see gold I enter, no matter how strong the chain may be. . . ." And Yosobe answers: "Your tale brings to mind my very own son. Because he was born on the koshin night, I was so worried I took him to the priest, who proclaimed that the baby had a streak of the thief in his face," and so forth. Not only were children born on koshin days thought to become thieves, but they were believed to be afflicted in varying degrees with naughtiness and stupidity as well.

Such beliefs were obviously closely connected with the interdiction

[2]*Joruri*, a kind of ballad-drama. [ed.]

against sexual activities on the koshin night, and a number of earthy satyrical verses exist from the Edo period to show this popular attitude. Moreover, the monkey figure used to represent the koshin would seem to show sexual overtones. The divinity is often shown in conjunction with a pair of monkeys, one holding a *gohei*[3] while the other holds a peach which, in Japan as in China, is a feminine sexual symbol....

To summarize. The koshin celebration present from the Heian period until the present day is celebrated six times a year on the day when, according to the Chinese sexagesimal cycle, the sign of the monkey is united with that of metal. Originally based on the religious, if not the philosophical, Taoist belief in the three Worms who report to Heaven on man's transgressions, the koshin practice was transmitted to Japan through the *ommyo-ji* certainly by the VIII century, and by the IX there are literary references to this observance. An aristocratic practice, largely Chinese in nature during the Heian and Kamakura periods, by the beginning of the Edo period, the koshin celebration had become popularized and concomitantly Japanized, with both Shinto and Buddhist elements. During the Edo period, koshin was to become firmly entrenched as a popular belief, and multiple references to it are to be found in the literature of the day. Consequently, the koshin celebration as it existed from the Tokugawa period to the present may properly be thought of as being Japanese for the most part, although it is undeniable that the beliefs rest on a basis of ancient Taoist concepts early transmitted to Japan. Today, koshin is most actively observed in the country areas, especially in the Tohoku and central Kanto regions, the obvious exceptions being the Daikyoji, devoted to Taishaku-ten, and the Kiho-in, ... Tokyo, as well as the famous koshin shrine (*koshindo*) of the Shitenno temple in Osaka.

15

ınfluence of Relıgıous taoısm on populaR Belıefs

Popular beliefs are those notions which are transmitted mainly by example and word of mouth rather than within the context of organized religion. Some popular beliefs may have originated within organized

---

[3]*Gohei,* a Shinto ritual wand, a stick with paper streamers. [ed.]

religion, but when they filter down to the people, they come to form parts of the nebulous world view by which the people live implicitly.

In the traditional life of Japan, almost every day, every act, every direction, and every aspect of the human career was somehow brought into harmony with this implicit world view of popular beliefs. This selection lists a number of examples of these beliefs, many of which are no longer followed.

Because popular beliefs are not organized into a system, beliefs from divergent sources often overlap or blend. After many centuries, it is almost impossible to distinguish between indigenous Japanese folk beliefs and beliefs borrowed from China. All the Chinese elements mentioned by Tokihiko Oto in this selection fall within religious Taoism understood in the broad sense. (*Ommyodo* is usually referred to in English literature as the Chinese theory of *yin* and *yang*.) Some of these notions and the corresponding practices are still found in contemporary Japan, but the ordinary person is not aware of their Chinese origin.

Reprinted by permission of the publisher from Tokihiko Oto, *Folklore in Japanese Life and Customs* (Tokyo: Kokusai Bunka Shinkokai [Japan Cultural Society], 1963).

Taboos

Even at this late date [1963], certain actions are tabooed in Japan as a matter of course. In affairs related to religious festivals especially, various taboos are scrupulously observed. The word for taboo in Japanese is *imi*, and the condition of a person subjected to such rules of avoidance is referred to as *mono-imi*. Of the current popular or superstitious beliefs, the majority are the survivals of taboos once seriously observed on the solemn occasions of a sacred or religious nature. The kinds of taboos are extremely numerous, but we shall examine some of the taboos concerning time, place, direction, action, and language.

First we may consider the taboos concerning dates. It is widely believed that certain days are intrinsically lucky, while certain other days are intrinsically unlucky. The traditional lore concerning good or bad luck largely derives from the teachings of the Ommyodo (Way of Positive and Negative Principles), Taoism and the school of thought based on the interpretation of the universe by laws of the sexagenary cycle and five natural elements, i.e., wood, fire, earth, metal and water. All of these theories have origins in the Chinese tradition. Intermixed with them are found some beliefs of apparently native Japanese origin. Few Japanese, for example, would start such enterprises as house construction, moving, marriage or prolonged travel on a day which is traditionally branded as unlucky. In farming, too, the day

of planting in particular is fixed with the greatest care as to its auspiciousness. In the sphere of domestic activities, sewing, cutting of the cloth, and manufacturing of *miso* (bean paste) used to be started on one of the so-called lucky days. Some of the other examples are the following.

The day called *Sanrinbo* (three-neighbor destroying) was avoided for starting a house-building project; if this rule was neglected, a fire would be sure to break out and the three neighboring houses as well as one's own burnt to ashes.

A journey was not to be started on the 8th of the month. It was extremely unlucky to come home from a trip on the 7th.

The day named *Taian* (Great Safety) was held as the luckiest day for marriage, and the custom of avoiding the day of *Tomobiki* (Friend-pulling) for a funeral is still nation-wide. Not a single exception is likely to be found for this latter rule even to this day. Both *Taian* and *Tomobiki* are considered because of the characters standing for these names: *Taian* means "safe and without mishaps," while *Tomobiki* is disliked for a possible recurrence of death.

In rice-planting, the Day of the Horary Sign of the Horse is eschewed. If seeds are sown on the Day of the Sign of Cock, the plants are sure to thrive. Soy beans for making bean-paste had better be cooked on the Day of the Monkey. Cloth is cut for making clothes on the Day of the Rabbit. If it is cut on the Day of the Monkey or the Horse, holes will be burnt in the dress. The first, the 15th and the 28th of every month were reserved as days to be devoted to deities, so that laundering was not done on these days.

Certain taboos concerned the ground. The precincts of a shrine or other sacred buildings were generally held holy and had to be kept ritually clean. Urinating on the ground was forbidden. No manure is used in cultivating the fields belonging to a Shinto shrine. Some of the fields in the village are often set aside as *toshibata*, which should not belong to any individual owners. Owning or cultivating such fields for private purposes may entail death or sickness. Similar prohibitions exist for some forested areas. The trees in such areas should not be cut down, nor should such places be claimed as private property. If these taboos are violated, it is believed that misfortunes come to the violator.

Another set of taboos pertain to directions. In the Heian Era (c. 11th century), a widely observed custom was that of *katatagai* (changing the directions). If one was going into a certain direction, and that direction happened to be an inauspicious one, one had to go to an intermediate place in another direction first and then proceed on one's destination from there. This rule was obeyed very strictly for journeys, trips for sightseeing, and picnics.

What is called *kimon* (devil's gate) in the popular architectural lore is another taboo concerning directions even to this day. This is a folk belief derived from the theories associated with the "Way of Positive and Negative

Principles." In this belief, the northeasterly direction identified as *Ushitora* (between the Signs of Ox and Tiger) is the exit and entrance for demons. Kitchens and privies should never be built in this direction. Northwest, or *Inui* (between the Signs of Dog and Wild Boar), is also a dangerous direction. A shrine of the house-god is often built in this corner of the family precincts as a safeguard.

The auspicious direction may change by years and months. Every year has its own "lucky" direction, which is called *Eho* (auspicious direction) or *Akinokata* (direction which is open). It was from this direction that the god of the New Year was supposed to come. In some parts of the Tohoku district, the direction in which the last thunder of the previous year pealed is made the auspicious direction of the New Year.

The direction with which the god called Konjin is associated is viewed as dangerous. Konjin changes his position from month to month, so that its location must be ascertained whenever construction work is to be started. Another unlucky direction known as *Kumauji* is held in fear by sailors and fishermen.

Certain natural objects, such as animals, plants and rocks, are also tabooed. It happens in many places that a certain tree is revered as a divine tree, especially as one consecrated to the mountain-god, and it is never cut down. Such a tree is often chosen for its curiously shaped branches. It may be a three-forked tree, or one with its branches growing in the form of a sedge hat.

A white stone or a striped one is considered something special which may never be picked up or brought home lest some member of the family should fall ill or the house burn down. Dogs and cats with a white stripe dividing the colored patches on their heads are called *hachiware* (broken crown) and are disliked. Such an animal is said to desert its keeper. Many people do not like cats with long tails.

None are perhaps more numerous than taboos concerning the minute details of everyday behavior. These rules are remembered in short proverbial expressions, which may be classified as superstitious or popular beliefs. They may be divided into two large categories: one compromising taboos on acts associated with holy or sacred objects and affairs, and the other including those avoided for their apparent or suspected relations to unlucky events. Going round and round a person, for instance, is detested in the extreme, probably because this is exactly what is done when a supernatural being is evoked; an assembly of people goes round and round a person who remains possessed at the center. It is said that a girl who wears a single flower in her hair may never marry. This seems to be based on the fact that priestesses as a rule wear single flowers as decorations for their hair and they are not supposed to marry.

On the occasion of a funeral, everything is to be done the opposite way of the ordinary. Therefore doing things in the opposite manner on ordinary

occasions is considered objectionable. Some of those manners are explained in the chapter on the Funeral Rites. Taking just one serving of rice, eating a single dumpling, or drinking just one cup and no more of tea on ordinary occasions is frowned upon for the same reason. Likewise, two people picking at one thing with their chopsticks or pulling at a single rice-cake to eat is disliked.

It is held dangerous for somebody to come into the house from a front entrance and leave through a back door, or for two persons to depart from a house together, going into two different directions at once. These people are believed to meet some misfortune. Putting a foot into the hearth is prohibited, especially on the night of January 14th, lest the seedling-beds should be ravaged by birds.

Many taboos are observed in farming and cultivation. For example, it is said that at seed planting if one furrow in the field is left unsown, some member of the family may die or run away from home.

16

transformation of religious taoism in a new religion

In the previous selection Konjin is mentioned casually as another force to be reckoned with in popular beliefs. Konjin is an evil force or divinity whose direction one must avoid on penalty of misfortune. This notion of Konjin as an evil force lives on in some parts of Japan, but for the founder of Konko Kyo, the encounter with Konjin was not casual; nor did it simply reinforce earlier notions of Konjin.

A number of new religious movements or New Religions arose in Japan during the 1800s around the dramatic religious experience of founders. Some of these movements, such as Konko Kyo, existed as officially recognized branches of Sect Shinto until the postwar period, when religious freedom made independent organization possible. For Kawate, founder of Konko Kyo, the crucial experience arose out of an apparently fatal illness, thought to be caused by the curse of Konjin. Then, miraculously cured, it was revealed to Kawate that Konjin was not a malevolent force but actually a benevolent deity. Kawate, formerly

energetic in his devout attempt to conform to every aspect of popular belief, now cast aside all these beliefs as mere superstitions. Instead, he elevated the reconceived Konjin as the uniting force of the universe who called for sincere unity between God and man.

This description of the founding of Konko Kyo shows how religious Taoism was transformed and transcended. Most of the content of the Chinese tradition was rejected outright, and even the nature of Konjin was radically revised. Religious Taoism plays a major role in the founding of a New Religion, but it is not directly transmitted in the process. (For examples of other New Religions, see Part 16.)

Reprinted by permission of the publisher from D. C. Holtom, *The National Faith of Japan: A Study in Modern Shinto* (New York: Paragon Book Reprint Corp., 1965).

Konko Kyo

The significance of the name which Konko Kyo bears can best be discovered by following the inner development of Kawate Bunjiro, the founder of the sect. Kawate was born September 29, 1814, the second son of peasant parents living in the village of Urami near the Inland Sea in the feudal district of Kibi, a territory which is now incorporated as part of Okayama Prefecture. He was adopted at an early age into a farmer family of the neighboring village of Otani. This latter place, grown to the size of a small city and given the name of Konko, thrives today as the national headquarters of the church which he created.

The records of the sect picture Bunjiro as a sensitive, retiring child, strangely alert to the need of helping others, who spent much time either busied with his own thoughts or visiting at shrines and temples and communing with the priests. As a young man and throughout his early years as husband and father he appears as an example of domestic kindness and patient thrift, yet ever oppressed by a sense of maladjustment to the spirit world in which he so profoundly believed. His excessive devotion to the jots and tittles of religious ceremony won for him among his neighbors the nickname of Shinjin Bun—"Pious Peter." At this time, his life, like the lives of those about him, was made bewilderingly difficult and full of apprehension by a maze of beliefs in lucky and unlucky days, in good and bad directions, in favorable and unfavorable auspices for all the endless details of household activity, in the strange potencies of the five natural elements, in occult astrological influences, in curses by evil spirits, in possessions by foxes and badgers, in the mysterious powers of a confused host of superhuman beings, good and bad.

Along with all the rest of the countryside he especially dreaded the curse of a certain calendar god named Konjin, a semi-demonic being who had been created originally in the superstitious folkways of China but who had found a congenial atmosphere in the fear and credulity of the Japanese peasants. So it was, then, that when loss of property, sickness and death among his children and other immediate relatives and, finally, a severe illness that threatened death to himself were visited upon him, his fears grew to the despaired conviction that he was being singled out by Konjin for dire punishment.

As Bunjiro lay waiting for death, his brother-in-law who had been faithful beyond all others in ministrations at his bedside, was seized with a god-possession and through him a revelation was received from the other world which announced that Bunjiro had not displeased the gods and that his recovery was assured. By this Bunjiro was convinced that some power in the spirit world was trying to do him good. The revelation took place on the evening of June 13, 1855. It marked the beginning of Bunjiro's entrance into a unified moral world. It was only a little light that he saw at the time, shining as it were far off in the midst of much darkness, but as he followed it, it widened before him into a clear flood of insight in which he saw all things in a new relationship. At first he seems to have thought that the calendar god Konjin was being revealed to him and that he had formerly misunderstood the real nature of this god. But as a succession of revelations—now made to Bunjiro directly—brought better perspective to his inner vision, he became convinced that he was being used as a medium of communication between man and the One True God of Heaven and Earth, furthermore, that God had no evil in his character but, on the other hand, was possessed of an unlimited love toward those that trusted him and, finally, that God and man became indissolubly united when man became really sincere toward God, an experience which he called the mutuality of God and man. In the end Bunjiro repudiated all the superstitions that had troubled his earlier years, gave up his property and retired to a little hut which he built at the foot of a mountain near Otani. He called his hut "The Sacred Business-place of God" and for twenty-five years lived there in fellowship with his new business partner, ministering to all who came to him. He died in the early morning of October 10, 1883. The date is commemorated annually in the great autumn festival of Konko Kyo.

In finding a proper designation for his supreme object of worship Bunjiro took the first element in the name of the old curse-god, Konjin, and gave to it the reading *kane* (*kon* in the sect name). It was true that this might be misunderstood by some in the sense of the ordinary word for metal, but with Bunjiro it carried the idea of a totally different term, namely, *kane*, or *kaneru*, meaning "to unite." God was the eternal spirit who comprehended and united all things in heaven and on earth. As his own experience deepened Bunjiro used various names for God. His final name, the one which has been

generally adopted by his church, was Tenchi Kane no Kami, "The God Who Gives Unity to Heaven and Earth." It was a unity which had first come to Bunjiro in his own moral world, but this unity, he believed, was only an aspect of the greater moral and spiritual unity of the entire universe.

Against the background of this brief outline of the inner development of the founder we are prepared to attempt a translation of the title, Konko Kyo. *Kyo* is "teaching"; *ko* is "light" or "glory"; *kon* has just been explained. Probably the best we can do for the sect name is to translate it: "The Teaching of the Glory of the Unifying God."

SELECTED READINGS

For works on various aspects of Taoism in Japan, see first the citations for each selection; some additional works are:

Clement, Ernest. "Calendar (Japanese)." In *Encyclopaedia of Religion and Ethics,* edited by James Hastings, 3, pp. 114-17. New York: Charles Scribner's Sons, 1908-27.

Erskine, William Hugh. *Japanese Festival and Calendar Lore.* Tokyo: Kyo Bun Kwan, 1933.

Hori, Ichiro, "On the Concept of *Hijiri* (Holy-man)." *Numen* 5 (1958), fasc. 2, pp. 128-60; fasc. 3, pp. 199-232.

Kubo, Noritada. "Introduction of Taoism to Japan." In *Religious Studies in Japan,* edited by the Japanese Association for Religious Studies, pp. 457-65. Tokyo: Maruzen, 1959.

Miller, Alan L., "Ritsuryo Japan: The State as Liturgical Community." *History of Religions* 11 (1971): 98-124.

pARt six

folk ReLigion

Japanese religion has never been as tightly controlled and centralized as religion in the West. Denominational patterns in Buddhism and Protestant Christianity may seem familiar, but what is more important is the fact that religious life for the Japanese was not so exclusively centered around ecclesiastical matters. While every family tended to be related to one Shinto shrine by geographical location and affiliated to one Buddhist temple by family tradition, many religious activities took place outside the temple and shrine without the benefit of professional religious leaders.

As can be seen in selection 15, many popular beliefs existed independently of organized religion, and many aspects of seasonal celebrations were not controlled by Shinto and Buddhism. The family and the home were centers of religious life, a theme which is taken up in Part 10. Folk religion is not simply an addition to organized religion but is a vital part of the religious life of the people.

Most folk religion in Japan is handed down orally and in the annual festivals. Usually this pattern of folk religion varies considerably with such factors as the local situation and the economic activities of the area. For example, farmers usually carry out some celebrations for transplanting and harvest, whereas fishermen observe their own ceremonies for safety and big catches. Urbanization and industrialization are causing much folk religion to disappear, but throughout Japan there are attempts to preserve the local color associated with all folk customs.

tRaditional celebRations at new yeaR's

One of the most distinctive features of Japanese religion is the way in which the passing of the seasons is marked by a round of celebrations. The organized religions also join in the celebrations, but many aspects of the celebrations are carried on by families and villages without the aid of leaders from organized religion. These annual celebrations form such an important part of religious life that there is a special Japanese term *(nenchu gyoji)* for them, and there are countless Japanese books describing the distinctive round of ceremonies or annual celebrations in each locale. (In Oto's account, *nenchu gyoji* has been translated as "annual functions.")

These popular celebrations are so numerous and so colored by local circumstances that they escape any attempt at systematic classification, but the Japanese generally single out five of these celebrations as *gosekku,* the five sacred festivals. This notion of five festivals apparently was borrowed from China, but it soon became an integral part of the Japanese religious tradition. The first festival, New Year's, is described in this selection. The second festival, the third day of the third month, is the girls' festival, usually known as the dolls' festival, for on this day girls made a display of their dolls in homes and enjoyed a special celebration. The third festival, the fifth day of the fifth month, the boys' festival, is marked by the boys' display of warrior dolls and the hanging of paper or cloth carp outside the home. The fourth festival, the seventh day of the seventh month, celebrates the Chinese legend that two celestial lovers meet only once a year; this day is marked by gay street decorations. The fifth festival, the ninth day of the ninth month, is the chrysanthemum festival; it is also linked with earlier Chinese notions but has come to be associated with the season of fall and the abundant chrysanthemum flowers. This list of five festivals and their conspicuous expressions gives only a brief glimpse of the many annual festivals and their colorful, joyful festivities.

Probably no annual celebration is more important than New Year's, and Oto describes all the details of a traditional New Year's celebration. It is interesting that every nook and corner of daily life is included in this celebration—from the decorations on the gate to the drawing of the first well water of the year and from the special food to the first dream of the year. Success in the family's economic activity is prayed for, but seriousness gives way to much merrymaking. As shown in figure 5, in a northern region of Japan the children enjoy the New Year by making a kind of igloo shrine for their own celebration. Another custom

of some northern regions is the playful terrorism of children by the demon called *namahage* (shown in figure 6). And all this happens without the benefit of organized religion. Even Japanese citydwellers enjoy the colorful display of these celebrations, and the distinctive local customs are being filmed for timely showing on national television. (See also Part 12.)

Reprinted by permission of the publisher from Tokihiko Oto, *Folklore in Japanese Life and Customs* (Tokyo: Kokusai Bunka Shinkokai [Japan Cultural Society], 1963).

Popular Ceremonies at New Year's

The annual functions in the ceremonial life of the Japanese people have a long history. Many of them can be traced to one or the other of the following three origins: rituals started by the court nobles centered around the Imperial Family, ceremonies deriving from traditions of the military caste during the feudal times, and those developed among the common people. These streams of traditions, however, are by no means distinct and independent of each other, for some of the customs associated with aristocracy or warrior classes have been adopted from the folk practices of people at large. In like manner, many of the ceremonial observances in the tradition of commoners have been more or less influenced by the customs and manners originated in the Imperial and aristocratic families or the military rulers of the feudal age.

A significant part of the customs in Japan has also been introduced from abroad, particularly from China. The Chinese traditions have exercised an especially strong influence on the ceremonial life at the Imperial Court, a fact that cannot be found in the annual functions of the people at large, at least not to the same extent. Here we must hasten to add that not all rituals of apparent similarity in China and Japan should be ascribed to Chinese origins. Some scholars tend to interpret them as being derived from Chinese traditions, but they are often grossly mistaken. Among the folk customs of Japan there have always been some very much like those observed by the Chinese.

In order to explain annual functions among the Japanese, it is necessary to know the changes which have taken place in the calendar of Japan. Three different calendars are in current use: the new Western (solar) calendar, the old (lunar) calendar, and the calendar lagging by one month. The present solar calendar was officially adopted at the beginning of the Meiji Era (1872), but the reckoning of days according to the lunar calendar or application of the new one month later calendar is still widely used in farming villages. This is because the farmers are accustomed to deciding on the dates of their

agricultural activities according to the lunar changes. Perhaps the most outstanding characteristic of the annually observed occasions in the rural areas is their close relationship to rituals performed for the purpose of ensuring a fruitful year, especially abundance in rice-crops. Ceremonies guaranteeing a prosperous year and those for thanksgiving at harvest times thus represent a considerable part of the annual functions. A total of 40 to 50 days or half-days are set aside during the year, on which one is supposed to rest from work and devote oneself to ritual observances. Some of the more important of these occasions are explained below in the order of the months.

January

New Year's Day is the time to worship the God of the Year with due ceremonies. This deity is identified sometimes with the God of Rice-fields, and at other times with the spirit of the ancestors of the family. The New Year celebrations include decorating the entrance of the house with pine boughs. The trees are the temporary seat for the God of the Year. Another seat for the same divinity is prepared in one of the rooms inside the house in the form of a shelf, called *toshi-dana* (year shelf). Thus the pine-decorations at the door and the year-shelf are somewhat overlapping in their functions, but this happens frequently in affairs related to ceremonial observances around the year. Early in the morning on New Year's Day, a representative male member of the family, or *toshi-otoko* (man of the year), goes out to the well for the first water, which is called *waka-mizu* (young water). In doing this, he takes some *mochi* (rice-cakes) with him and throws half of them into the well, bringing back the rest. This signifies that he has made an offering to the Water-god. In many towns and villages, women are relieved of their duties of preparing meals for the first three days of the New Year. Instead, the head of the house gets up early on these mornings and cooks the prescribed dish of the occasion, *zoni* (soup containing meat, rice-cakes and vegetables).

On the 2nd day of the New Year, everyone should celebrate a ceremonial beginning of his or her own work: the first rope-making, first sewing, and first writing by a brush. A merchant opens his business for the year on this day, which is called *hatsuni* (first cargo). The dream dreamt on this night is called *hatsuyume* (First Dream of the Year), which foretells the fortunes for the coming year. The 7th is celebrated with a special dish called *nanakusa* (seven herbs), a porridge cooked with seven kinds of herbs.

On the 11th is observed a ceremonial start of tilling the ground. On this day *mochi* is thrown to the crows to foretell the harvest. If they eat it, the harvest will be good; if not, it will be a poor harvest. The 15th is called *ko-shogatsu* (little New Year), when more rites and ceremonies are scheduled than for any other single day. It used to be New Year's Day according to the lunar calendar. Rice-cakes are served not only to people of the household, but also to the cattle, "*mochi* for the oxen" and "*mochi* for the horses." For

the New Year of implements, mortars, pestles, sickles and hoes are washed clean and small rice-cakes are fastened to them. This is to let them celebrate the New Year, too. The majority of ceremonies performed on this day is aimed at praying for a fruitful year. A willow-tree, or some such graceful-looking plant, is erected on the family precincts and decorated with *mochi* fastened on its branches very much in the same manner as a Christmas tree is set up in the Western countries. This is a symbolic representation of a flowering rice-plant. If the family happens to be regularly in sericulture, the *mochi* is made in the shape of cocoons, called *mayu-dango* (cocoon dumplings), praying for abundant production of cocoons.

The people in Akita prefecture celebrate *ko-shogatsu* by digging cellars in the massive snowfall. In the cellars, known as *Kamakura*, they enshrine *Suijin-sama* (the God of Water) and children assemble to enjoy *mochi* and *amazake* (figure 5).

Figure 5. Kamakura Festival, Akita Prefecture. Reprinted by permission of the publisher from Tokihiko Oto, *Folklore in Japanese Life and Customs* (Tokyo: Kokusai Bunka Shinkokai [Japan Cultural Society], 1963).

Other objects are made on this day, including whittled wooden wands; *kezurikake* (called *awa-bo* and *hie-bo;* millet and barn-yard-grass ears), likened to the ripe ears of these grains. A persimmon tree in the garden may be prodded by somebody making light cuts in the trunk by an axe, saying "Will you or will you not bear fruit?" Somebody will answer for the tree, "I will, I will." In snowy regions of northern Japan, they perform a ceremony called "rice-planting." Imitating making seedling-beds, they set pine-needles on the snow. The rite is conducted in the hope of ensuring a year of abundance.

Families may expect visitors on this night. In the Tohoku and Hokuriku districts, young men of the village put on masks of demons, impersonating supernatural beings known as *Namahage* or *Namomitakuri,* and make their rounds of village houses (figure 6). These imaginary beings are believed to

Figure 6. Namahage, Tohoku district. Reprinted by permission of the publisher from Tokihiko Oto, *Folklore in Japanese Life and Customs* (Tokyo: Kokusai Bunka Shinkokai [Japan Cultural Society], 1963).

come to the villages in order to punish their laziness and take away the callous places formed on their shins as a result of staying by the fireside too long. The head of the family receives these visitors with courtesy, entertaining them with rice-cakes and other foods. Children are scared and try to run away from them. A visitor by the name of *hoto-hoto* or *koto-koto* is known throughout the country. He is also impersonated by village youths. They bring a straw "treasure ship" to the houses, leaving it somewhere without being seen. The family is expected to put some rice-cakes or money in it, but if they see the young men they splash water on them as they run off. The name, *hoto-hoto* or *koto-koto*, seems to have derived from the sound of knocking on the door. It is surmised that these customs originally represented the visitation of the God of the New Year.

The most impressive ceremony of the season is the bonfire on the 15th. In some regions this is celebrated on the 4th, but in Kyushu, where it is generally called *onibi* (spirit fire), it is on the 7th. This is often a festival for the *Doso-jin* or *Sae no Kami* (God of the Crossroads) and is known by various names such as *onbe, sagicho,* and *tondo-yaki.* All the New Year decorations are collected from the entrances and are burnt in this bonfire at which children are active. A conical hut of bamboo and straw is constructed on tall piles, and the children are allowed to stay in it for the entire night. They toast the rice-cakes donated by various families and pass their time eating and singing. The hut is also burnt finally, and the God of the New Year is believed to go home on the smoke of its burning. If one warms oneself well by this fire, one is not likely to catch colds, it is said. Everyone will bring a rice-cake or dumpling stuck to a willow twig to toast over it and then eat it.

18

Japanese shamanism

The most prominent aspects of folk religion are the communal celebrations that involve whole families and entire villages or even the whole country in such major events as greeting the New Year. But folk religion also includes occasions when the individual makes a particular request on his own. In traditional Japan one could appeal to various popular religious practitioners for help concerning sickness, worries, or communicating with the dead. These practitioners gained their qualifications

and performed their rites mainly outside the confines of organized religion.

One of the most interesting of these careers in folk religion is the female shaman, or shamaness, who was sought for various special requests but especially for communicating with the dead. Ichiro Hori describes the role of the shamaness in Japanese history and the clearly defined steps for training as a shamaness. The thorough training and symbolic initiation attest to the seriousness of the occupation.

Shamans are found in many cultures, and their religious services to the community vary considerably. However, in Japan as elsewhere, the shaman is generally believed to possess the superhuman ability to leave the body and go to the other world. This means that he (or she) can even talk with the dead. In some parts of Japan, especially in the north, shamanesses still exist, and their "ministry" is much more serious than the rather playful seances of the West.

Reprinted by permission of the author and publisher from Ichiro Hori, *Folk Religion in Japan: Continuity and Change*, edited by Joseph M. Kitagawa and Alan Miller (Chicago: The University of Chicago Press, 1968). Copyright © 1968 by the University of Chicago.

Shamanesses in Japan

Japanese shamanism has persisted throughout a long period of religious history without having been institutionalized in a strict sense, though it commingled with Shinto and Buddhism and underwent many changes.

The leading role in Japanese shamanism has been played by shamanesses. . . . In Japanese, the general term for a shamanic figure is *miko*, which means explicitly a shamaness. There is no special term for a male shaman. . . .

According to the classification of Taro Nakayama, Japanese shamanesses are divided into two categories. The first category he calls the *Kan-nagi*, which include the *miko*, who belong to the imperial court and Shinto shrines. These shamanesses retain roles only in certain formal Shinto rituals but have lost almost all their original functions and techniques. The second category is the *Kuchiyose*, including shamanesses who settle down in their own villages or migrate from village to village in compliance with the requests of the residents. They utilize techniques of trance and engage in telepathy, mediumship, divination, and fortunetelling, employing flexible but predictable forms. Their most frequently requested service is to communicate with guardian deities or spirits or with wraiths and spirits of the dead. The most popular name for the first category is *miko* or *jinja-miko* (Shinto shrine shamaness) ; for the second category, *ichiko* or *sato-miko* (city or village shamaness) . The shamanesses of these two categories are semi-institutionalized. The *jinja-*

miko (or *kan-nagi*, using Nakayama's term) are usually chosen from among daughters of hereditary families of Shinto priests or of hereditary parishioners of particular Shinto shrines. By contrast, the *sato-miko* (or *kuchiyose-miko*, using Nakayama's term) become shamanesses through certain initiatory ordeals and training directed by a teacher or elders.

I must add a third category, which includes both male and female shamans, in order to clarify the shamanic elements of contemporary religious phenomena in Japan, such as the newly arisen religions, and the functions of many independent sorcerers and magicians. I shall call this category the *jussha* (magician) or *gyoja* (practitioner) system—that is, the magico-shamanic system. The Japanese *jussha* and *gyoja* are chosen by their guardian spirit, deity, or ancestral shaman. . . .

Until the beginning of the twentieth century there were many wandering shamanesses (*aruki-miko*) in rural society and even in Yedo (the former name of Tokyo), Kyoto, and Osaka. They were called *ichiko, ezusa-miko* as well as *Shinano-miko, Agata-miko* and *nono*. *Shinano* (the old name of present-day Nagano prefecture) and *Agata* (a country name in Nagano prefecture) are from the sites of the largest headquarters of these wandering shamanesses. They visited from village to village within their territories immediately following the harvest in autumn, traveling in groups of five or six. Their main functions were: communication with spirits, deities, wraiths, and the dead; divination and fortunetelling through trance; prayers for recovery of the sick; and purification of new buildings, wells, stoves, and hearths. They might give their own fetish to a parishioner's child so that he would grow up in good health; sometimes they held memorial services for a parishioner's ancestors. Some were said to have practiced clandestine prostitution, especially in the urban societies.

These wandering shamanesses have almost disappeared in present-day Japan, though many settled village shamanesses belonging to the *kuchiyose* system are still active in various provinces, notably in the Tohoku (northeastern) area of Honshu. In the Tohoku area they are not genuine shamanesses in the strict sense, not having been elected or chosen by their deity or spirit but rather, voluntarily or involuntarily, adopted by an elder shamaness master and bound to her in the relationship of master and apprentice. In the Tohoku area almost all the shamanesses are blind. Blind girls in this area have usually become the apprentices of the older shamanesses who lived near their native village. The novices undergo training disciplines such as cold-water ablution, purification, fasting, abstinence, and observance of various taboos. They are taught the techniques of trance, of communication with superhuman beings or spirits of the dead, and of divination and fortune-telling; they also learn the melody and intonation used in the chanting of prayers, magic formulas, and liturgies, and the narratives and ballads called *saimon*. After three to five years' training, they become full-fledged shamanesses through the completion of initiatory ordeals and an initiation ceremony which includes the use of symbols of death and resurrection.

When the novice has completed her training, she is initiated into the shamanic mysteries by her mistress. Before the initiation ceremony, as preliminary preparation, the novice puts on a white robe called the death dress and sits face to face with her mistress on three rice bags. Several shamaness elders assist in the ceremony. They chant and utter the names of deities, buddhas, and several magic formulas in unison with the mistress and the novice. In this mystical atmosphere, the novice's joined hands begin to tremble slightly. Observing carefully the novice's change of behavior, the mistress perceives the climax of inspiration and suddenly cries in a loud voice to the novice: "What is the name of the deity that possessed you?" Immediately the novice answers: "So-and-so deity (or sometimes buddha or bodhisattva) possessed me." When the mistress hears this answer, she throws a large rice cake at the novice, and the novice falls off the bags and faints. Sometimes the elders dash water on top of the novice's head 3,333 times at a wellside or at the seashore. The novice in a dead faint is warmed by the body heat of shamaness elders who share her bed, and finally regains consciousness. The novice is said to be newborn and is then initiated. She changes her white death dress to a colorful so-called wedding dress and performs the ceremony of the traditional wedding toast by exchanging nine cups of *sake* with her mistress. This exchange of cups is the most important part of the traditional wedding ceremony of Japan. After ritually practicing the first communication with her ancestral spirit and other spirits of the dead, the novice is given a large feast to certify her proficiency as an independent shamaness. Her mistress, shamaness elders, parents, brothers and sisters, relatives, and friends are all invited. After a week or ten days' isolation at her tutelary shrine as a rite of recovery, or *agrégation,* she becomes a professional shamaness. . . .

The shamanesses of the Tohoku area are usually requested to communicate with and transmit the will of superhuman beings and the spirits of the dead. They are often invited to visit a family in mourning, because the first communication with the spirit of the newly dead person is thought to be an important part of the funeral. They call it the *hotoke-no-kuchiake* ("opening of the dead person's mouth"). *Hotoke* originally meant "Buddha," but in colloquial speech now indicates any dead person. Especially when a person has met an unnatural death or died in difficult childbirth, the ceremony of opening the dead person's mouth is the most important service for the salvation of his soul. The relatives collect a sum of money and rice from seven neighboring villages and invite a shamaness to perform a special and complicated service called *nana-kura-yose* (séance together with the seven divine seats) . . . .

One interesting custom is the large gathering of shamanesses held once a year, on the day of *Jizo-bon,* at several sacred mountains and temples in northern Honshu, such as Mount Osore, the Jizo hall in Kanagi-machi in Aomori prefecture, Hachiyo-ji temple in Fukushima prefecture. *Jizo-bon* is a festival for the bodhisattva Kshitigarbha, whose Japanese name is Jizo (Ti-tsang in Chinese). Jizo, popular bodhisattva among the Japanese since

the tenth century, is believed to be a savior of spirits of the dead, who otherwise would be suffering tortures in hell, as well as a guardian deity of children.

Mount Osore is a dormant volcano and is believed to be the Other World by the inhabitants of the area, who believe that there is a terrestrial paradise as well as a terrestrial hell on the mountaintop with its crater lake. From early morning on the twenty-fourth day of the sixth month of the lunar calendar—the festival day of Jizo—old men and women from various villages climb Mount Osore carrying special rice dumplings to offer at each of the stone statues of Jizo and stupas and mounds along the mountain paths. Since ancient times the common people have believed that dead children are required to heap up small stones to build a stupa, goaded by the ogres of hell, if they died without having offered any service to their parents or community. Accordingly, any woman who has lost a child heaps small stones in the shape of a stupa as a substitute for her child on this day.

More than thirty shamanesses also climb the mountain for the festival and occupy a special corner near the main hall of the temple in order to fulfill the worshippers' requests. Old women who have been deprived of husband, son, daughter, or grandchild ask one of the shamanesses to communicate with this spirit as a part of the indispensable memorial service. They sit on the ground around a shamaness and listen with rapt attention to the voice of the dead relative who speaks through the shamaness. From morning till midnight these shamanesses fall into trances to communicate with departed spirits upon each request. A shamaness's income on that day alone might amount to more than eight thousand yen (approximately twenty-five dollars) at the rate of a hundred (about thirty cents) for each request. Each trance for a single spirit continues for five or ten minutes on the festival day; on ordinary days, it lasts an hour or more.

19

Japanese folk tales

Folk tales are an important part of the Japanese cultural heritage, a popular mixing of religious beliefs and historical events with local color and pride in antiquity. As handed down in Japan, folk tales represent a dimension of culture not so prominent in the West; these tales are not really "believed in," as with religious scriptures, yet they are treasured much more than the Western fairy tales.

The Japanese are very proud of their long national heritage, and are equally jealous of the distinctiveness of local traditions. For example, if there is a "Saint Kobo's Well" in the district it will be pointed out to a visitor. Even a local historian who knows that Saint Kobo (the founder of the Buddhist Shingon sect) could not have visited the village might still take pride in the antiquity of this legend. What is crucial is not so much what actually happened long ago but how the local people relate themselves to the memorable personages and events of Japanese history.

Some of the brief tales printed here are specifically religious, such as the reference to Saint Kobo and "The Serpent Suitor" and "Human Sacrifice to the River God." In fact, these stories might be called folk legends, because they tell of the religious significance of local institutions, particularly the local shrines. The main point of "The Revengeful Spirit of Masakado" is how prior historical events still affect us today; this is most true of the curse of the dead and family ties. The tale of Benkei recounts superhuman aspects of the life of this famous warrior, who forms one of the most important topics for art and plays.

All of the tales in selection 19 have been reprinted from *Folk Legends of Japan,* by Richard M. Dorson, with permission of the publisher, Charles E. Tuttle Co., Inc.

Saint Kobo's Well

There is a spring by the name of St. Kobo's Well in the village of Mura-matsu, Ninohe-gun. The following story concerning this well is told in this district. A girl was once weaving alone at her home. An old man, staggering, came by there and asked her for a cup of water. She walked over the hill more than a thousand yards away and brought back water for the visitor. The old man was pleased with her kindness and said that he would make her free from painful labor. After saying this, he struck the ground with his cane. While he was striking, water sprang forth from the point struck by his cane. That spring was called St. Kobo's Well.

The old man who could do such a miraculous deed was thought to be St. Kobo, however poor and weak he might look.

The Revengeful Spirit of Masakado

Masakado fought against Hidesato at Nakano-ga-hara in Musashi Province in the third year of Tenkei [940]. He was shot in the shoulder by Taira Sadamori and grappled down by Fujiwara Chiharu, and his head was cut off.

Therefore Masakado's spirit remained on the field of Nakano and caused

suffering to the people of the vicinity in many ways. In the eastern districts of Japan, Masakado's spirit effected various miracles, but to the people who had some blood connection with Hidesato, his spirit caused fierce spells. Especially in the Sano family it was forbidden to go to the Kanda Myojin Shrine, because the Sano were the descendants of Hidesato. The Sano house at Ogawa-machi in Kanda was very near the Kanda Myojin, so on the festival day at this shrine the gate of the house was not opened to anyone; on ordinary days every person of the Sano house was forbidden to walk in front of the shrine.

During the Anei era [1770-80], a samurai named Kanda Oribe lived at Kobinatadai-machi. This man was a descendant of Masakado and wore his crest. His close companion Sano Goemon lived at Yushima. One day Sano dropped in at Kanda's on his way back from his official duties, as they were intimate friends. They had a good time together, and after a while Kanda said: "I shall take you to a fine place." And he took Sano to a *yujoya*[1] named Kashiwaya, near Agaki Shrine.

At the time Sano had been wearing ceremonial dress. But it was ridiculous to go to a *yujoya* dressed thus, so Kanda lent Sano an informal cloak with the Masakado crest on it.

While they were making merry at the *yujoya*, Sano's face suddenly turned pale, sweat poured from his brow, and he fainted in agony. In a moment the circumstances were entirely changed. In confusion, they called for doctors and medicine. Kanda hired a sedan and sent Sano to his home.

Kanda was so anxious about his friend that he hurried over early next morning to see him. However, Sano came briskly out of his room and said: "Last night I shivered and fainted. After shivering and fainting I fell unconscious until they took off that cloak of yours I was wearing. When I went into bed, I immediately recovered. And now I feel just as well as usual. This probably happened because I borrowed your cloak with your crest on it. Maybe Masakado's spirit put a spell on me."

So Kanda was also convinced of the power of his ancestor's spell, and he apologized to Sano for his carelessness.

The Serpent Suitor

Once there lived a village headman named Shiohara in Aikawa-mura, Ono-gun. He had a lovely daughter. Every night a nobleman visited the daughter, but she knew neither his name nor whence he came. She asked him his name, but he never told her about himself. At length, the girl asked her nurse what to do. The nurse said: "When he comes next time, prick a needle with a thread through his skirt, and follow after him as the thread will lead you. Then you will find his home."

The next day the girl put a needle in the suitor's skirt. When he de-

[1]*Yujoya,* a brothel. [ed.]

parted, the girl and the nurse followed him as the thread led them. They
passed through steep hills and valleys and came to the foot of Mt. Uba, where
there was a big rock cave. As the thread led inside, the girl timidly entered
the cave. She heard a groaning voice from the interior. The nurse lighted a
torch and also went into the cave. She peered within and saw a giant serpent,
bigger than one could possibly imagine. It was groaning and writhing in
agony. She looked at the serpent carefully, and she noticed that the needle
which the girl had put in her lover's skirt was thrust into the serpent's throat.

The girl was frightened and ran out of the cave, while the nurse fainted
and died on the spot. The serpent also died soon. The nurse was enshrined
in Uba-dake Shrine at the foot of Mt. Uba, and the cave of the serpent is
also worshiped. . . .

If a man enters this cave with something made of metal, or if many
people go into the cave at the same time, the spirit of the cave becomes
offended and causes a storm.

Relics of Benkei

There is a hill called Benkei-mori in Nagami, Honjo-mura, Yatsuka-gun,
A small shrine formerly called Benkichi's Shrine, which is now in the pre-
cinct of Nagami Shrine, stands there. According to a document kept in the
shrine, the woman named Benkichi was the daughter of a samurai in the
province of Kii [now Wakayama-ken]. She was born on May 5, in the third
year of Taiji [1129]. For some reason she came to Nagami in Honjo-mura in
the third year of Kyuan [1147] and stayed there. After three years she met a
tengu[2] on a mountain path and conceived a child. In the thirteenth month
she gave birth to Benkei.

When Benkei was seventeen years old his mother died. He enshrined her
as the goddess Benkichi and left this place. These things are written in detail
in Benkei's letter, which is said to have been presented to the shrine by
Benkei. Near Benkei-mori there is a well. Tradition says that Benkei took his
first bath with water from this well.

A small island called Benkei-jima is in the sea off the coast of Nohara in
Honjo-mura. Trees grow very thick on its mountains. According to tradition,
Benkei was a very naughty boy and in his ninth year he was abandoned on
this island. Benkei played the game of fox and geese with the *tengu*. While
they were playing, the *tengu* taught Benkei many tactics. The stone base
which they used for the game was later carried by boat to another place. But
the boat was overthrown by a sudden storm and the stone base sank into
the sea.

This island is connected to the mainland by a narrow sand path. It is
said that Benkei made this path, by dropping little stones which he carried
in his sleeves and skirt, for the purpose of escaping from the island. There

[2]*Tengu*, a mountain goblin. [ed.]

is also a place called Benkei's Smithy at Shinjo in the same village, where Benkei is said to have had his sword forged.

Human Sacrifice to the River God

An old wise-woman came from Miyanome in Ayaori-mura and settled at Yazaki in Matsuzaki-mura, Kamihei-gun. She had a daughter whom she cared for lovingly. The girl grew up and was married to a man who came to live with them. The young couple loved each other, but the mother disliked the son-in-law and wanted to get rid of him.

In those days the dam which supplied the villagers with water from the Saru-ga-ishi River would give way several times every year, and people were troubled by floods. It happened again that the dam broke when the villagers were in need of water. Thrown into confusion, they gathered together and talked the matter over. At last they decided to consult the wise-woman. She, on her part, thought this a good opportunity to destroy her son-in-law. Accordingly, she told the people to catch a person who would be dressed in white and riding a gray horse to Tsukumoshi-mura the next morning, and to throw him into the river as a sacrifice. The villagers assembled at the dam and waited from midnight on for a person in white dress to come by on horseback.

Early next morning the old woman's son-in-law, unaware of impending disaster, dressed himself in white, as he had been told to do by the mother, and rode off on his gray horse. When he came to the dam, many villagers stood in his way to catch him. The son-in-law was surprised and asked them: "Why are you all here?"

The villagers were surprised in their turn to see that the person was none other than the wise-woman's son-in-law, whom they all knew well. When the son-in-law heard about the matter he said: "If it is the god's word, I must obey. I will drown myself in the bottom of the river and sacrifice myself for the sake of the villagers. But a human sacrifice cannot be made by one person. A couple, man and woman, are needed to satisfy the god. I will have my wife die with me."

Just then the wise-woman's daughter, who knew of the mother's evil plot, rushed to the scene, riding on a gray horse and dressed in white. The husband and wife rode into the river together and sank down to the bottom. The old wise-woman regretted that her plan had miscarried. She also jumped into the water, weeping.

All at once the sky darkened and a fierce thunderstorm lashed the heavens. For three days and nights it rained ceaselessly, and the river overflowed its banks. After the flood had subsided, the people noticed a big stone that they had never seen before. The villagers used this stone as the foundation in reconstructing the dam. This stone was called the Wise-woman's Stone.

The son-in-law and his wife were deified as gods of the dam [*seki-gami*]. There is also a shrine called Bonari Myojin where the old wise-woman died.

SELECTED READINGS

For works on various aspects of folk religion, see first the citations for each selection; some additional works are:

Bownas, Geoffrey. *Japanese Rainmaking and Other Folk Practices.* London: George Allen & Unwin, 1963.

Casal, U. A. *The Five Sacred Festivals of Ancient Japan: Their Symbolism and Historical Development.* Tokyo: Sophia University and Charles E. Tuttle Co., 1967.

Fairchild, William P. "Shamanism in Japan." *Folklore Studies* 21 (1962): 1-122.

Ouwehand, C. *Namazu-e and Their Themes: An Interpretative Approach to Some Aspects of Japanese Folk Religion.* Leiden: E. J. Brill, 1964.

Visser, Marinus William de. "The Fox and Badger in Japanese Folklore." *Transactions of the Asiatic Society of Japan* 38, Pt. 1 (1909): 1-17.

part seven

christianity

Christianity has always had a difficult time in Japan. It arrived rather late in Japanese history, after the major religious traditions had already interacted to form a distinctive Japanese religious heritage. In addition, Christianity sharply contrasted with the Japanese heritage. The career of the Christian church in Japan generally can be characterized by two features: on one hand, Christianity has emphasized its distinctiveness and uniqueness, resisting mixture with the Japanese tradition; on the other hand, no more than a small percentage of the population has assumed church membership, so that Christian influence in Japan has often been outside the church and has never been dominant.

Christianity was present in Japan for about one hundred years (1550 - 1650) before being completely proscribed, and then it reentered Japan in the last half of the nineteenth century. The Jesuits who introduced Catholicism in the mid-sixteenth century faced great obstacles in their missionary efforts, but they gradually won sincere converts. Some descendants of these first Japanese Christians secretly maintained their faith in spite of persecution and contacted Roman Catholic priests who entered Japan in the 1860's.

For over a century, Catholic and Protestant missions from the entire Western world have been active in Japan. In fact, one of the problems facing Christianity in Japan has been the extreme proliferation of institutions and denominations arising out of European and American experience but not necessarily suitable for the Japanese experience. At several times, there has been optimism for mass conversion to Christianity— during the enthusiasm for Western culture in the 1870s and during the disorientation after World War II, for example—but in both cases the optimism was unfounded. Christianity is respected in various ways—in recognition of Jesus as a religious leader, in the reading of the Bible, and in praise of Christianity's role in education and social reform. However, Japanese Christian churches still are a minor influence in the country's religious life when compared with Shinto shrines and Buddhist temples. (One interesting aspect of Christianity adopted by the Japanese is the popular celebration of Christmas, described in selection 52.)

20

the introduction of roman catholicism into japan

The Jesuit order was the major missionary agent to introduce Roman Catholicism into Japan, and this selection provides a glimpse of the attitudes and conduct of these sixteenth century missionaries. It is remarkable how soon and how thoroughly the Jesuits were able to recognize and attune themselves to Japanese language and culture. We must remember that in the sixteenth century there were no language schools, not even grammars or dictionaries to guide them; nor were there any historical or cultural studies of Japan to help acculturate them. The Jesuits assessed their own position in Japanese society as parallel to that of Zen monks, so they carried out their conversations and social relations from this level. (Complicated language and etiquette patterns force a person to act in accordance with some understanding of his own social position.) In short, as much as possible, the Jesuits tried to compromise and adapt their own life style to that of the Japanese. Modern Westerners may be surprised that Japan in the 1500s and 1600s emphasized cleanliness much more than Europe of the same time, and one Jesuit compromise meant more rigorous rules for personal and domestic cleanliness.

At the end of this selection is the translated text of the edict which finally signaled the end of the Christian century. Christianity was proscribed as a foreign religion, and severe punishment was promised for unrecanting Japanese Christians *(Kirishitan)*. Catholic priests *(bateren)* and all Europeans (known as Southern Barbarians) were expelled. The only exception was closely controlled commercial trade with Europeans at special ports. The strong opposition of the Japanese tradition to this foreign religion can be seen in selection 23.

Reprinted from C. R. Boxer, The Christian Century in Japan, 1549-1650, 1967; originally published by the University of California Press; reprinted by permission of The Regents of the University of California.

Jesuits in Sixteenth Century Japan

The Company of Jesus[1] has often been termed the most militant and uncompromising of all the Roman Catholic religious orders, but, like most generalizations, this verdict is only partly correct. . . .

The truth is (or was) that the Company, although fundamentally militant, was by no means equally uncompromising. The manner in which the sons of Loyola[2] adapted themselves to the Japanese way of life is another instance of their genius for compromise. It also affords an interesting indication of the mutual reactions of intelligent but prejudiced Europeans and Asiatics when confronted with another civilization, equal in most ways and superior in some, to their own. A study of "the daily round, the common task," of the Jesuit missionaries in Japan is particularly enlightening in this respect; since for reasons which I need not go into, their colleagues of the China mission did not mix quite so freely with the different grades of society in the Middle Flowery Kingdom.[3]

The adaptability of the Jesuits was evinced by the founder of the Japan mission, the apostolic Francis Xavier. After Xavier's preliminary and Franciscan-like humility had failed to produce any impression on the haughty daimyo,[4] the Jesuit made a more fruitful use of pomp and ceremony with the aid of his seafaring friend, Duarte da Gama. But the attitude of the Jesuits toward Japanese culture and civilization was really clarified by Valignano, who, in this manner as in so many others, clearly laid down the policy and methods to be followed. He decided, probably at the suggestion of Luis Frois and other veteran missionaries, that the Jesuits should arrogate to themselves the status and standing of the Zen priests, as the most potent, intelligent, and respected members of the Buddhist clergy. . . .

The Jesuits in Japan could be divided into three groups. First came the fathers (padres) with whom the real authority was vested, and who, up to Valignano's time, were all Europeans. Next came the brothers (irmaos), most of whom were Europeans, but who included about seventy Japanese in 1592. Lastly came the dojuku or native acolytes and catechists, of whom there were about a hundred in 1582, and two hundred and sixty in 1604. Strictly speaking, these last were not members of the Company, but for practical purposes they can be considered as such, since Valignano repeatedly

[1]The Company of Jesus, in other words, the Jesuit order. [ed.]
[2]Sons of Loyola, meaning Jesuits. [ed.]
[3]Middle Flowery Kingdom, a literal translation of the term for China. [ed.]
[4]Daimyo, a feudal lord. [ed.]

stressed that they were an essential part of the mission organization. There were also the household servants and caretakers who performed menial but useful tasks. They were not Jesuits, but were a charge on the Company's pay roll. The Japanese commonly termed the fathers *bateren* and the brothers *iruman* from a corruption of the corresponding Portuguese words. Perhaps the best way to understand the working of the Jesuit mission during its heyday in the Keicho period, is to consider each of these categories in turn before looking at the picture as a whole.

Although Cabral's[5] policy of "keeping the Japanese in their place," was overruled by Valignano in favor of one of racial equality, the fact that no Japanese brothers were ordained as priests in the Society for many years, automatically ensured that the control of the mission remained with the European padres. Since the Jesuit mission in Japan came in the sphere of the Portuguese padroado or Crown Patronage in the East, the majority of these missions were Portuguese claims, and since the mission largely depended for its existence on the resources and facilities furnished by Goa, Macao, and Malacca, Portuguese influence was naturally predominant. Portuguese was the lingua franca of the missionaries themselves, and most of their official correspondence with Goa, Lisbon, and Rome was written in this language. The rivalry with the Spanish friars from the Philippines tended to strengthen the Lusitanian cast of the Japan mission, which it retained throughout the whole time that it functioned in the island empire. The fact that its founder, Xavier, was a Basque, and its great organizer, Valignano, was Italian, does not affect the general accuracy of this statement. The local chroniclers of the mission, Luis Frois and Joao Rodriguez Tcuzzu were both Portuguese, as was Padre Diogo de Mesquita, the "bear leader" of the Kyushu envoys to Rome in 1582–1590. From the beginning to the end, Portugal contributed more in men and money to the Japan mission than did any other country.

The chief native protectors of the padres, old Otomo of Bungo, and the daimyo of Arima and Omura, had always been insistent on the advisability of the European Jesuits conforming to the Japanese way of life so far as they possibly could. Valignano accepted and enforced this principle, which was laid down in the local Jesuit code of behavior, as instanced by the "Advertimentos" of 1583, the "Addiciones" and "Obediencias" of 1592, and Pasio's final revision of the "Obediencias" in 1612. These sources give a clear idea of the way the mission functioned during the Keicho period, and of the motives which supplied the main springs for many of its actions.

Valignano stated that nowhere was the proverb of "When in Rome, do as the Romans do" more applicable than in Japan. He insisted that the padres make detailed study of the minutiae of Japanese etiquette, and conform closely to Japanese customs in this respect. He stressed the vital necessity of understanding the delicately graded differences and the subtle distinctions

[5]Cabral, a Jesuit missionary. [ed.]

between the various classes of society in Japan. He insisted on the correct use of honorifics in the colloquial and written languages. He ruled that the padres should exact the deference that was due to them as priests on a level with those of Zen sect, but added that they should not allow overzealous Christians to give them more than their due. Padres were to be addressed by the term *sama* (lord) as a sign of respect, and were always to be treated as social superiors by the brothers and dojuku.

Similarly, he stressed the importance of the European padres addressing daimyo and samurai with due deference and politeness, but warned them against overdoing this, for excessive politeness was likewise taken amiss in Japan, and did the speaker more harm than good. He continually reiterated the importance of Europeans always keeping their tempers, even under insult and provocation, since nothing was so demeaning in the eyes of Japanese as lack of self-control or any outward display of feeling. Boisterous laughter and gesticulation were also to be carefully avoided; and any rudeness from a daimyo or noble was not to be openly resented, but met with a display of mingled politeness and firmness in order to shame the offender. Japanese etiquette in the serving of *saké* to guests and casual callers was also adopted, as was the formal tea ceremony, chanoyu. The implements for this social rite were always kept on hand in the larger Jesuit establishments which were also provided with a *chashitu*, or ceremonial tea room, for the entertainment of guests.

The complicated code of present giving, formal calls on New Year's Day, and similar national customs were also adopted by the Jesuits, although they were directed to exercise due economy wherever practicable in the selection of gifts. Buddhist or Shinto holidays were to be ignored by the missionaries. Intensive language study was decreed for all newcomers from Europe, a year and a half being usually allowed for this purpose. Owing to shortage of personnel (there were less than fifty ordained priests in Japan in 1598), this study was not always done. Padre Joao Rodriguez complained in 1598 that several of the padres had only a rudimentary grasp of the language, and that other new arrivals were too old to make more than very slow and unsatisfactory progress in this difficult tongue. Xavier had asked for Basques and Flemings to be sent out to Japan, since he thought that they would become acclimatized more readily than would southern Europeans. This suggestion was not carried out and the mission continued to be predominantly staffed by Portuguese. Incidentally, it is amusing to find Rodriguez further complaining that some of the local superiors and rectors had become too bureaucratic and set in their ways. He added slyly that once these reverend gentlemen had given up office, they were likely to display a reluctance for the daily drudgery of ordinary missionary work, and their religious ardor noticeably cooled. Rodriguez was a decidedly carping critic and there is no need to take his strictures too seriously, but they are not without significance in the light of later Franciscan and Dominican accusations that the Jesuits were liable to neglect the end for the means.

The influence of the Japanese code of behavior is also evident in Valignano's rule that erring sinners of good social standing should not be admonished directly by a padre, but through a third person, preferably a Japanese brother or senior native convert of the same social standing as the offender. Likewise the padres were to be very careful in fault finding or in reproving their Japanese inferiors, for the latter were prone to react violently if admonished in other than a kindly paternal fashion.

Unlike contemporary Europe, cleanliness emphatically came next to godliness in Japan, and of this the Jesuits were early aware. Physical dirt and religious poverty tended to be closely associated in Catholic Europe, where lice were regarded as the inseparable companions of monks and soldiers. The Japanese craze for fastidious cleanliness formed a sharp contrast. The Jesuits soon realized that in this they had something to learn from the Buddhist bonzes;[6] and Valignano repeatedly stresses the importance of scrupulous cleanliness in the dress and housing of Jesuits in Japan. He could not shake off his inherent European prejudice against washing, and approve of the Japanese custom of a daily hot bath, but in other respects he insisted that Jesuits conform to local standards of cleanliness.

Their houses were built and furnished in Japanese style, from plans drawn by native architects in consultation with the Jesuit superiors. Guest chambers were included for the reception of distinguished travelers, but the "Obediencias" of 1612 contain a warning against indiscriminate hospitality, and the abuse thereof by *itazura-mono*, or idlers who were merely bent on cadging a free meal and bed. Since women were not so secluded in Japan as they were in most Asiatic countries (or in sixteenth-century Spain and Portugal for that matter), the Jesuits were permitted to receive female visitors, although in a *zashiki* or a room with sliding doors ajar so that the occupants were visible to those elsewhere in the building.

Text of the Sakoku, or Closed Country Edict of June, 1636

1. No Japanese ships may leave for foreign countries.
2. No Japanese may go abroad secretly. If anybody tries to do this, he will be killed, and the ship and owner(s) will be placed under arrest whilst higher authority is informed.
3. Any Japanese now living abroad who tries to return to Japan will be put to death.
4. If any Kirishitan believer is discovered, you two [Nagasaki bugyo[7]] will make a full investigation.
5. Any informer(s) revealing the whereabouts of a bateren will be paid 200 or 300 pieces of silver. If any other categories of Kirishitans are discovered, the informer(s) will be paid at your discretion as hitherto.

---

[6]*Bonzes*, priests. [ed.]
[7]*Nagasaki bugyo*, government administrators at the port of Nagasaki. [ed.]

6. On the arrival of foreign ships, arrangements will be made to have them guarded by ships provided by the Omura clan whilst report is being made to Yedo, as hitherto.

7. Any foreigners who help the bateren or other criminal foreigners will be imprisoned at Omura as hitherto.

8. Strict search will be made for bateren on all incoming ships.

9. No offspring of Southern Barbarians will be allowed to remain. Anyone violating this order will be killed, and all relatives punished according to the gravity of the offence.

10. If any Japanese have adopted the offspring of Southern Barbarians they deserve to die. Nevertheless, such adopted children and their foster-parents will be handed over to the Southern Barbarians for deportation.

11. If any deportees should try to return or to communicate with Japan by letter or otherwise, they will of course be killed if they are caught, whilst their relatives will be severely dealt with, according to the gravity of the offence.

12. Samurai are not allowed to have direct commercial dealings with either foreign or Chinese shipping at Nagasaki.

13. Nobody other than those of the five places (Yedo, Kyoto, Osaka, Sakai and Nagasaki) is allowed to participate in the allocation of *ito-wappu*[8] and the fixing of silk import prices.

14. Purchases can only be made after the *ito-wappu* is fixed. However, as the Chinese ships are small, you will not be too rigorous with them. Only twenty days are allowed for the sale.

15. The twentieth day of the ninth month is the deadline for the return of foreign ships, but latecomers will be allowed fifty days grace from the date of their arrival. Chinese ships will be allowed to leave a little after the departure of the [Portuguese] galliots.

16. Unsold goods cannot be left in charge of Japanese for storage or safekeeping.

17. Representatives of the five [shogunal] cities should arrive at Nagasaki not later than the fifth day of the long month. Late arrivals will not be allowed to participate in the silk allocation and purchase.

18. Ships arriving at Hirado will not be allowed to transact business until after the price allocations have been fixed at Nagasaki.

Nineteenth day of the fifth month of the thirteenth year of Kwanei [June 22, 1636].
Addressed to Sakakibara Hida-no-kami and Baba Saburozayemon, the joint bugyo of Nagasaki, and signed by Hotta Kaga-no-kami, Abe Bungo-no-kami, Sakai Sanuki-no-kami and Doi Oi-no-suké, the four great councillors or Go-roju.

---

[8]*Ito-wappu,* the monopoly for dealing in raw silk. [ed.]

21

the plea for an authentic japanese christianity

One of the problems that has plagued Christianity, especially Protestantism, in modern Japan is the proliferation of European and American
church organizations. Some of the difficulty may lie within the Japanese
religious experience, which tends to emphasize loyalty to small social
groups (as seen in selection 31); however, in this case the fragmentation
originates mainly from outside Japan. This problem is not simply the
number of denominations but also that they force the identity of the
Japanese Christian into the mold of a particular denominational tradition.
As Uchimura points out so well in the following excerpt, most Christian
denominations arise out of and express the national character of people
or even the regional character within a nation, as with Cumberland
Presbyterianism. But since no Japanese Christian was born and raised in
the Cumberland region of Kentucky, his social, political, economic, and
artistic sensitivities are not nurtured by the same factors that influence
the Cumberland resident. In short, Uchimura says that it is hypocritical
for a Japanese Christian to ape the mannerisms of Kentucky; a person
who has been brought up in Japan cannot "jump out of his skin" and
become a Cumberland Presbyterian.

Uchimura advocates that Japanese Christians must express their
Christianity in distinctively Japanese fashion, through the forms of Japanese culture. For this reason he talks about the "two J's," Japan and
Jesus. The Japanese person who is truly committed to Jesus as a religious
leader will be able to express his commitment through Japanese culture.
Uchimura presents a high ideal for Protestant Christianity in Japan, an
ideal which is still pursued but has not yet been widely attained.

Reprinted by permission of the publisher from *Sources of Japanese Tradition*, edited by Ryusaku Tsunoda, Wm. Theodore de Bary, and Donald Keene (New York: Columbia University Press, 1958), paperback edition, Vol. 2, pp. 348-350.

Japanese Christianity

I am blamed by missionaries for upholding Japanese Christianity. They say that Christianity is a universal religon, and to uphold Japanese Christianity is to make a universal religion a national religion. Very true. But do not these very missionaries uphold sectional or denominational forms of Christianity which are not very different from national Christianity? Are they sure that their Methodism, Presbyterianism, Episcopalianism, Congregationalism, Lutheranism, and hundred other Christian isms—they say that in Christiandom there are above six hundred different kinds of Christianity—are they sure that all these myriad kinds of Christianity are each of them a universal religion? Why blame me for upholding Japanese Christianity while every one of them upholds his or her own Christianity? If it is not a mistake to uphold any one of these six-hundred different forms of Christianity, why is it wrong for me to uphold my Japanese Christianity? Please explain.

Then, too, are these missionary-critics sure that there is no national Christianity in Europe and America? Is not Episcopalianism essentially an English Christianity, Presbyterianism a Scotch Christianity, Lutheranism a German Christianity, and so forth? Why, for instance, call a universal religion "Cumberland Presbyterianism"? If it is not wrong to apply the name of a district in the state of Kentucky to Christianity, why is it wrong for me to apply the name of my country to the same? I think I have as much right to call my Christianity Japanese as thousands of Christians in Cumberland Valley have a right to call their Christianity by the name of the valley they live in.

When a Japanese truly and independently believes in Christ, he is a Japanese Christian, and his Christianity is Japanese Christianity. It is all very simple. A Japanese Christian does not arrogate the whole Christianity to himself, neither does he create a new Christianity by becoming a Christian. He is a Japanese, and he is a Christian; therefore he is a Japanese Christian. A Japanese by becoming a Christian does not cease to be a Japanese. On the contrary, he becomes more Japanese by becoming a Christian. A Japanese who becomes an American or an Englishman, or an amorphous universal man, is neither a true Japanese nor a true Christian. Paul, a Christian apostle, remained an Hebrew of the Hebrews till the end of his life. Savonarola was an Italian Christian, Luther was a German Christian, and Knox was a Scotch Christian. They were not characterless universal men, but distinctly national, therefore distinctly human, and distinctly Christian. . . .

I have seen no more sorrowful figures than Japanese who imitate their American or European missionary-teachers by being converted to the faith of the latter. Closely examined, these converted "universal Christians" may turn out to be no more than denationalized Japanese, whose universality is no more than Americanism or Anglicanism adopted to cover up their lost nationality.

"Two J's"

I love two J's and no third; one is Jesus, and the other is Japan.

I do not know which I love more, Jesus or Japan.

I am hated by my countrymen for Jesus' sake as *yaso*, and I am disliked by foreign missionaries for Japan's sake as national and narrow.

No matter; I may lose all my friends, but I cannot lose Jesus and Japan.

For Jesus' sake, I cannot own any other God than His Father as my God and Father; and for Japan's sake, I cannot accept any faith which comes in the name of foreigners. Come starvation; come death; I cannot disown Jesus and Japan; I am emphatically a Japanese Christian, though I know missionaries in general do not like that name.

Jesus and Japan; my faith is not a circle with one center; it is an ellipse with two centers. My heart and mind revolve around the two dear names. And I know that one strengthens the other; Jesus strengthens and purifies my love for Japan; and Japan clarifies and objectivises my love for Jesus. Were it not for the two, I would become a mere dreamer, a fanatic, an amorphous universal man.

Jesus makes me a world-man, a friend of humanity; Japan makes me a lover of my country, and through it binds me firmly to the terrestrial globe. I am neither too narrow nor too broad by loving the two at the same time.

O Jesus, thou art the Sun of my soul, the saviour dear; I have given my all to thee!

O Japan,

> Land of lands, for thee we give,
>   Our hearts, our pray'rs, our service free;
> For thee thy sons shall nobly live,
>   And at thy need shall die for thee."
>   —J. G. WHITTIER

> *To Be Inscribed Upon My Tomb*
> I for Japan;
> Japan for the World;
> The World for Christ;
> And All for God.

SELECTED READINGS

For works on various aspects of Christianity in Japan, see first the citations for each selection; some additional works are:

Drummond, Richard H. *A History of Christianity in Japan*. Grand Rapids, Mich.: William B. Eerdmans Publishing Co., 1971.

Iglehart, Charles W. *A Century of Protestant Christianity in Japan*. Rutland, Vt.: Charles E. Tuttle Co., 1959.

Ikado, Fujio, and McGovern, James R., comps. *A Bibliography of Christianity in Japan: Protestantism in English Sources (1859-1959)*. Tokyo: Committee on Asian Cultural Studies, International Christian University, 1966.

Kitamori, Kazoh. *Theology of the Pain of God*. Richmond, Va.: John Knox Press, 1965.

Laures, Johannes. *The Catholic Church in Japan: A Short History*. Rutland, Vt.: Charles E. Tuttle Co., 1954.

Ohata, Kiyoshi, and Ikado, Fujio. "Christianity." In *Japanese Religion in the Meiji Era*, edited by Hideo Kishimoto, translated by John F. Howes, pp. 171-309. Tokyo: Obunsha, 1956.

pARt eight

syncretism in japanese religious life

Religion in Japan is characterized both by a plurality of religious traditions and by mutual influence among these traditions. With the possible exception of Christianity, all the major religious lines within Japan have interacted to form a distinctive national heritage. This means that although it is possible to distinguish between the formal traditions of religions such as Buddhism and Shinto, each tradition is shaped in part by the other. What is more important, in the life of the people there has been no neat pigeonholing of religions. For example, in selections 11 and 14, we see that individuals are more interested in the totality of a ritual or cult than in its historical influences. (For a description of religious syncretism in one village, see selection 38.)

Japanese people have usually experienced religion in terms of an overall world view and mutually reinforcing acts of worship. Selections in this part show how individuals naturally integrated parts of several traditions into a total philosophy of life. Several authors state specifically that there is no difference between Shinto, Buddhism, and Confucianism. This has been the majority opinion in Japanese history, although some religious leaders and some groups (such as Nichiren Buddhism) have assumed exclusive commitment to one tradition. (For a Buddhist interpretation of syncretism in Japanese religion, see selection 7.)

22

RELIGIOUS LIFE IN MEDIEVAL JAPAN

It has long been the practice in Japan to participate simultaneously in several religious traditions with no sense of contradiction. The extracts from the will of a tenth century nobleman in this selection illustrate this practice. The will offers simple advice to the nobleman's heirs, showing concretely how several religious traditions are interwoven in a person's daily life. According to this will, one should be aware of astrological and calendrical concerns as soon as he arises in the morning. Even a small matter such as washing one's hands has a specific procedure—facing west, the direction of Buddhist paradise. Other restrictions concerning personal cleanliness are in conformity with the calendar. The author of the will recommends chanting the name of Buddha and *kami*, but he feels no need to label the source of these diverse elements—it is enough that they define a total personal world view.

Advice on personal behavior—especially concerning frugality and filial piety—is indirectly Confucian. On the other hand, daily devotion to a specific divinity is advisable, as is the chanting of Buddhist mantra (formulas). And just as one cares for his family during life, so should he set aside money for his own memorial services. George Sansom, a noted historian and author of the following extract, points out how Buddhist, Confucian, and even Shinto elements interact freely in this will. Of course, this last testament sets a very high ideal of personal conduct and devotion, which the average person might not attain, but the document is valuable for showing how several traditions are blended in the religious life of an individual.

Reprinted from *A History of Japan to 1334,* by George Sansom, with the permission of the publishers, Stanford University Press. © 1958 by the Board of Trustees of the Leland Stanford Junior University.

The Will of a Tenth Century Nobleman

The ascetic motive, the feeling for simplicity, purity, frugality, is as characteristic of Heian taste as is the strong sense of form and colour expressed by contrast in brilliant costume and elaborate ceremonial. It is an integral part of the great aesthetic tradition, which is perhaps rooted in early ideas of ritual purity. It is certainly an aspect of Japanese social ideals which should not be overlooked, and we may therefore turn for a little while to the circles of high-minded statesmen and severe moralists. Their standards of propriety are set forth in many diaries and injunctions to posterity, notably

of the tenth century, some of which have already been cited. It is significant that one of the most important of these is a document known as *Kujo-den no Goyuikai*, the Testamentary Admonitions of Kujo-den, who was none other than the great Fujiwara leader Morosuke, Minister of the Right at his death in 960. Though it is too long for full quotation here, the following extracts will give a fair idea of its quality. It must be read as setting forth a rule of life followed by Morosuke and recommended by him to his heirs and successors.

*

"Upon arising, first of all repeat seven times in a low voice the name of the star for the year. [There are seven—the seven stars of the Great Bear.] Take up a mirror and look at your face, to scrutinize changes in your appearance. Then look at the calendar and see whether the day is one of good or evil omen. Next use your toothbrush and then, facing West [i.e., in the direction of Paradise], wash your hands. Chant the name of Buddha and invoke those gods and divinities whom we ought always to revere and worship. Next make a record of the events of the previous day. [Throughout the document much stress is laid on the careful use of the calendar for noting engagements and on the accurate recording of the day's business as soon as possible after the event.]

"Now break your fast with rice gruel. Comb your hair once every three days, not every day. Cut your fingernails on a day of the Ox, your toenails on a day of the Tiger. If the day is auspicious, now bathe, but only once every fifth day. There are favourable and unfavourable days for bathing.

"Now if there is any business upon which you must go abroad, put on your clothes and cap. Do not be sluggish in attending to your duties.

"When you meet people do not talk a great deal. And do not discuss your personal affairs. State your opinion, and say what is necessary, but do not repeat what others have said. The disasters of mankind proceed from the mouth. Beware, be on your guard. [Note that most works of this kind emphasize the importance of reserve, of circumspection in speech and gesture.] And when you read documents concerned with state affairs always treat them with discretion.

"At the morning and evening meals you must not make a habit of eating and drinking to excess. Nor should you eat except at proper times. [This rule is supported by a slightly garbled quotation from the Odes.]

"Careful planning can secure the future. In general as you get on in years and become well-acquainted with affairs, you should read classical literature in the morning, next practise handwriting, and only after this indulge in games or sports. But an excessive addiction to hawking and hunting is positively wrong.

"After receiving your manly robes [this refers to the ceremony called "genbuku," the donning of the toga virilis] and before you embark on an official career, conduct yourself in this manner: Early in life select a divinity as the object of your devotion and chant his holy name, after cleansing your

hands in a basin of water. One may judge how near a man is to salvation from the frequency with which he recites the mantra [the invocations and spells of the mystic sects].

"There are many warning examples close at hand of disaster and calamity overtaking our irreligious colleagues. Thus the Third Regent, the Lord Tadahira [Morosuke's father], has told us: 'In the eighth year of Encho (930) when a thunderbolt struck the Pure Cool Hall, the courtiers went pale. I, having taken refuge in the Three Treasures [the Buddhist faith], found in this event nothing to be frightened about. But the Great Counsellor Kiyoyuki and the Vice-Counsellor Mareyo, who had never paid homage to the Law of the Buddha—these two were struck dead.' From this we may draw our lesson, that the grace bestowed upon us by our faith in the mantra will save us from misfortune. Moreover, many of the clergy, men of faith, purity, and wisdom, can according to their spiritual power bear witness to similar events. But faith is not of help only in this life, for it will indeed ensure for us the life to come.

"If you would learn something of literature, let your attention be devoted especially to the histories and chronicles of our native land.

"In all things render always the utmost loyalty and upright service to your Lord. Always devote the fullest degree of filial piety to your parents. Let your deference to your elder brother be like that which you pay to your father, and your love for your younger brother like that which you feel for your child; so that in all things great or small your hearts may be all one, and the aspirations of all [members of the family] so united that they do not differ by a hair's breadth.

"Cherish your defenceless sisters with all care. . . .

"In general, so long as you are not ill, you should always wait upon your father once every day. Should there be some obstacle, send word and enquire whether it would be suitable to call in the evening. The son and heir of King Wen will serve exceedingly well as a model of filial behaviour. [This is the celebrated Duke of Chou, regarded by Confucius as the paragon of all virtues.] . . .

"Let the income of your house as it is received be divided first into ten parts, and let one part be devoted to alms.

"Make complete plans beforehand for the conduct of your affairs after your death. . . . When this is not done you invite all manner of inconvenience for your wife, your children, and your servants, who then must ask favours of those from whom they ought not to expect them, or will lose that which they ought not to lose, thus leading to the ruin of your house and to censure by others.

"Always put by a portion of your income to provide for the Seven Requiem Masses,[1] for the repose of your spirit, beginning with the cost of the funeral itself.

• • •

[1] Requiem masses were always conducted by Buddhist priests. [ed.]

"Do you who come after me reflect fervently on these things, and always devote yourselves to public and private affairs with the utmost diligence."

*

These cold injunctions to posterity do not sound like the sentiments of a great noble presiding over an extravagant and dissolute aristocracy. They are more akin to the utterances of a prophet deploring the evils of his day. But they are not really moral principles. Rather they are rules for success in life, calling for extreme self-control, and the observances of a very strict code of behaviour exacted by Buddhist faith and Confucian piety. Perhaps their most notable feature is the great weight given to filial duty, together with a disapproval of all social intercourse beyond what is required for the due performance of public obligations. The family is the unit, the means, and the purpose of life. It is self-contained and independent of, if not hostile to, other families. In public what is to be prized is gravity and solemnity. Only in the bosom of the family may one abandon something of the reserve which distinguishes a· man of breeding, and relax in an atmosphere of humanity and love.

What seems at first sight surprising is the repeated stress upon frugality and simplicity. It is, of course, in part of Confucian origin, for the Sage must always avoid excess of any kind; but it comes also from a persistent strain in the Japanese character which finds expression in the earliest Shinto ritual and is visible throughout Japanese social history. It is interesting to note that the passage recommending simple clothing and furniture and condemning display is quoted in later literature as a classical dictum on frugality.

23

unity of shinto, confucianism, and Buddhism as the Rationale of the government

The previous selection illustrates the interaction of religious traditions in the life of the individual; this selection illustrates similar interaction on the level of government. The occasion for this letter from the sixteenth century Japanese military ruler (civil dictator) Hideyoshi was an earlier letter from the Roman Catholic viceroy of India. The tone of the letter pictures a bold, powerful leader who is proud of his national heritage and not timid about criticizing foreign traditions.

First Hideyoshi outlines his political ambitions, such as ruling China (called here the great Ming nation and the Middle Kingdom). Then he describes the foundation of the Japanese heritage, drawing freely upon Shinto, Confucian, and Buddhist notions. For example, his opening statement, "Ours is the land of the Gods, and God is mind," derives from Shinto—the idea that Japan is the land of the Gods—and from Neo-Confucianism—the more philosophical principle that God is mind. But the document specifies for the foreign reader that this "God" is identical in Japan's three major traditions, and "To know Shinto is to know Buddhism as well as Confucianism."

This official government document demonstrates the strong sense of unified religious world view as a distinctive Japanese heritage, in clear opposition to foreign "heresies." Especially to be protected is the Confucian ethical and political notion of humanity, which the Catholic priests have allegedly tried to destroy. Christianity is criticized as preaching but one doctrine "to the exclusion of others." Hideyoshi turns the tables on the Christians by offering to send instruction in Japan's "profound philosophy."

Reprinted by permission of the publisher from *Sources of Japanese Tradition*, edited by Ryusaku Tsunoda, Wm. Theodore de Bary, and Donald Keene (New York: Columbia University Press, 1958), paperback edition, Vol. I, pp. 316-318.

Letter to the Viceroy of the Indies

Reading your message from afar, I can appreciate the immense expanse of water which separates us. As you have noted in your letter, my country, which is comprised of sixty-odd provinces, has known for many years more days of disorder than days of peace; rowdies have been given to fomenting intrigue, and bands of warriors have formed cliques to defy the court's orders. Ever since my youth, I have been constantly concerned over this deplorable situation. I studied the art of self-cultivation and the secret of governing the country. Through profound planning and forethought, and according to the three principles of benevolence, wisdom, and courage, I cared for the warriors on the one hand and looked after the common people on the other; while administering justice, I was able to establish security. Thus, before many years had passed, the unity of the nation was set on a firm foundation, and now foreign nations, far and near, without exception, bring tribute to us. Everyone, everywhere, seeks to obey my orders. . . . Though our own country is now safe and secure, I nevertheless entertain hopes of ruling the great

Ming nation. I can reach the Middle Kingdom aboard my palace-ship within a short time. It will be as easy as pointing to the palm of my hand. I shall then use the occasion to visit your country regardless of the distance or the differences between us.

Ours is the land of the Gods, and God is mind. Everything in nature comes into existence because of mind. Without God there can be no spirituality. Without God there can be no way. God rules in times of prosperity as in times of decline. God is positive and negative and unfathomable. Thus, God is the root and source of all existence. This God is spoken of by Buddhism in India, Confucianism in China, and Shinto in Japan. To know Shinto is to know Buddhism as well as Confucianism.

As long as man lives in this world, Humanity will be a basic principle. Were it not for Humanity and Righteousness, the sovereign would not be a sovereign, nor a minister of state a minister. It is through the practice of Humanity and Righteousness that the foundations of our relationships between sovereign and minister, parent and child, and husband and wife are established. If you are interested in the profound philosophy of God and Buddha, request an explanation and it will be given to you. In your land one doctrine is taught to the exclusion of others, and you are not yet informed of the [Confucian] philosophy of Humanity and Righteousness. Thus there is no respect for God and Buddha and no distinction between sovereign and ministers. Through heresies you intend to destroy the righteous law. Hereafter, do not expound, in ignorance of right and wrong, unreasonable and wanton doctrines. A few years ago the so-called Fathers came to my country seeking to bewitch our men and women, both of the laity and clergy. At that time punishment was administered to them, and it will be repeated if they should return to our domain to propagate their faith. It will not matter what sect or denomination they represent—they shall be destroyed. It will then be too late to repent. If you entertain any desire of establishing amity with this land, the seas have been rid of the pirate menace, and merchants are permitted to come and go. Remember this.

As for the products of the south-land, acknowledgment of their receipt is here made, as itemized. The catalogue of gifts which we tender is presented on a separate paper. The rest will be explained orally by my envoy.

Tensho 19 [1591]: Seventh Month, 25th Day [signed] The Civil Dictator

24

BleNòInG of RelIgIous traòitions in popular teaching

As can be seen in selection 22, the Japanese people tended to inter-relate several religions in their daily lives, even though leaders of Shinto and Buddhism tried to maintain the distinctiveness of their respective traditions. In the late Tokugawa period, however, a number of popular teachers attempted to lead the people with a mixture of notions from several traditions.

One teacher who gained great fame was Ninomiya, described in this selection by one of his disciples. Ninomiya tried to simplify the doctrines of Shinto, Confucianism, and Buddhism so that they would form a unified practical guide for the common people. Therefore, he relied not so much on abstract argument as on precepts for frugality and virtue in an agrarian setting.

Ninomiya attempted to resolve what he thought were artificial differences between the three great religions of Japan and blended them into one prescription, or 'pill.' Each ingredient in the pill was effective for a specific area of the Japanese tradition, yet when in the form of a compounded prescription, the several ingredients could not be distinguished. The thrust of Ninomiya's teaching was that because man is indebted to nature, he should repay this debt with virtue, and in his view, each of the three traditions supported the repayment of virtue. Ninomiya's basic idea combines the Shinto sense of gratitude toward nature (in the sense of cosmic rhythm) and the Confucian sense of respect for superiors in a hierarchical society.

Reprinted by permission of the publisher from *Sources of Japanese Tradition*, edited by Ryusaku Tsunoda, Wm. Theodore de Bary, and Donald Keene (New York: Columbia University Press, 1958), paperback edition, Vol. 2, pp. 79-80.

The "Pill" of the Three Religions

Old Ninomiya once said, "I have long pondered about Shinto—what it calls the Way, what are its virtues and what its deficiencies; and about Confucianism—what its teaching consists in, what are its virtues and deficiencies;

and also Buddhism—what do its various sects stand for, and what are their virtues and deficiencies. And so I wrote a poem:

> The things of this world
> Are like lengths
> Of bamboo rod
> For use in fish nets—
> This one's too long,
> That one too short.

"Such was my dissatisfaction with them. Now let me state the strong and weak points of each. Shinto is the Way which provides the foundation of the country; Confucianism is the Way which provides for governing the country; and Buddhism is the Way which provides for governing one's mind. Caring no more for lofty speculation than for humble truth, I have tried simply to extract the essence of each of these teachings. By essence I mean their importance to mankind. Selecting what is important and discarding what is unimportant, I have arrived at the best teaching for mankind, which I call the teaching of Repaying Virtue. I also call it the 'pill containing the essence of Shinto, Confucianism and Buddhism.' ". . .

Kimigasa Hyodayu asked the proportions of the prescription in this "pill," and the old man replied, "One spoon of Shinto, and a half-spoon each of Confucianism and Buddhism."

Then someone drew a circle, one half of which was marked Shinto and two quarter-segments labeled Confucianism and Buddhism respectively. "Is it like this?" he asked. The old man smiled. "You won't find medicine like that anywhere. In a real pill all the ingredients are thoroughly blended so as to be indistinguishable. Otherwise it would taste bad in the mouth and feel bad in the stomach."

SELECTED READINGS

For works on various aspects of syncretism in Japanese religion, see first the citations for each selection; some aditional works are:

Earhart, H. Byron. *A Religious Study of the Mount Haguro Sect of Shugendo: An Example of Japanese Mountain Religion.* Tokyo: Monumenta Nipponica, Sophia University, 1970.

Kamstra, Jakob H. *Encounter or Syncretism: The Initial Growth of Japanese Buddhism.* Leiden: E. J. Brill, 1967.

Matsunaga, Alicia. *The Buddhist Philosophy of Assimilation: The Historical Development of the Honji Suijaku Theory.* Tokyo: Sophia University and Charles E. Tuttle Co., 1969.

part nine

closeness of man, gods, and nature

Japanese religion comprises a half dozen different traditions which interact with one another, so that the Japanese people have tended to participate in all these traditions simultaneously. Therefore, in order to understand the sum of these traditions, we need to define the nature of Japanese religion as a whole, or the nature of the overall Japanese religious world view. One way is to recognize the persistent themes which characterize Japanese religion throughout most of its history, cutting across most of its religious traditions. In Japan at least six persistent themes can be distinguished; one theme forms the topic of each of Parts 9 through 14. (For the presence of these six themes in the New Religions, see selection 49.)

One of the major features of Japanese religious life is the way in which man, gods, and nature are closely interrelated on the same plane. The term *gods* can mean *kami*, Buddhist divinities, or even venerated human beings and souls of the dead. *Nature* means not an objective and inert collection of substance but the sacred rhythm of the cosmos as a living unity. From the earliest times to the present, the Japanese people have celebrated their closeness to the *kami* and their intimate relationship to nature. (For the notion of *kami* see selection 1.) As seen in Shinto mythology (selection 2), the *kami* express their sacredness and power through their embodiment in nature, such as the wind, trees, rivers, and mountains. This idea contrasts sharply with the Judaic and Christian traditions, which tend to emphasize the distance between God and man and the inferiority of nature to man.

This triangular relationship of gods, man, and nature is found in Japanese Buddhism as well as in Shinto; in fact, some of the best examples of this theme are in Zen Buddhism. Zen masters encourage individual enlightenment and the person's identity with the natural world rather

than the relationship of a person to God. Even art forms such as landscape painting and the poetry of haiku contain the notion of conformity to nature, which in the Japanese world view is an important religious orientation. (This is a good illustration of Kishimoto's statement that Japanese religious and artistic values are closely related [see Part 1].) In this chapter the illustrations are chosen from artistic materials to show how religion and art intertwine in Japan, but examples from explicitly religious materials could also be mentioned. (For example, see selection 30 for a discussion of how the dead become *kami* and selection 47 for a description of a foundress who is treated as a "living-*kami*" in her own lifetime.)

25

Religious sentiment in ancient poetry

The *Manyoshu,* compiled in the eighth century, is the oldest collection of Japanese poetry. This work contains more than a thousand poems of diverse subject matter, and because it is respected as an ancient watershed of Japanese poetic and religious expression, it is still widely read today.

As explained in the modern introduction to the *Manyoshu,* the inspiration for this poetry is usually ascribed to the many spirits (or *kami*) which inhabited the natural world. There was no attempt to distinguish between the forces of nature and the power of the *kami,* they were so closely related. As man participated in and appreciated the beauty of the natural world, he acknowledged the presence of the *kami.* This intuitive and aesthetic (rather than rational) approach to the divine is typical of ancient Japan and Shinto in general.

In the stanzas of this collection, lyric poetry and religious sentiment intertwine, even when the subject matter is rather fanciful. For example, the poem "The Three Hills" retells the age-old account of how two (male) mountains competed for the love of another (female) mountain. Here not only aesthetic and religious but also romantic subjects are blended. For the Japanese audience, it also recalls the landscape of the

Yamato plain, the setting for much of early Japanese culture. The poem of "Lady Otomo of Sakanoe" expresses her earnest prayer in seeking communion with the ancestral *kami*. The final selection shows that already in the eighth century the Japanese possessed their curious sorrow and delight in the evanescence of life. Usually this awareness is described in the idiom of Buddhism, but in this case the essence of life is captured completely with only the image of a boat which passes out of sight.

Reprinted by permission of the publisher from *The Manyoshu* (New York: Columbia University Press, 1965).

The Manyoshu: "Collection for a Myriad Ages"

The Manyo man lived in a world peopled by multitudes of gods and spirits, genii and fairies. And it is noteworthy that despite the wide acceptance of Confucianism and Buddhism, almost all the gods whom he sang, or who fed the well-spring of his lyric inspiration, were purely Japanese. They were gods of the indigenous cult which was named Shinto, or the Way of the Gods, in contradistinction to Buddhism.

There is here no need of attempting to explore the whole field of Shinto mythology. So far as the *Manyoshu* is concerned, it suffices that on the one hand there were the spirits, which had survived from the remote past in folklore, and which still affected daily life; and on the other, those whose influence was steadily rising as gods of the clan or nation. When analyzed historically, it will be seen that the Manyo idea in this connection was really an admixture and fusion of concepts which had different origins and which were in various stages of development. There were mysterious powers which moved and had their being in nature but which were too vaguely felt to be personified: lands and provinces, mountains and rivers, trees and herbs, and even human acts such as speech, were believed to be endowed with spirits, and as such were made objects of reverence or fear. There were gods possessing full personalities, namely the ancestors of the Imperial House and of various clans, the patrons of arts and industries, the tutelary deities of communities and the spirits of nature. Thus, individual objects of nature in their various capacities, sometimes as mediums through which gods manifested themselves to man, sometimes as gods in themselves, and sometimes as divine property or demesne, occupied their respective places in the religious life of the nation. . . .

Emperor Tenji

The Three Hills

Mount Kagu strove with Mount Miminashi
  For the love of Mount Unebi.
Such is love since the age of the gods:
As it was thus in the early days,
  So people strive for spouses even now . . . .

Lady Otomo of Sakanoe

Chanted at a Religious Service to Her Ancestral God

Oh, our heaven-born god,
Descended from the heavenly plains—
With the *sakaki*[1] branch
Fresh from the inmost hill,
Tied with white paper and mulberry cloth,
With a wine-jar set in the purified earth,
With a cord of many bamboo-rings
Hanging from my neck,
With my knees bent like the deer's,
With my maiden's scarf flung over me,—
Thus I entreat thee, our god,
Yet can I not meet him? . . .

Manzei

To what shall I liken this life?
It is like a boat,
Which, unmoored at morn,
Drops out of sight
And leaves no trace behind.

---

[1]*Sakaki,* an evergreen tree sacred to Shinto and grown around Shinto shrines.

the Role of nature in zen Buddhism

D. T. Suzuki was the first interpreter of Zen to the West, and his English books on Zen are probably still the most widely read in the Western world. One interesting aspect of his interpretation is the way in which he contrasts Zen with Western notions. As in the following selection, this contrast often involves him in provocative, or even polemic, arguments, but for this very reason they point out some distinctions between the basic assumptions of Zen and Western religions.

The main point in this selection is the divergent notions of nature in Zen and Western thought: "To the Western mind Nature and Man are separated"; by contrast, in Zen "there is perfect identity of Man and Nature, of God and Nature." Suzuki shows how this contrast results in different religious goals. For Western man, he claims, the struggle is to become united with God, and nature is seen as an enemy in this struggle. In Zen, nature is seen as a friend in the attempt to become aware of one's own true character in relationship to the fullness of the world.

In this brief selection Suzuki has not exhausted the Western concept of nature; in fact, he seems more concerned with describing his own anti-Western viewpoint than the facts of Western cultural history, and there is room to disagree with his analysis of Judeo-Christian religion. But there is no doubt that he is expressing a generically Japanese viewpoint: nature is not an obstacle but a friendly aid in religious fulfillment. One might even say further that nature in this broad sense provides much of the content of the religious goal in Japan; to be harmoniously related to nature is one of the highest aims in Japanese religious life. Suzuki advances some abstract Buddhist reasoning to validate this goal, but the same goal is expressed more concretely in art and poetry.

Reprinted by permission of the publisher from Daisetz T. Suzuki, "The Role of Nature in Zen Buddhism," in *Eranos Jahrbuch*, 1953, Eranos Foundation, and by permission of Matsugaoka Bunko.

Nature in Zen and in the West

... We can summarize the following as characteristic of the Western attitude towards Nature.

1. Nature is something hostile to Man and drags him down when he is struggling to reach God. The temptations of Nature symbolized as "the

flesh" are often too irresistible and make Man exclaim, "The spirit is willing but the flesh is weak."

2. While Nature and God are warring against each other, Nature and Man are also at war. Or rather, as commanded by God, Man is always striving to exercise his dominating power over Nature.

3. There is no way for Man to approach Nature in a conciliatory, friendly, fraternal spirit. If the one does not destroy the other, the other is sure to destroy and dominate over the one. There is nothing in Nature that will help Man in his spiritual advancement.

4. Nature is a material world and the material world is meant for exploration and exploitation and also experimentation.

5. In another sense the material world is brute fact, stands as the *pour-soi* against the *en-soi*. Intellect cannot do anything with it, but has to take it as it is and to make the best of it.

6. The dichotomy of Nature-and-Man implies hostility, even an utter irreconcilability, and is, therefore, mutually destructive.

7. No idea seems to be present here which is indicative or suggestive of human participation in, or identification with, Nature. To the Western mind Nature and Man are kept separate....

Nature is sometimes treated by Western people as something already "there" into which Man comes and which he finds himself confronting, rather inhospitably, because he feels he does not belong in it. He is conscious of his situation in which he is placed, surrounded by all kinds of inert matter and brute fact. He does not know why he is here, nor does he realize what is coming to him. Endowed with consciousness, however, he thinks he can make decision as to what his future course will be, and further, he feels he is entirely responsible for his decision. He is lonely and helpless because Nature is threatening and ready to swallow him down into its own maw....

There is, however, another way of considering Nature and Man. Inasmuch as Nature stands before Man as an unknown quantity and Man comes to it with his consciousness from somewhere else than Nature itself, Nature and Man cannot be friendly and sociable, for they have no way to communicate with each other. They are always strangers. But we must not forget that the very fact that Man finds himself encountering Nature demonstrates that they cannot be said to be totally unknown to each other. If this were the case there would be no encountering of any character between the two. To this extent, then, Nature is already telling Man something of itself and Man is understanding Nature that much. Then Man cannot be said to be entirely an outsider but is somehow standing in a relationship to Nature and perhaps coming out of Nature itself. Man must be after all an insider.

Here is a room for Zen Buddhism to enter and to give its own views on the relationship of Nature and Man.

While separating himself from Nature, Man still is a part of Nature, for the fact of separation itself shows that Man is dependent on Nature. We can

say this: Nature produces Man out of itself; Man cannot be outside of Nature, he still has his being rooted in Nature. Therefore, there cannot be any hostility between them. On the contrary, there must always be a friendly understanding and a sympathetic communication between Man and Nature. Man came from Nature in order to see Nature in him, that is, Nature came to itself in order to see itself in Man.

This is a kind of objective thinking—to say that Man comes from Nature and that Man sees himself through Nature, or that Nature sees itself through Man. There is another way of seeing into the situation. We here shift our position from objectivity to subjectivity. This probing into subjectivity is also probing into the very basis of Nature as it is in itself.

To turn into subjectivity means to turn from Nature to Man himself. Instead of considering Man objectively in opposition to Nature, our task is now to make Man retreat as it were into himself and let him see what he finds there in the depth of his being. The probing of Nature thus becomes the problem of Man: Who or what is Man? . . .

. . . The point that I am trying to make is that Zen starts from where time has not come to itself, that is to say, where timelessness has not negated itself so as to have a dichotomy of subject-object, Man-Nature, God-world, etc. This is the abode of what I call "pure subjectivity." Zen is here and wants us to be there too. In terms of Nature, Zen is where one of the masters remarked, "When I began to study Zen, mountains were mountains; when I thought I understood Zen, mountains were not mountains; but when I came to full knowledge of Zen, mountains were again mountains."

When the mountains are seen as not standing against me, when they are dissolved into oneness of things, they are not mountains, they cease to exist as objects of Nature. When they are seen as standing against me as separate from me, as something unfriendly to me, they are not mountains either. The mountains are really mountains when they are assimilated into my being and I am absorbed in them. As long as Nature is something differentiated from me and is displayed before me as if it were an unknown quantity and a brute fact, Nature cannot be said even to be unfriendly or actively hostile.

On the other hand, Nature becomes part of my being as soon as it is recognized as Nature, as *pour-soi*.[1] It can never remain as something strange and altogether unrelated to me. I am in Nature and Nature is in me. Not mere participation in each other, but there is a fundamental identity between the two. Hence, the mountains are mountains and the rivers are rivers; they are there before me. The reason I can see the mountains as mountains and the waters as waters is because I am in them and they are in me, that is *tat tvam asi*.[2] If not for this identity, there would be no Nature as *pour-soi*. "The primary face" or "my nose" is to be taken hold of here and nowhere else.

---

[1] *Pour-soi*, for itself. [ed.]
[2] *Tat tvam asi*, "you are that (ultimate reality)," a statement from the *Chandogya Upanishad*. [ed.]

Identity belongs in spatial terminology. In terms of time, it is timelessness. But mere timelessness does not mean anything. When Nature is seen as confronting me, there is already time, and timelessness now turns itself into time. But time-serialism has its sense only when it goes on in the field of timelessness which is the Buddhist conception of *sunyata* ("emptiness"). In this *sunyata* the mountains are mountains and I see them as such and they see me as such—my seeing them is their seeing me. It is then that *sunyata* becomes *tathata* ("suchness") or that *tathata* is *sunyata* and *sunyata* is *tathata.*

When we come to this stage of thinking, pure subjectivity is pure objectivity, the *en-soi*[3] is the *pour-soi:* there is perfect identity of Man and Nature, of God and Nature, of the one and the many. But what we have to remember here is that the identity does not at all imply the annihilation of one at the cost of the other. The mountains do not vanish, they stand before me, I have not absorbed them, nor have they wiped me out of the scene. The dichotomy is there, which is suchness, and this suchness (*tathata*) in all its suchness is emptiness (*sunyata*) itself. The mountains are mountains and yet not mountains. I am I and you are you, and yet I am you and you are I. Nature as a world of manyness is not ignored and Man as a subject facing the many remains conscious of himself.

27

Religious aspects in painting

If traditions such as the Shinto *kami* and Zen Buddhism describe the religious content of nature, then the fullest expression of nature in concrete form is through art. The way in which men relate to nature is seen in their artistic depiction of the natural world. In this selection we encounter yet another form of the Japanese appreciation of nature—a painter's own theory of the nature of painting. The description of Mitsuoki's theory of art and translations from his writings provide a fascinating illustration of the sacredness of nature in traditional art.

The gist of Mitsuoki's theory is that art is poor when it is a bad copy of nature and even when it is a good copy of nature which stops at being

[3]*En-soi,* in itself. [ed.]

simply a copy. To be most successful, to be ranked as a Divine Work, art must capture the spirit or motion of life. To attain this level a man needs more than ordinary human skill and craftsmanship—he needs the gift of heaven. This means that the artist, to be successful, must live in accord with the rhythm of the universe, so that he can express the same rhythmic spirit in his painting.

This theory draws on Chinese precedents, so that it is difficult to label its religious sources. It is as close to Taoistic ideas as it is to those of Shinto and Zen Buddhism. But the historical source of the theory is not as significant as the impact of the theory in artistic and religious life. The goal of the traditional artist painting a landscape or a housewife practicing flower arrangement is the same: to bring one's own life into conformity to the rhythm of nature in such a way that artificiality is avoided and a pleasant harmony is attained. Sesshu (1420 - 1506) is considered by many to have expressed this rhythm of nature better than any other Japanese artist. (See the photograph of his work *Winter Landscape*, figure 7.)

The Art of Painting

...It was not until the last years of the seventeenth century that any effort was made toward the formulation of a Japanese theory of painting. One of the earliest who attempted this was a renowned court painter, Tosa Mitsuoki (1617–91). The title of his book, *The Authoritative Summary of the Rules of Japanese Painting* ("Honcho Gaho Taiden"), itself suggests his conception of Japanese painting as independent of Chinese art....

What type of art theory emerges through these sections? Its central thesis seems to be summarized by Mitsuoki in a passage that appears in "The Essentials of the Theory of Painting": "Among works of painting that delineate various kinds of objects, some are mediocre because they are exceedingly lifelike, and others are mediocre because they are not lifelike. If there is a painting which is lifelike and which is good for that reason, that work has followed the laws of life. If there is a painting which is not lifelike and which is good for that reason, that work has followed the laws of painting. Herein lies the essence of my precepts." Mitsuoki is here clarifying the relationship between nature and art in a fourfold argument. Art should imitate nature, but a mere duplication of an object of nature does not neces-

Figure 7. *Winter Landscape*, by Sesshu. Reprinted from Robert Treat Paine and Alexander Soper, *The Art and Architecture of Japan*. © Robert Treat Paine and Alexander Soper, 1955. Reprinted by permission of Penguin Books Ltd.

sarily produce a good work of art. The artist must at some point depart from, or even distort, nature. But of course a casual distortion of nature would not bring forth a good work of art, either; such a work, being not lifelike, would be lifeless. All good works of art are lifelike, not so much in the sense that they copy all the outward details of real life, as in the sense that they observe all the inward laws of nature. The painter may omit some external particulars in order to stress a certain invisible law of nature, thereby making his work more lifelike in effect. A superb artist might go even further; his painting may not appear lifelike but has a forceful effect for that very reason. He has gone beyond the laws of life; he has entered a sphere governed solely by the laws of art. According to Mitsuoki, such is the ultimate of the art of painting.

It should be noted that Mitsuoki here conceives the laws of nature and of art not as mutually exclusive or contradictory, but as complementary. The artist must first observe the laws of nature before he comes to cope with the laws of art; otherwise his work would not resemble life but become lifeless. To observe the laws of nature and to follow them faithfully are, in fact, the two most elementary laws of art. Details of an object of nature should never be overlooked. A student in painting should start his training by learning how to depict the way things are in real life. Mitsuoki's advice to beginners is very revealing: "Anyone who wishes to learn the art of painting should first study the way of things in nature. He should then proceed to learn how to use the brush in outline-drawing. Finally he should come to have a good grip of the spirit. On the last point there is a good deal that cannot be said in word." The study of nature comes even before learning how to handle the brush. Without thoroughly knowing how things are in real life, one cannot draw their outlines. A careful observation of objects in actual life is an absolutely necessary preliminary for anyone who wishes to learn drawing, and eventually, the spirit of painting. . . .

Closely following Hsia Wen-yen, Mitsuoki classifies into three categories all the works of painting above the acceptable level: the Competent work, the Marvelous Work, and the Divine Work. On the first of the three Mitsuoki remarks: "A painting which succeeds in reproducing the original figure and which follows all the technical rules of painting may be called a Competent Work. The painter has well observed the disciplines and mastered an established style. Such is commonly called a skillful artist. One can reach this stage through training. No ordinary painter can attain the ranks of the Divine Work and the Marvelous Work." In other words, a painter who has learned all the rules and techniques of painting necessary for an exact reproduction of color and shape can produce a Competent Work, which, although itself a fine accomplishment, still leaves much to be desired.

The next higher in rank is the Marvelous Work. Mitsuoki explains: "A painting in which the brushwork is superb, the coloring is perfect, and the meaning overflows, may be called a Marvelous Work. The painter has tran-

scended established styles, for his art is now fully mature; even though he paints independently of the rules, he never breaks the rules. This is because he paints the meaning rather than the shape." The student of painting, as he advances in his training, must try to go beyond the rules after completely mastering them. He will go beyond the mere copying of color and shape, beyond a faithful reproduction of the external appearance. If he successfully does this, his work will show a charm not so much through its outward life-likeness as through its meaning, for the meaning of a painting lies not in the shape or color of the object but in the way in which the painter delineates it. There are therefore cases where the artist departs from ordinary rules and does not copy the exact shape or color. An advanced painter can do this because he, thoroughly knowing the objective of his work, paints the meaning rather than the shape. . . .

When the painter pursues this principle to the ultimate, he will reach the realm of the Divine Work, the highest of the three ranks. Mitsuoki, again quoting from Hsieh, writes: "This is a work which has 'the spirit's circula-tion—life's motion.' It springs from heavenly nature and surpasses any or-dinary man's skill. It is therefore called the Divine Work." The painting of the highest order is a product of inborn nature given by heaven, something even a painter of the most meticulous craftsmanship cannot attain. For this reason it cannot be learned by training: there is some superhuman quality accessible only to a limited number of geniuses. Mitsuoki tries to explain this mysterious quality by referring to a well-known Chinese aesthetic term, Hsieh Ho's "the spirit's circulation—life's motion." The term has aroused a great deal of controversy as to its precise meaning, and painters and critics in China and Japan have given scores of different interpretations. Mitsuoki felt it imperative to explain the term in his own words and to clarify what he meant by it. This he does in the very first paragraph of the *Summary*. He writes:

"The spirit's circulation" means that the painter, as he sets out to work, lets the spirit of his soul circulate through his body. When his soul is small and his spirit insufficient, his brushwork will be stunted, feeble, and always unsatisfactory. The painter's brushwork should become gentle and soft upon grief, coarse and strong upon anger, mellow and carefree upon joy; it is essential that the painter choose the precise emotion. He should first enter into a calm frame of mind, a mind devoid of nervousness or excitement; he should let the spirit expand through his body, with his soul filling up heaven and earth; in such a mindless state he will begin a work of painting. "Life's motion" means that a painting, whether of a god or a devil or a man, whether of a beast or a bird or a tree, contains the spirit of the object and thereby makes the spectator feel as if the object were standing before his eyes. A warrior should show his martial glory, a court lady her elegant charm, a Buddhist priest an appearance of his holy mission. A bird should have the force of soaring and singing, a beast the vigor of howling and scampering. A pine or cypress tree should show the mysteriously venerable shape with which it stands through the snow and frost; a dragon or a tiger should dis-play the force by which it catches the spirit of the wind and the clouds, moving

even heaven and earth. Spring flowers, ready to burst open, have the air of warmth and resourcefulness; summer trees, with their cool verdure, have the potentiality of powerful growth; autumn grass, with wilted dryness in the atmosphere, has an appearance of harsh desolation; and winter flowers, with the snow and frost, have the color of withstanding the cold. The foremost principle in the art of painting lies in a successful rendering of the spirit each object has. Particularly important is the case of painting men and human life. Unless the painting successfully transmits the spirit of the object, it will have nothing divine in it, and, if that is the case, the work is like a shrine with no god in it. No ordinary artist can transmit such a spirit into his work; but, unless the student strives with this aim in mind from the first day of his training, how could he expect to attain the ultimate of the art of painting eventually? The same is true of all other paintings. There would be no need for talking about principles of painting, if painting were no more than an art of copying the shape. The ultimate aim of painting is to represent the spirit of the object. In every work of painting, whether it is of human life, a bird, a beast, an insect, or a fish, the spirit of a living object can be represented only by putting eyes into the painting. A portrait, whatever fine complexion or shapely figure it may have, will suffer from the lack of a living spirit if it is dead in the eyes.

Mitsuoki has given the age-old Chinese term an interpretation typical of medieval Japanese aesthetics.

In essence the so-called Divine Work is a further development of the Marvelous Work. The meaning, which was essential to the Marvelous Work, is now replaced by the spirit. But the spirit is really the source of the meaning; each object has its meaning, its *raison d'etre,* because of its spirit given by nature. The spirit is the life-force of the object. It is not an attribute but a potential power. An artist who paints a bird should do it in such a way as not merely to copy all the attributes of a bird but to transmit the "bird-ness" of it; otherwise his bird will neither fly nor sing, it will be devoid of spirit and of life. One who paints the portrait of a man should of course reproduce his complexion and appearance with precision, yet far more important is the making of the eyes, for it is the eyes that reflect the spirit of the man. Without the spirit the portrait is soulless and lifeless; the man is a corpse. That painting, in other words, would have no "life's motion."

How, then, could the artist put life into his work? Through "the spirit's circulation," Mitsuoki would answer. The painter can give spirit to his painting only by growing into the object of the painting himself—that is to say, by identifying his spirit with the spirit of the object in his painting. In order to do this, he would first have to unite himself in one spirit; his whole being, and not his intellect alone or his emotion alone, should be inspired. However, this does not mean that his mind is all in excitement; on the contrary, he will be in a most tranquil state of mind, with no interference of his ego. His body fully pervaded with the spirit, is empty of the spirit; the maximum of fullness is void. The mind of the artist in such a state can fill up the whole of heaven and earth; it can transform itself to any outside object with ease. Himself a bird, the painter can paint a bird that has its true spirit, a bird ready to fly

or sing at any moment. Himself liberated from his personal grief, he can paint a grieving man with life and spirit, for the grief he paints is not his own but that of the particular man he is painting. The artist must paint a precise emotion, Mitsuoki has said; in painting an emotion, the artist ought to exclude all emotions of his own. Only then will the painting have an emotion of its own, a life of its own; it will have "life's motion." "The spirit's circulation" is the creative process, and "life's motion" its resulting product.

28

Religious content in haiku

The short, "telegraphic," seventeen-syllable haiku has rapidly become an international art form. Western poets often write haiku in English and other Western languages, and several haiku magazines are printed in America. But it is well to remember that the haiku developed first in Japan (where composing the short, disciplined poems is still an important personal experience), and many people who are familiar with this poetry feel that the haiku of Matsuo Basho, a seventeenth century poet, have never been surpassed.

In the following selection, Harold Henderson provides background on the life of Basho and commentary on several of his haiku so that we can better appreciate the poet and his work. The crucial juncture in Basho's life was his practice of Zen, which seemed to add a new dimension to his poetry. Zen emphasizes a sudden enlightenment, one result of which is the realization of the intimate tie between man and nature. (This is also discussed by Suzuki in selection 26.) In many haiku, especially those of Basho, the flash of poetic insight is an artistic counterpart to the Zen moment of enlightenment. One of the difficulties Westerners may have in first reading haiku is the extreme compactness and suggestive character of these miniature poems. Henderson helps us see the utter simplicity yet the vast profundity in such haiku as Basho's "frog" poem, which illustrates the religious character of nature in Japan. Although not all haiku are explicitly religious in content, this poetry generally forms a bridge between artistic and religious activities.

The second excerpt quotes Basho more broadly on the nature of art as depending on "the creative power of the universe." Thus, for

painter and poet alike, as well as the perceptive beholder, the crucial factor is to have "spirit." This teaches us that Basho's poetry was not a pedantic sophistication but rather an insight into the essence of art and even a statement of man's relation to the universe. In this, Basho is in sympathy with the art theory of Mitsuoki (in selection 27).

From *An Introduction to Haiku* by Harold G. Henderson, copyright © 1958 by Harold G. Henderson. Reprinted by permission of Doubleday & Company, Inc.

The Haiku of Basho

... Basho was consciously looking for the poetic beauty to be found in things not themselves particularly beautiful. He was still developing both his technique and his poetic insight. Two years later, in 1681, something happened to him. He announced that his life, simple as it was, was "too worldly," and he began the serious study of Zen—the Buddhist sect which gives most attention to contemplation. It was after this, in the last ten years of his life, that nearly all of his finest poetry was written.

Early in 1686 Basho wrote what is probably the best-known haiku in the Japanese language—one which he himself considered as marking the most important turning point in his poetic life. The poem itself is deceptively simple. Literally translated, it is:

> Old pond:
> frog jump-in
> water-sound.

Many competent critics have found in this a deep and esoteric meaning; others have considered it too darkly mysterious to understand at all. Perhaps some light may be thrown by the fact that the last two lines were the first to be composed. The circumstances seem well attested. Basho was sitting in the garden of his little house in Edo with some friends and pupils, when suddenly a sound was heard, necessarily during a period of silence. Basho, without premeditation, looked up and said: *"Kawazu tobikomu mizu no oto"* (frog-jump-in water-sound). This was immediately recognized as a possible ending for a haiku, and after the others had made various suggestions, Basho completed it with "old pond" for the first line. If this story is correct, the closest possible English for the poem would seem to be:

> Old pond—
> and a frog-jump-in
> water-sound . . .

If this were the only poem that Basho had ever written, one might wonder whether the poet really put into it all the deep meaning that one finds. But the proof is overwhelming that, consciously or unconsciously, Basho did put into most if not all of his later haiku all the meaning that anyone can find, and probably much more. It has been my own experience that the more one reads them, the more one finds depths in each single one, even in those that appear most trivial. One gets a feeling that they are somehow all parts of one whole. Japanese who have had the same experience have explained it by saying that Basho was so imbued with the spirit of Zen that it could not help showing in everything he wrote. This is quite possibly true, but as an explanation it suffers from the fact that nobody has yet been able to define what the "spirit of Zen" actually is. Zen "illumination" *(satori)* is apparently a strong emotional experience for which there are no words. It has been called a "realizing of reality," and some Christian theologians have praised it as being "the highest form of natural mysticism." About all that non-Zen people can do is to observe its effects on Basho and on his poems. Among the qualities which are often considered as indicative of his Zen are a great zest for life; a desire to use every instant to the uttermost; an appreciation of this even in natural objects; a feeling that nothing is alone, nothing unimportant; a wide sympathy; and an acute awareness of relationships of all kinds, including that of one sense to another. Whether or not these qualities are due to Zen, they do exist in Basho's haiku, at least in the originals.

Only comparatively few of Basho's poems are obviously religious, though several seem to be records of semi-mystic experiences. For example, in his *Sarashina Journey* Basho records that while he and his pupil Etsujin were journeying through the mountains of Kiso, they found themselves climbing a steep and dangerous path. On their left was a deep gorge, and at its bottom, thousands of feet below, a rushing river. They took each step in terror, until they came to the fragile ivy-covered rope bridge which spanned the gorge and which they had to cross. Basho gives no details of his feelings, but appends the haiku:

> Around existence twine
> (Oh, bridge that hangs across the gorge!)
> ropes of twisted vine.

There are also other poems, which would be obviously religious to a Japanese Buddhist of any sect:

> Octopus traps: how soon
> they are to have an end — these dreams
> beneath the summer moon.

Octopus traps are earthenware pots, set horizontally in shallow water, into which during the nighttime the animal backs as if it were a crevice in the rocks. In the morning it is unable to get out. In the original, which is prefaced with the words: "On board the boat," the effect of *wo* is to make the

moon the subject, and suggest that it looks down on the whole sea- and landscape, and all its "ephemeral dreams." Here the religious implications are obvious, even if we do not go into the Buddhist symbolism of the boat and the moon. It is, however, worthy of note that whenever Basho uses the word "dream" he seems also to be thinking of human life; and perhaps it is even more noteworthy that to him the "illusion" of the world does not seem to mean that it is in any sense unreal, but rather, as with St. Thomas Aquinas, that it is far more real than it seems.

The vast majority of Basho's haiku are not obviously religious, whatever the Zen content may be. They are for the most part simple descriptions of actual scenes and events, with just enough detail given to allow the reader to put himself in Basho's place and so share his emotions....

In 1694 Basho died, and died as he would have wished, on one of his beloved wanderings, and surrounded by many of his friends and pupils. During his last illness he was constantly discussing religion and philosophy and poetry (three things that were almost one to Basho), and when it became evident that he was dying his friends asked him to give them a "death poem" —the sum of his philosophy. Basho refused, on the ground that every poem in his last ten years, starting with the "old pond" haiku, had been composed as if it were a death poem. But on the next morning he called them to his bed- side, saying that during the night he had dreamed, and that on waking a poem had come to him. And he gave them:

> On a journey, ill,
> and over fields all withered, dreams
> go wandering still.

To get the force of *kakemeguru*, "go wandering" should be given its most active sense. For those who wish to go back to the original I must add that the word "still" is used, not only because it seems definitely implied, but also because of Basho's subsequent reference, as reported in the "Oi Nikki," to *nao kakameguru yume*, dreams which run about "still" or "still more." Surely as lovely a farewell as any poet ever gave to the world.

Reprinted by permission from *Literary and Art Theories in Japan*, Makoto Ueda (Cleveland: The Press of Western Reserve University, 1967), copyright © 1967 by The Press of Western Reserve University.

Basho and the Poetic Spirit

In truth, the poetic spirit was conceived by Basho on an even grander scale. He believed that this spirit went far beyond the realm of the Haiku, that, indeed, it pervaded all areas of creative arts. Basho says this in his own writing:

There is a common element permeating Saigyo's lyric poetry, Sogi's linked verse, Sesshu's painting,[1] and Rikyu's tea ceremony. It is the poetic spirit, the spirit that leads one to follow the ways of the universe and to become a friend with things of the seasons. For a person who has the spirit, everything he sees becomes a flower, and everything he imagines turns into a moon. Those who do not see the flower are no different from barbarians, and those who do not imagine the flower are akin to beasts. Leave barbarians and beasts behind; follow the ways of the universe and return to nature.

Somewhat metaphysically Basho has here conceived a spirit that underlies all creative activities. It is a spirit that produces all works of art, and ultimately it goes back to the creative power of the universe. The universe creates beautiful flowers and the lovely moon, and so does the artist; they are both creative, and appreciative, of things beautiful. The creation and appreciation of beauty is essentially what distinguishes civilized men from barbarians and beasts; it is the prime factor of culture. Thus Basho's poetic spirit comes to assume a form of cultured primitivism; his concluding words are fittingly enough, "return to nature."

SELECTED READINGS

For works on various aspects of the theme of closeness of man, gods, and nature in Japanese religion, see first the citations for each selection; some additional works are:

Casal, U. A. *The Five Sacred Festivals of Ancient Japan: Their Symbolism and Historical Development.* Tokyo: Sophia University and Charles E. Tuttle Co., 1967.

Earhart, H. Byron. "The Ideal of Nature in Japanese Religion and Its Possible Significance for Environmental Concerns," *Contemporary Religions in Japan* 11, Nos. 1-2 (1970), 1-26.

Hori, Ichiro. *Folk Religion in Japan: Continuity and Change.* Edited by Joseph M. Kitagawa and Alan L. Miller. Chicago: University of Chicago Press, 1968. See pp. 141-79.

Matsudaira, Narimitsu. "The Concept of Tamashii in Japan." In *Studies in Japanese Folklore.* Edited by Richard M. Dorson, pp. 181-97. Bloomington: Indiana University Press, 1963.

Matsunaga, Alicia. "The Land of Natural Affirmation: Pre-Buddhist Japan." *Monumenta Nipponica* 21, Nos. 1-2 (1966): 203-9.

[1]See the photograph of one of Sesshu's works in selection 27. [ed.]

part ten

Religious significance of the family, living and dead

In America, religious life tends to focus on the church or synagogue, but in Japan, the family is at least as important as the shrines and temples of organized religion. Indeed, in selection 30 George DeVos says that certain types of psychological security found in a relationship to a personal God in the West are found only in relation to the family in Japan. Until modern times Japanese people always participated in religion primarily as families and only secondarily as individuals.

In ancient Japan the head of the clan was both a political and a religious leader, since he had the all-important right and duty of leading the rites for the ancestors. In other words, the clan itself constituted a religious group, with its own objects of veneration, its own rituals, and its own religious leaders. The general outlines of the family as a religious institution continued into later history; for example, in the system of main families and branch families, a major characteristic of the main family is its right to house the memorial tablets and to conduct rituals for the ancestral spirits.

In recent times the traditional home would often feature a *kamidana* (*kami-* or god-shelf) for Shinto-style offerings as well as a *butsudan* (Buddhist altar) for commemorating the family dead. The family as a group was affiliated to at least one Shinto shrine by its geographical location and to a parish Buddhist temple by the succession of a family tradition. Families participated in shrine life mainly through seasonal festivals and in temple life through annual celebrations and memorials for the family dead. Only when he made a special prayer (for help in crisis or relief from sickness) did an individual make a trip to specific shrines and temples. However, in contemporary Japan, as in most modern industrialized, urbanized countries, the family and its traditional practices are undergoing considerable change.

29

the family as the basis for religious activities

In traditional Japan, one participated in religion not so much on the basis of individual decision as on the basis of group membership; a person saw himself primarily as a member of a group of interrelated families, and this group set the tone for religious activities.

An important family unit in earlier Japan which still exists in some regions is the *dozoku,* an arrangement of branch families around one main family. The religious character of this social group is borne out by the fact that "in principle each has its own particular shrine and its own cemetery." Members of any *dozoku* are bound together by the obligation of participating in both annual and special ceremonies (such as funerals). In this selection Ichiro Hori describes a *dozoku* and the religious calendar it follows. This yearly round of ceremonial observances throws light on traditional religious life in Japan. For example, professional religious leaders are conspicuously absent, because the head of the main household is automatically the family religious leader. His leadership is demonstrated in the facts that the most important memorial tablets are in his home and that he conducts the annual memorial rites. (The dominant role of the two annual festivals of New Year's and Bon is also discussed in selections 17 and 34.)

Reprinted by permission of the author and publisher from Ichiro Hori, *Folk Religion in Japan: Continuity and Change,* edited by Joseph M. Kitagawa and Alan Miller (Chicago: The University of Chicago Press, 1968). Copyright © 1968 by the University of Chicago.

Dozoku and Its Belief System

Dozoku is the smallest family unit in contemporary rural Japan and is, so far as we know, the smallest unit in which collective beliefs lie. The term *dozoku* denotes a family grouping of a main family (*hon-ke*) and branch families (*bun-ke*) which are linked by patrilineal kinship. The *dozoku* group which one may find exemplified in several districts at the present time seems to have a historical connection with the clan system of antiquity and the kinship system of the medieval period. The *dozoku* is thought to have been the basic unit of Japanese rural society. One of the oldest and most common Japanese terms for the *dozoku* group is the word *maki* (literally "an enclosure"), which is a group having the same surname. Even today, the main family is called *maki-gashira,* which means "head of the *maki.*"

The *dozoku* is the smallest economic, social, and cultural unit in the

village. The religious unity of any given *dozoku* group is shown by the fact that in principle each has its own particular shrine and its own cemetery. The members of the *dozoku* group must take part in the annual festivals and the memorial services for ancestors under the leadership of the head of the main family. The main family, or its head, possesses political, economic, and spiritual authority, and has the responsibility of overseeing the daily life of all the branch families. In turn, members of the branch families are obliged to serve the main family spiritually and materially. . . .

The Saito *dozoku* group in Iwate prefecture offers a typical example of an actual *dozoku* system. It consists of thirty-four families: a main family, five patrilineal branch families, two patrilineal sub-branch families, and twenty-six non-consanguineally related ("fictive") branch families and their sub-branch families promoted from servant status. . . .

The relationship between the main family and the branch families in the Saito *dozoku* group is reflected in mutual aid in daily life. This corporation is especially apparent on such occasions as the building or thatching of a house, well sinking, and at the times of births, marriages, and deaths. There is also a custom that the members of branch families must periodically greet, or in some way help, the main family as the following calendar shows:

Thirtieth day of the twelfth month of the lunar year.—*One person from each branch family goes to the main family to help make rice cakes* (mochi) , *the most important and sacred food at the New Year and other festival days and ceremonies in Japan. About this time, the main family gives gifts to the branch families, who in turn offer their small, hand-made goods to the main family* (seibo-rei) .

First day of the first month.—*The men of the branch families usually visit the main family to give greetings on the New Year; the host and hostess of the main family give them special food and sake in return. On the next day, the same greetings are performed by the women of the branch families.*

Fifteenth of the first month.—*Members of the branch families gather at the house of the main family to make rice cakes for the Little New Year* (koshogatsu) . *After dinner, there is a mock celebration of rice planting in the garden of the main family's house.*

Nineteenth of the first month.—*Sacred rice cakes for the New Year are ceremonially distributed. The members of the branch families take pieces of sacred cakes and dine together at the main family's house.*

Thirteenth to sixteenth of the seventh month.—*This is the time of the Bon festival (memorial services for the spirits of ancestors and all souls of the dead). Members of branch families clean the ancestors' tombs (usually stone monuments) in the main family's graveyard on the thirteenth day. Early in the morning of the fourteenth day, members of branch families gather at the main family's house in order to celebrate the Bon festival; they clean the house and prepare the ornaments and new altars for the coming spirits or souls from the other world. After this, all members of the* dozoku *group go to the graveyard with offerings and worship at their ancestors' tombs. Breakfast and lunch are served by the host of the main family. On the afternoon of the sixteenth day, members of the branch families again gather with the main family to honor the ancestors' spirits as well as all the souls enshrined in the special altars and to say good-bye to those who are returning to the other world.*

Centering in the New Year and the Bon festival, ceremonial gatherings or *visitings at the main family's house take place on the third day of the third month*

(so-called Hina-matsuri *or Doll festival), on the third day of the fourth month, on the fifth day of the fifth month (so-called* Tango-no-Sekku *or Boys' festival), on the fifteenth day of the eighth month (the Harvest Moon), on the twenty-ninth day of the ninth month (Twenty-ninth Day festival) and on the twentieth day of the tenth month (Twentieth Day festival).*

The customs are not unique to this *dozoku* group, but are universal in *dozoku* groups in Japanese rural society. The ancestral tablets are often in the Buddhist altar of the main family's house, and therefore members of branch families usually gather with the main family to take part in the services. I suppose that underlying these customs are deep-rooted and ancient feelings of ancestor worship which are reflected in the New Year festival, in the ancestor worship at the equinoctial week in spring and autumn, and in the Bon festival.

The spiritual and religious center of the *dozoku* group is symbolized by the *kabu-ko* or *senzo-ko. Kabu* is a synonym for *maki* and essentially means *dozoku.* Thus, the *kabu-ko* is the religious association of the *dozoku* group, and the *senzo-ko* is the association governing the ritual meeting for common ancestor worship. One of the significances of these *ko* is that the privilege of joining them is limited to members of the *dozoku* group and never extended to members of families which are related only by marriage. Presumably it reflects the prototype of ancestor worship, basic to the social structure in Japan.

Ancestor worship in *senzo-ko* or *kabu-ko* gradually deteriorated with the rise of the tutelary kami or deities of these *dozoku* which attained social prominence, and these newly emergent kami ultimately became the ordinary village kami *(mura-uji-gami)* of today. The beliefs which evolved from the *dozoku* groups are of basic importance in the structure of contemporary Japanese village society. These beliefs center in the idea that the spirit becomes deified thirty-three years after death, and becomes subject to ancestor worship along with the kami who have some connection with the ancestor of the *dozoku* group.

30

where the family of god is the family

The previous selection focused on the family system as a base for religious activities, but this selection singles out the significance of veneration of the dead in family religion. There is no clear counterpart to

so-called ancestor worship in modern Europe and America, and that is probably why erroneous stereotypes have arisen. As David Plath mentions, Westerners tend to emphasize the morality aspect of ancestor worship and to exclude the equally important sense of security and comfort the dead provide.

Westerners tend to think that the Japanese (and Chinese) must pay respect to the ancestors and that if it were not for their moral conscience, they would dispense with these formalities. However, the family circle of living and dead provides a sense of belonging that is almost as important to the Japanese as the relationship to God is to Westerners. Plath also points out that this concern for ancestors does not mean simply a dead weight from the past and conservative orientation; on the contrary, holding one's head up before the ancestors means to perform effectively in the present, which may mean changing old modes of behavior for new.

In making an anthropological analysis of the "family of God," Plath chooses the three categories of the departed, the ancestors, and the outsiders and describes the various forms and periods of worship designated for each. These activities are not curious phenomena of interest solely to scholars but are the ground rules taken for granted in the religious life of the traditional family, much of which continues into the present. Concern for the dead has been a prominent part of Japanese religion since prehistoric times (as can be seen in selection 36), and some popular religious practitioners specialize in communicating with the dead (as illustrated in selection 18). (Buddhist rites for the dead are described in selection 11. The status of *kamidana* and *butsudan* in contemporary family life is described in selection 45.)

Reprinted from David W. Plath, "Where the Family of God Is the Family: The Role of the Dead in Japanese Households," reproduced by permission of the American Anthropological Association from *American Anthropologist*, Vol. 66, No. 2, 1964. Also by permission of the author.

Ancestors — and Other Souls

I find it useful to distinguish three categories of souls in Japanese household religion. Like most abstract categories these three have their fuzzy edges. But with a few exceptions the living members of a household treat souls in each of the three categories in distinctively different ways. Like most social categories these three can be defined by their conditions of recruitment, tenure, and retirement. Although these conditions are by no means spelled out in equal detail for all three categories, the degree of detail itself is a clue to the emotional gravity of the category.

1. *The Departed.* The departed are primarily the souls of household members who died in recent memory, secondarily the souls of non-members whom the living choose to honor. I state it in this way to stress household bonds: the living may hold rites for non-members, for members they must. . . .

All such regular members should upon death be recruited into the departed. The survivors prepare a tablet sacred to the departed's personal memory (except that husband and wife frequently share the same tablet). The tablets are preserved in the house on a shelf or in a cabinet reserved for them. Here is where one usually meets the departed, although on occasion one may meet them at a temple, graveyard, crossroads, hilltop or elsewhere.

As the tablet shows, the departed soul retains selfhood within the collective otherness of death. It is remembered as an individual by at least one of the living. Like all members of the household it has a right to continued affection and "human feeling" from the others. It joins all the members, living and dead, at periodic household gatherings, especially at New Year's and Midsummer. More importantly, the living help the departed soul celebrate the anniversaries of its death-day. This may continue for upwards of 50 years—practice varies widely—or until no one remains among the living who knew the departed personally. At this point the departed is retired into the ranks of the nameless ancestors. Personal tablet and selfhood are destroyed.

Significantly, there is no generic Japanese term for the departed. The departed can be subsumed under broader categories of spirits, gods, buddhas, ancestors, etc. But they stand out primarily as individuals. By contrast the other two categories are recognized explicitly.

2. *The Ancestors.* The ancestors are all the departed regular members of a household who have been expunged from living memory. Non-member departed presumably retire to join the ancestors of some other family line or else are relegated among the homeless wandering souls.

For the ancestors recruitment and tenure are specified, but there is no provision for retirement. This is literally a dead end. Recruitment here is the obverse of retirement from departed-ship. The soul melts into the household "choir invisible," an everlasting and unnumbered plurality. Usually the ancestors share a single generic tablet on the family shelf. They continue to have the same rights and duties of membership as the living and the departed. But now these rights and duties are impersonal, atemporal, and ethereal. The distinction between the personal ties one has with the departed and the impersonal ties one has with the ancestors has important implications which we will examine later. . . .

Japanese definitions of the ancestors usually offer a formula composed of (1) the founder of a household, plus (2) all subsequent souls who were regular members at death. The second category thus includes, in my terms, both departed and ancestors. However it does not include the soul of any

natal member of the household who was married out, adopted out, or left to found a new household. . . .

3. *The Outsiders*. The outsiders form a residual category. They are at the fringes of institutionalization, where conditions of membership are not easy to state with precision. They include all homeless souls who are not regularly affiliated with any household line, or whose line has lapsed. But they also may include the souls of dead guests, probationary members, etc. who remain nearby but who eventually should return to join the departed in their own household.

Outsiders are not usually admitted to the household shelf. Some families provide a separate shelf for them, outside the house or on a veranda. Usually this is a temporary shelf, erected only on a few ceremonial occasions during the year. The household shelf, by contrast, is permanent. Nor is there ordinarily a household tablet for the outsiders, although communities sometimes collectively honor their unknown dead. Retirement is undefined, and about all that can be said of tenure is that the outsiders are generally suspect. Presumably they are quite unhappy over their situation—e.g. having died away from home, or having no heirs to care for them—and they deserve at least an occasional charitable nod. . . .

Worship — and Other Sentiments

1. *The Living and the Dead*. As a corporation, the Japanese household includes both living and dead members, and both are essential to its existence. All members are responsible for the welfare and continuity of the corporation, and all should be mutually concerned for their co-members. The dead provide a spiritual charter guaranteeing the right of their household line to a separate existence. The living provide the material stuff, both productive and reproductive, that keeps the line in motion. The living actively carry out household business. The dead remain passive except episodically; they serve mainly as moral arbiters and as sources of emotional security.

Western stereotypes of ancestor worship tend to favor the morality aspect: the dead as conscience. This is part of the Japanese view and needs no emphasis. In Japan as in many other cultures the living strive for success lest they be ashamed to stand before the dead, who are informed of all memorable events, especially of transitions in the domestic and personal cycles. What does need emphasis, for it is less common in Western stereotypes, is the security aspect: the dead as comfort. In the Japanese view this is equally fundamental. It is becoming ever more clear that emotional security in Japanese life rests primarily upon the maintaining of household ties. As George DeVos has put it, "certain types of psychological security found in a relationship to a personal God in the West are found only in relation to the actual family in Japan." Nakamura Hajime speaks of this propensity as one of "uncon-

ditional belief in a limited human nexus." "Ancestor reverence" can readily be seen as a religious expression of this dependence....

At death the soul enters a period of uncertainty that has many parallels the world over. The flesh is disposed of in a few days; but the spirit, polluted by death and potentially dangerous, may wander for many weeks. It is purified and made safe by a series of rites that ordinarily culminate on the 49th day after death. However, sometimes the living find it necessary to later perform additional rites to make certain that the soul has securely entered the ranks of the departed.

At the far shore, the soul enters the clean and peaceful world of the departed and the ancestors....

The world beyond cannot be described in any but equivocal phrases. Spatially it is both here and there, temporally both then and now. The departed and ancestors always are close by; they can be contacted immediately at the household shelf, the graveyard, or elsewhere. Yet when they return "there" after the midsummer reunion they are seen off as for a great journey. They are perpetually present. Yet they come to and go from periodic household foregatherings.

2. *The Living and the Departed*. The souls of all household members should be treated as though alive. For the unknown and impersonal ancestors this treatment is understandably nebulous, but toward the intimately known departed it can be highly specific. The wants of a departed soul can be catered to directly. It is very common for the living to prepare dishes or to gather flowers that the departed prefers. In the words of the famed eighteenth century scholar, Hirata Atsutane, "It goes without saying as regards father and mother, but in fact making offerings to anyone, we ought to offer what they liked when alive, or should we at any time be eating any tasty thing they would fancy, then we should offer it: In speaking of my own wishes I intend of course to ask my children that after my death they will give me plenty of fish and vegetable offerings of all kinds." This can be done at any time but perhaps is most common when celebrating death-day anniversaries....

One can visualize the departed in explicit form. One also can use photographs to heighten the effect, and they frequently are set upon the household shelf, or hung in the parlor, or even inset in tombstones. In his novel, *An Adopted Husband* (1919) Futabatei says of the illegitimate daughter, Sayoko, who has come back as widow to her father's house: "When, as an unfortunate widow, she returned home, her unmotherly mother and her sister, with whom she could not agree, treated her as if she were in the way. Though they always acted as if they wished her to leave, alas! she had no place to go, and she could only stay patiently on. Each time she felt sad, she keenly missed her real mother, whose face even she did not know; and she hungered after the dreamy memory of her father, who had been so tender; sometimes she would speak to his photograph."

The response can be of comfort or of conscience. As an example of the former, Dore tells that one woman remarked to him, "For us old people, visiting the graves is like going to the pictures and so on for the youngsters. You go to meet your dead; you can see their faces in your mind's eye and you can talk to them—you don't get any reply, of course, but it feels good." And as an example of the latter, the widowed mistress of the Kubo household in *The Sound of Waves,* is reflecting upon the possibility of remarriage. " 'Like this, I could still have four or five children more.' But at the thought her virtuous heart became filled with contrition. Quickly tidying her clothing, she bowed before her husband's memorial tablet."

In Japanese ideals, the living and the departed are full of mutual affection. Hostility is suppressed. The success or failure of any individual redounds to all. Therefore the living should be grateful for the legacy left them by the departed and the ancestors, while the departed and the ancestors should be pleased to hear that their line continues to prosper....

3. *The Living and the Ancestors.* As we have seen, the ancestors are known and related to only in the mass. They usually are made visible only in a communal tablet and perhaps communal gravestone. Nothing happens to them as individuals. They are not capricious as the wandering souls may be. But they have nothing in the way of portrayable characteristics. They cannot be visualized either physically (as e.g. the demon with the long red nose) or behaviorally (as e.g. the badger spirit who loves to sit in the treetops throwing sand at people). The only thing that clearly sets them apart from the myriads of gods and souls is their concern for the continuity of their household line. They do worry lest the living grow negligent. Standing before them the sluggard is shamed. However, this shades into a highly general and impersonal ethical concern. So that if the ancestors represent their particular household line, at the same time they also are moral representatives for society as a whole. We can see both of these aspects in the following excerpt from a recent book of popular sociology:

> You probably all have had the experience of having graduated from school and gotten a job, and when you received your first pay your mother took the pay envelope, displayed it on the household shelf, and offered a candle. This probably is a survival of rites to indicate that you have come of age and been added as one link in the social bonds of the household as a unit.
>
> Or a more extreme situation is when we often are dragged by dad or mom to the front of the household shelf and asked "Do you think you can give any excuse to the ancestors for doing that?" The shelf is associated with the household and with society, so that rebelling before it is like rebelling against the whole world; and this is why a lecture in front of the shelf has such potency (Yomiuri Shimbun Shakaibu 1962:35-36) .

There is a further point. In the usual Western views of ancestor worship the ancestors are seen as a kind of deadweight from the past. They are supposed to foster a past-time orientation and a solidly conservative stance

among the living. This may hold for other societies, but I think it misleading in the Japanese instance. In the Japanese view the ancestors do not demand that life continue exactly as they knew it. What they expect is not so much specific performance as effective performance—effective meaning whatever will assure the continuity of the household line. Far from hindering change, ancestor worship in Japan at least can be a spur to it. And the general Japanese concern for pragmatic adaptation has been recognized and commented upon many times over.

31

ınòıvıòuaL anò famıly ın japanese Relıgıon

The tight network of social groups such as *dozoku* and families and their dominance in religious life tends to diminish individual initiative in religious life. The two previous selections interpret mainly the dominance of social groups, whereas this selection points out the relative docility of individual members of these groups. The individual participates in religious life as a member of his group rather than on the basis of his individual decision (although the New Religions sometimes constitute an exception to this general rule; see Part 16). Hajime Nakamura points out that this tendency strengthens social stability, but it can also result in blind support of the authorities and existing social institutions.

However, if the individual as member of a socioreligious group is rather weak, the individual as source of authority and object of devotion is very strong, because another characteristic of Japanese religion is the way in which belief and devotion are directed toward powerful personalities rather than toward transcendent divinities or abstract doctrines. For example, even when Japanese founders of Buddhist sects placed their faith in the Lotus Sutra or in recitation of the name of Amida, they did so because of their trust in the person who advised them. Then the person revered with absolute trust becomes a symbol in his own right—what Nakamura calls "absolute devotion to a specific individual symbolic of the human nexus."

A perennial example of this characteristic is the attitude toward the Japanese emperor and in premodern times the attitude toward the military ruler *(shogun)*. More recent and dramatic instances of this ten-

dency are the founders (and foundresses) of the New Religions, some of whom are seen as actual living *kami*. (The life of a foundress forms the topic of selection 47.) Therefore, we understand that this Japanese "absolute devotion to a specific individual" is not an isolated aspect of the whole tradition but is directly tied to the broad notion of *kami* (which is explained in selection 1).

Reprinted from *Ways of Thinking of Eastern Peoples: India-China-Tibet-Japan*, by Hajime Nakamura, (© 1964 by East-West Center Press, Honolulu) by permission of The University Press of Hawaii.

Absolute Devotion to a Specific Individual Symbolic of the Human Nexus

The tendency to confine values to a limited human nexus reveals itself in Japan in absolute devotion to a specific individual as a concrete symbol of Japanese social values. The Japanese, unlike the Indians and Chinese, prefer not to conceive of a human nexus in an abstract way. They are apt rather to follow an individual as a living representative of that nexus. As I have previously indicated, the "family" in ancient Japan was not an abstract concept, but was embodied in the person of the living family head. There is also a tendency to identify the *shogun* with the *bakufu* (shogunate government), the Emperor with the State. In the feudalism of the West, relations between lord and vassal were extremely complex, and the notion of contract played an important part in such relations. In feudal Japan, however, this relationship was a simple one; the vassal devoted his entire existence to his lord. This gave rise to the motto "a loyal vassal does not know two masters." This way of thinking, characteristic of Japanese society in general, manifests itself among Japanese thinkers in an attitude of absolute devotion and obedience to a specific individual.

Most Japanese thinkers of the past were either Buddhists or Confucianists. Now, of course, religion is apt to base itself upon some authority. However, Indian and Chinese thinkers do not rely on a specific individual, but tend rather to establish and follow universal laws. Japanese thinkers, on the contrary, were likely to disregard universal laws in favor of the authority of a specific individual.

For some 700 years after the adoption of Buddhism, it was customary for Buddhists to explain the doctrine and expound their theories in the Chinese language. Japanese Buddhism, therefore, was in a sense an extension of Chinese Buddhism. This does not mean, however, that the Japanese merely took over the universal teachings of Buddhism as it was practiced in China at the time of adoption. Japanese scholar-monks received their doctrines

from one specific Chinese teacher, and that is precisely what they wanted to do. Saint Dengyo (767–822), for example, wished to travel to China so that he might discover the true significance of the Lotus Sutra (*Hokke-kyo*). In his letter requesting admittance to China, he writes as follows: "I have long regretted the absence of a commentary which would explain the profound import of the Lotus Sutra. By good fortune I have procured a copy of the excellent discourse of the T'ien t'ai sect. I have studied it a number of years, but errors and omissions in the text make it impossible to grasp the fine points. If I do not receive instruction from a master, then, even if I were to get (the meaning), I should be unable to believe in it." Thus, he went to China, studied under Tao-sui (c. 800), and returned to Japan.

The attitude of absolute devotion to a specific individual became still more pronounced in Kamakura Buddhism, which is especially representative of Japanese Buddhism. The Pure Land doctrine of Honen (1133–1212) was based exclusively upon one master, Shan-tao (613–681). At the same time Honen exalted the authority of the teacher. He says, "To view the doctrine of the Pure Land without the aid of oral tradition is to lose sight of one's share in the rebirth." Shinran (1173–1262), too, was absolutely devoted to his master, Honen. "As far as I, Shinran, am concerned, the sole reason I have faith is that a good man explained to me that in order to be saved by Amida I had only to recite the invocations (*nembutsu*). I do not know whether the *nembutsu* is actually the means to rebirth in the Pure Land, or whether perhaps it is the road to Hell. Even though I were cajoled by Saint Honen that I should go to Hell through the *nembutsu*, I should do so and not regret it."

Wishing to establish rationally the authority of his personal interpretation of Buddhism, Shinran makes the major premise of his reasoning rest on the absolute authority of the teacher. "If the original view of Amida is true, then the teachings of Sakyamuni are true, and the commentaries of Shan-tao cannot be false; if the commentaries of Shan-tao are true, the teachings of Honen cannot be false; if the teachings of Honen are true, how would it be possible for me, Shinran, to utter a falsehood."

This is cast in the form of a complex syllogism, but in each of the component syllogisms there is a hidden premise, namely, "the word of a disciple faithful to his teacher is as true as that of the teacher." Such a proposition is very questionable. The Japanese, however, consider it perfectly natural. They even pass over it in silence as not requiring overt explanation....

At any rate, Shinran himself had not the slightest thought of originating a new sect. His proposed aim was merely to elucidate the true purport of his master Honen's teachings. "My master Genku (Honen), being well versed in Buddhism, took pity on common people, both good and bad. He began to teach the doctrine of the true religion (*shinshu*) in the provinces, and spread the chosen original vow (of Amida) throughout this corrupt world." By "true religion" Shinran refers to the Pure Land sect (*jodo-shu*) of Honen, and not to the so-called True Pure Land sect (*jodo-shinshu*). The attitude

of dependence upon the master was also influential among the followers of Shinran. "When I take council with myself and consider in my fumbling way the past and present, I must regret the differences (that have sprung up) in the true faith as taught orally by our master. I fear that future students will fall into an unbroken series of errors, for, unless one is fortunate enough to be grounded upon knowledge derived from the original source, how can he possibly gain entrance to the Easy Way *(Amidian nembutsu)*? One's own insight of one's own private views should in no wise be confounded with the doctrine of Another's Strength *(tariki)*. Therefore I shall note down here the gist of the sayings of the late Saint Shinran, which remain in my mind. I hope thereby to dissipate the doubts of my coreligionists."

This tendency is also apparent in Nichiren (1222–1282), who attacked the Pure Land teachings. At the end of the scriptures of Mahayana Buddhism, it is said that Sakyamuni entrusted the scriptures to various persons, but according to Nichiren the true transmission of the Lotus Sutra is revealed only by the specific person who had received its guardianship. It is for this reason that Nichiren called himself the reincarnation of the Bodhisattva Jogyo to whom the Lotus Sutra had been entrusted.

It is especially Nichiren's conviction that he was a reincarnation of Buddha which distinguishes him from the other Chinese and Japanese who studied the Lotus Sutra. "I, Nichiren," he says, "am like the messenger of the Bodhisattva Jogyo. . . . Indeed I teach this doctrine. . . . I feel that I must be a reincarnation of the Bodhisattva Jogyo."

This differs considerably from the interpretation of the Lotus Sutra by Chinese Buddhist commentators. . . .

Whereas Chinese Buddhist commentators gave absolute value to the absolute taken as a basic principle, in Japan, Nichiren attributed this absolute authority to a specific person in certain particular circumstances. . . .

The attitude of absolute submission to a specific person is one of the distinct features of the way of thinking that can be commonly observed among the Japanese of the past. And, as we can see in the warrior's motto "a loyal vassal does not know two masters" or in the code of "morals" even among gamblers, the actual mores of most Japanese people reflect this feature of their way of thinking. As we have seen above, this can be by no means treated simply as a social phenomenon of a feudal society.

The attitude of total submission to a specific authority is not restricted to the Japanese of the past, but can still be clearly observed among contemporary Japanese. Even in those self-styled "progressives" who are very severe toward conventional ideas, this trend is tenaciously adhered to. One reason for this is that the Japanese are always sensitive to efforts to establish compact relations among the individuals within a small closed community. This endeavor for mutual relationship serves to create a sense of unity and sympathy among the Japanese. But, at the same time, it sometimes leads them to accept blindly the principle of authority at the expense of individuality.

Although not an exhaustive study, my discussion opens a way, I hope, to a deeper understanding of the great influence which leaders, especially religious leaders, have had on the Japanese people in the past and are still having in the present. The figure of the *kyoso* (founder or foundress) of modern religious movements is one instance of the fascination which a certain type of man or woman can have for the masses.

Emperor Worship

The Japanese way of thinking, which pays the highest respect to some particular living person and at the same time bows down to hierarchical distinctions of social status, culminates in ascribing absolutely divine attributes to the individual at the top of the hierarchy of Japanese society. Emperor worship is thus established. Emperor worship, however, is not the only product of this tendency of thought. At times *shoguns* or their ancestors were recognized as having a claim to divine authority. For example, in the Tokugawa period, Ieyasu Tokugawa (1542–1616), the founder of the Shogunate Government, was given the appellation *"tosho daigongen"* (literally, "great incarnate Deity of the eastern light"), and was referred to often as *"Gongen-sama"* ("The Incarnate God"). At the same time the Dutch referred to the Tokugawa Shogun as the "Kaiser." Therefore we ought to treat Emperor worship and *Shogun* worship as a single tendency, examining it first as ruler worship (*Kaiserkultus*) and subsequently examining it in the special sense of Emperor worship. . . .

Weak Awareness of Religious Values

There was no distinct concept of god among the primitive Japanese. As to the origin of the word *"kami"* (God), there are conflicting views among scholars, and none of them has yet produced any conclusive evidence. *"Kami"* in Japanese may mean "above," "one's superior," or "hair," and the political ruler was once called *"okami"* (the one that is above us). Everything placed above one both in space or in the hierarchical order is called *"kami."* Even if the etymological origin of each *"kami"* is different, the difference is not discernible in daily usage. For the Japanese, therefore, God was not a distinct entity complete in itself, but was diffused in all, that is, above and beyond ordinary human beings. It was the custom of Shintoism from antiquity to deify those persons who rendered distinguished services to a particular human nexus such as a family, a village, or a native community. . . .

A salient feature of Japanese religions is that members of religious organizations were customarily not individual persons but families, and even now this feature can be noticed in many cases. "The importance of the family group orientations appears even in religion. Here the unit of worship is not the individual but the family group. Instead of being concerned with

personal creed or individual salvation, the religion of Japan has traditionally supported the social system based on familial value. The basic group orientations of the Japanese were reinforced by the Buddhist Confucian doctrines; general life views differ profoundly from those of Puritan or Protestant religious teachings."

SELECTED READINGS

For work on various aspects of the theme of the religious significance of the family in Japan, see first the citations for each selection; some additional works are:

Hozumi, Nobushige. *Ancestor Worship and Japanese Law*. 6th ed., rev. Tokyo: Hokuseido Press, 1940.
Ooms, Herman. "The Religion of the Household: A Case Study of Ancestor Worship in Japan." *Contemporary Religions in Japan* 8, Nos. 3-4 (1967): 201-333.
Smith, Robert J. "Ihai: Mortuary Tablets: The Household and Kin in Japanese Ancestor Worship." *Transactions of the Asiatic Society of Japan*, Third Series, 9 (1966): 83-102.

part eleven

Importance of purifications, Rituals, and charms

In comparison with the Christian tradition, the practices of traditional Japanese religion are more similar to the Old Testament than to the New Testament, especially the Japanese emphasis on purification and rituals. The Japanese do not have a pattern of sin and forgiveness, in the sense that sin means disobeying a monotheistic God and forgiveness means that God bestows grace on a repentant man. Rather, in Japanese religion the crucial pair of terms is closer to defilement and purification; defilement means a kind of impurity or unclean condition, and purification means restoring purity by ritual procedures.

The ideal is a cosmic harmony in which men, the *kami,* and nature all participate in total unity. In early times, sickness, childbearing, blood (especially menstrual blood), death, and ritual mistakes all tended to upset the triangular balance of the sacred. Purification procedures were a very important part of religious life in premodern Japan. For example, in the home there were special procedures at the end of the year for cleaning the house of impurities and purifying it by lighting a new fire. Similar procedures were followed when a death occurred in the family. Many of these traditional practices have fallen into disuse in modern times, but even today the Japanese people are concerned with personal cleanliness, as evidenced by the hot face towel *(o-shibori)* provided in good restaurants and the ubiquitous hot bath.

Not just purification alone but a host of specific rituals and charms characterize Japanese religion. Religious life is carried out by means of these special charms and rituals rather than through regular worship services. Some rituals and charms were found only in religious institutions, but many were used in the home and in informal groups without professional religious leadership.

32

purification in the ritual prayers of ancient shinto

Purification is important on many occasions in Japanese religion, but probably the most widespread and most formal occasion is the semiannual ceremony of purification at Shinto shrines. The translation of the ancient *norito* (ritual prayer) which follows is the age-old text of the Shinto ritual for dealing with impurities on a nationwide basis. Of the numerous *norito* which have been handed down, the one for Great Exorcism was performed at midyear and at year's end. On these two days, most local shrines carried out the "great purification," reciting prayers, making offerings, and thereby purifying the surrounding people and land.

The "sins," or impurities, to be purified are described in terms of the ancient mythology rather than as contemporary actions. These mythological allusions are difficult to grasp without a knowledge of the *Kojiki* and *Nihongi*, but we can readily understand the prayers and offerings for purification and the purifying images of wind and water. The precedent for purification is the mythological incident when the great *kami* descended to earth and pacified the land. In accord with this precedent, the deities are invoked to descend once more and with their power to remove impurities from the land. The purifying *kami* are symbolized as the cleansing force in water and wind.

This highly formal rite of purification expresses a main theme of Japanese religion which is echoed in various popular and family practices. The Japanese have always held cleanliness important; the sixteenth century Jesuit missionaries to Japan commented that Japanese hygienic standards were much higher than those in Europe of the same age (see selection 20). Traditionally, every Shinto shrine provided water with which worshipers washed their hands and rinsed their mouths—ritual purification—before approaching the shrine itself. These examples, which could be multiplied endlessly, demonstrate that purification is a crucial ceremonial experience in the religious life of the Japanese.

Reprinted by permission of the publisher from Donald L. Philippi, translator, *Norito: A New Translation of the Ancient Japanese Ritual Prayers* (Tokyo: Institute for Japanese Culture and Classics, Kokugakuin University, 1959).

Great Exorcism of the Last Day of the Sixth Month

This is the exorcism formula read at the Great Exorcism (Oho-harahe) held twice a year: on the last days of the sixth and twelfth months. Its purpose was, of course, to remove all sins from the entire kingdom; however, it would seem that sin (*tumi*) referred more precisely to what we would call pollutions. The sins of the nobles, courtiers, and palace functionaries were all rubbed off onto 'sin-bearers'—the 'heavenly narrow pieces of wood' and the 'heavenly sedge reeds' which figure in the ritual—which were taken and thrown into the river.

The *norito* was recited in the presence of a great assembly of courtiers and nobles; it was spoken by either a Nakatomi or an Urabe. . . .

Hear me, all of you assembled princes of the blood, princes,
    court nobles, and all officials. Thus I speak.

The various sins perpetuated and committed
    By those who serve in the Emperor's court,
        The scarf-wearing women attendants,
        The sash-wearing men attendants,
        The quiver-bearing guard attendants,
        The sword-bearing guard attendants,
    As well as all those who serve in various offices—
These sins are to be exorcised, are to be purified
    In the great exorcism of the last day of the sixth month
        of this year—
Hear me, all of you. Thus I speak.

By the command of the sovereign Ancestral Gods and Goddesses,
    Who divinely remain in the High Heavenly Plain,
The eight myriad deities were convoked in a divine convocation,
    Consulted in a divine consultation,
    And spoke these words of entrusting:
        'Our Sovereign Grandchild is to rule
        'The Land of the Plentiful Reed Plains of the Fresh Ears
            of Grain[1]
        'Tranquilly as a peaceful land.'

[1]A poetic reference to Japan. [ed.]

Having thus entrusted the land,
    They inquired with a divine inquiry
    Of the unruly deities in the land,
    And expelled them with a divine expulsion;
They silenced to the last leaf
    The rocks and the stumps of the trees,
    Which had been able to speak,
And caused him to descend from the heavens,
    Leaving the heavenly rock-seat,
    And pushing with an awesome pushing
        Through the myriad layers of heavenly clouds—
Thus they entrusted [the land to him].[2]

The lands of the four quarters thus entrusted,
    Great Yamato, the Land of the Sun-Seen-on-High,
    Was pacified and made a peaceful land;
The palace posts were firmly planted in the bed-rock below,
    The cross-beams soaring high towards the High Heavenly Plain,
    And the noble palace of the Sovereign Grandchild constructed,
      Where, as a heavenly shelter, as a sun-shelter,
        he dwells hidden,
      And rules [the kingdom] tranquilly as a peaceful land.

The various sins perpetrated and committed
    By the heavenly ever-increasing people to come into existence
    In this land which he is to rule tranquilly as a peaceful land:
First, the heavenly sins:
    Breaking down the ridges,
    Covering up the ditches,
    Releasing the irrigation sluices,
    Double planting,
    Setting up stakes,
    Skinning alive, skinning backwards,
    Many sins [such as these] are distinguished and called the
      heavenly sins.
The earthly sins:
    Cutting living flesh, cutting dead flesh,
    White leprosy, skin excrescences,
    The sin of violating one's own mother,
    The sin of violating one's own child,
    The sin of violating a mother and her child,
    The sin of violating a child and her mother,

[2]All bracketed material in this selection is provided by the translator in the original
publication. [ed.]

> The sin of transgression with animals,
> Woes from creeping insects,
> Woes from deities of on high,
> Woes from the birds of on high,
> Killing animals, the sin of witchcraft—
> Many sins [such as these] shall appear.

When they thus appear,
By the heavenly shrine usage,
> Let the Great Nakatomi cut off the bottom and cut off the top
> > Of heavenly narrow pieces of wood,
> And place them in abundance on a thousand tables;
> Let him cut off the bottom and cut off the top
> > Of heavenly sedge reeds
> And cut them into myriad strips;
> And let him pronounce the heavenly ritual, the solemn
> ritual words.
When he thus pronounces them,
> The heavenly deities will push open the heavenly rock door,
> And pushing with an awesome pushing
> > Through the myriad layers of heavenly clouds,
> Will hear and receive [these words].
Then the earthly deities will climb up
> To the summits of the high mountains and to the summits of
> the low mountains,
> And pushing aside the mists of the high mountains and the
> mists of the low mountains,
> Will hear and receive [these words].

When they thus hear and receive,
Then, beginning with the court of the Sovereign Grandchild,
> In the lands of the four quarters under the heavens,
> Each and every sin will be gone.
As the gusty wind blows apart the myriad layers of heavenly clouds;
> As the morning mist, the evening mist is blown away by the
> morning wind, the evening wind;
> As the large ship anchored in the spacious port is untied
> at the prow and untied at the stern
> > And pushed out into the great ocean;
> As the luxuriant clump of trees on yonder [hill]
> > Is cut away at the base with a tempered sickle, a sharp sickle—
As a result of the exorcism and the purification,
> There will be no sins left.

They will be taken into the great ocean
 By the goddess called Se-ori-tu-hime,
  Who dwells in the rapids of the rapid-running rivers
   Which fall surging perpendicular
   From the summits of the high mountains and the summits
    of the low mountains.
When she thus takes them,
 They will be swallowed with a gulp
  By the goddess called Haya-aki-tu-hime,
   Who dwells in the wild brine, the myriad currents
    of the brine,
    In the myriad meeting-place of the brine of
    the many briny currents.
When she thus swallows them with a gulp,
 The deity called Ibuki-do-nusi,
  Who dwells in the Ibuki-do,
  Will blow them away with his breath to the land of Hades,
  the under-world.
When he thus blows them away,
 The deity called Haya-sasura-hime,
  Who dwells in the land of Hades, the under-world,
  Will wander off with them and lose them.
When she thus loses them,
 Beginning with the many officials serving in the Emperor's court,
 In the four quarters under the heavens,
 Beginning from today,
 Each and every sin will be gone.
Holding the horses
 Which stand listening,
  Pricking up their ears towards the High Heavenly Plain,
Hear me, all of you:
Know that [all the sins] have been exorcised and purified
 In the great exorcism performed in the waning of the evening sun
 On the last day of the sixth month of this year. Thus I speak.

Oh diviners of the four lands,
 Carry them out to the great river
 And cast them away.   Thus I speak.

33

a rite of possession

Of the various rites in traditional Japanese religion, perhaps none is more fascinating for the Western reader than the rite of possession. Possession is the religious ceremony whereby a divinity is invoked to enter, or "possess," a person; the person then acts or speaks not for himself but as the agent of the divinity which temporarily possesses him. The reverse of possession is *exorcism*, driving out the divinity of possession. In this selection Percival Lowell refers to one of the actors as an "exorcist"; however, exorcism usually refers to the driving out of evil spirits which have entered a person and caused sickness or mental problems (as seen in selection 47).

Lowell provides a quaint description of how he observed three Japanese pilgrims practicing a rite of possession while climbing the sacred mountain Ontake. It is well to remember that Lowell encountered these climbers in 1895, and much has changed in Japan since this time, but some temples and festivals still feature possession as a regular event. A large section of the populace was formerly able to become possessed, even without any formal training. (Shamans constitute a special category of trained religious leaders; their possession was part of the professional role, as seen in selection 18. Another example of sudden possession is the experience of the foundress of Tenrikyo, discussed in selection 47.)

Such rites of possession also reflect the closeness of man and *kami*. The *kami* may temporarily enter a person for simple divination, as in this selection, or the *kami* may permanently possess a person, as in the case of Tenrikyo's foundress and the founder of Konko Kyo (as related in selection 16).

Reprinted from Percival Lowell, *Occult Japan or the Way of the Gods: An Esoteric Study of Japanese Personality and Possession* (Boston, Houghton Mifflin Company, 1895).

Religious Possession During a Mountain Pilgrimage

We had reached, after various vicissitudes, as prosaically as is possible in unprosaic Japan, a height of about nine thousand feet, when we suddenly came upon a manifestation as surprising as it was unsuspected. Regardless of us, the veil was thrown aside, and we gazed into the beyond. We stood face to face with the gods.

The fathoming of this unexpected revelation resulted in the discovery of a world of esoteric practices as significant as they were widespread. By way of introduction to them, I cannot do more simply than to give my own. Set as the scene of it was upon the summit of that slumbering volcano sunk in trance itself, a presentation to the gods could hardly have been more dramatic.

We had plodded four fifths way up the pilgrim path. We had already passed the first snow, and had reached the grotto-like hut at the eighth station—the paths up all high sacred mountains in Japan being pleasingly pointed by rest-houses; we were tarrying there a moment, counting our heartbeats, and wondering how much more of the mountain there might be to come, for thick cloud had cloaked all view on the ascent, when three young men, clad in full pilgrim white, entered the hut from below, and, deaf to the hut-keeper's importunities to stop, passed stolidly out at the upper end: the hut having been astutely contrived to inclose the path, that not even the most ascetic might escape temptation. The devout look of the trio struck our fancy. So, leaving some coppers for our tea and cakes, amid profuse acknowledgment from the hut-keeper, we passed out after them. We had not climbed above a score of rods when we overtook our young puritans lost in prayer before a shrine cut into the face of the cliff, in front of which stood two or three benches conspicuously out of place in such a spot. The three young men had already laid aside their hats, mats, and staffs, and disclosed the white fillets that bound their shocks of jet-black hair. We halted on general principles of curiosity, for we had no inkling of what was about to happen. They were simply the most pious young men we had yet met, and they interested us.

The prayer, which seemed an ordinary one, soon came to an end; upon which we expected to see the trio pack up and be off again. But instead of this one of them, drawing from his sleeve a *gohei*-wand,[1] and certain other implements of religion, seated himself upon one of the benches facing the shrine. At the same time another sat down on a second bench facing the first, clasped his hands before his breast, and closed his eyes. The third reverently took post near by.

No sooner was the first seated than he launched into the most extraordinary performance I have ever beheld. With a spasmodic jerk, pointed by a violent guttural grunt, he suddenly tied his ten fingers into a knot, throwing his whole body and soul into the act. At the same time he began a monotonic chant. Gazing raptly at his digital knot, he prayed over it thus a moment; then, with a second grunt, he resolved it into a second one, and this into a third and a fourth and a fifth, stringing his contortions upon his chant with all the vehemence of a string of oaths. Startlingly uncouth as the action was, the compelling intentness and suppressed power with which the paroxysmal pantomime was done, was more so.

[1]*Gohei,* a Shinto ritual wand, a stick with paper streamers. [ed.]

His strange action was matched only by the strange inaction of his vis-a-vis. The man did not move a muscle; if anything, he grew momentarily more statuesque. And still the other's monotoned chant rolled on, startlingly emphasized by the contortion knots.

At last the exorcist paused in his performance, and taking the *gohei*-wand from beside him on the bench, placed it between the other's hands, clenched one above the other. Then he resumed his incantation, the motionless one as motionless as ever. So it continued for some time, when all at once the hands holding the wand began to twitch convulsively; the twitching rapidly increased to a spasmodic throe which momentarily grew more violent till suddenly it broke forth into the full fury of a seemingly superhuman paroxysm. It was as if the wand shook the man, not the man it. It lashed the air maniacally here and there above his head, and then slowly settled to a semi-rigid half-arm holding before his brow; stiff, yet quivering, and sending its quivers through his whole frame. The look of the man was unmistakable. He had gone completely out of himself. Unwittingly we had come to stand witness to a trance. [See figure 8.]

At the first sign of possession, the exorcist had ceased incanting and sat bowed awaiting the coming presence. When the paroxysmal throes had

Figure 8. "A possession by the gods upon Ontake." Reprinted from Percival Lowell, *Occult Japan or the Way of the Gods: An Esoteric Study of Japanese Personality and Possession* (Boston: Houghton Mifflin Company, 1895).

settled into a steady quiver—much as a top does when it goes off to sleep—he leaned forward, put a hand on either side of the possessed's knees, and still bowed, asked in words archaically reverent the name of the god who had thus deigned to descend.

At first there was no reply. Then in a voice strangely unnatural, without being exactly artificial, the entranced spake: "I am Hakkai."

The petitioner bent yet lower; then raising his look a little, preferred respectfully what requests he had to make; whether the peak would be clear and the pilgrimage prove propitious, and whether the loved ones left at home would all be guarded by the god? And the god made answer: "Till the morrow's afternoon will the peak be clear, and the pilgrimage shall be blessed."

The man stayed bowed while the god spake, and when the god had finished speaking, offered up an adoration prayer. Then leaning forward, he first touched the possessed on the breast, and then struck him on the back several times with increasing insistency. Under this ungodly treatment the possessed opened his eyes like one awaking from profound sleep. The others then set to and kneaded his arms, body, and legs, cramped in catalepsy, back to a normal state.

No sooner was the ex-god himself again than the trio changed places; the petitioner moved into the seat of the entranced, the looker-on took the place of the petitioner, and the entranced retired to the post of looker-on. Then with this change of persons the ceremony was gone through with again to a similar possession, a similar interview, and a similar awakening.

At the close of the second trance the three once more revolved cyclically and went through the performance for the third time. This rotation in possession so religiously observed was not the least strange detail of this strange drama.

When the cycle had been completed, the three friends offered up a concluding prayer, and then, donning their outside accoutrements, started upward.

Revolving in our minds what we had thus so strangely been suffered to see, we too proceeded, and, being faster walkers, had soon distanced our god-acquaintances. We had not been long upon the summit, however, when they appeared again, and no sooner had they arrived, than they sat down upon some other benches similarly standing in the little open space before the tip-top shrine, and went through their cyclical possessions as before. We had not thought to see the thing a second time, and were almost as much astounded as at first.

Our fear of parting with our god-friends proved quite groundless. For on returning to the summit-hut after a climb round the crater rim, the first thing to catch our eyes amid its dim religious gloom was the sight of the pious trio once more in the full throes of possession. There were plenty of other pilgrims seated round the caldron fire, as well as some native meteor-

ologists in an annex, who had been exiled there for a month by a paternal government to study the atmospheric conditions of this island in the clouds. Up to the time we met them the weather had been dishearteningly same, consisting, they informed us somewhat pathetically, of uninterrupted fog. The exorcists, however, took no notice of them, nor of any of the other pilgrims, nor did the rest of the company pay the slightest heed to the exorcists; all of which spoke volumes for the commonplaceness of the occurrence.

SELECTED READINGS

For works on various aspects of the theme of purifications, rituals, and charms in Japanese religion, see first the citations for each selection; some aditional works are:

Bownas, G. "Shinto." In *The Concise Encyclopedia of Living Faiths,* edited by R. C. Zaehner, pp. 348-64. Boston: Beacon Press, 1967.
Buchanan, Daniel C. "Some Mikuji of Fushimi Inari Jinja." *Monumenta Nipponica* 2 (1939): 518-34.
Earhart, H. Byron. "Four Ritual Periods of Haguro Shugendo in North-eastern Japan." *History of Religions* 5, No. 1 (1965): 93-113.
Hildburgh, W. L. "Charms and Amulets (Japanese)." *Encyclopaedia of Religion and Ethics,* edited by James Hastings, 3, pp. 449-51. New York: Charles Scribner's Sons, 1908-27.
Starr, Frederick. "Ema." *Transactions of the Asiatic Society of Japan* 48 (1920): 1-22.

part twelve

prominence of local festivals and individual cults

Neither Shinto shrines nor Buddhist temples observe a weekly day of worship like the sabbath of Jews and Christians. What characterizes Japanese religion is the yearly round of festivals which enliven family activity and participation in both shrine and temple celebrations. In modern times the government has declared a number of national holidays, but still the typical festival (matsuri) is the shrine affair organized and celebrated by the local shrine and villagers. The most important annual celebration is New Year's, and a close second is Bon, the late summer festival for the dead.

Another characteristic feature of traditional Japanese worship is the organization of voluntary organizations for honoring specific kami or Buddhist divinities. A regular (usually monthly) meeting of the members was held by rotation in a member's home, featuring a joint worship service, a meal, and social relaxation. (Such a cult which happens to focus on a Taoist divinity is seen in selection 14.)

34

festivals at new year's and bon

A Shinto reference work defines festivals *(matsuri)* as "ceremonies offering prayers, thanksgiving, or reports to, praising the virtues of, and presenting offerings to a deity or deities" but adds that "generally the ceremonies of a *matsuri* are made up of solemn rituals, followed by celebrations of wild, frantic joy." Japanese festivals usually have these two sides—the formal ritual and the popular festivities. "The solemn rites center around presentation of . . . food offerings, recitation of *norito,* music, and worship, and are followed by a feast . . . at which the sake and food offered to the god are consumed. The joyous celebrations include a procession with the deity, dancing, theatrical performances, . . . wrestling contests, and great feasts." The festival is even seen as a sacred principle of life for Shinto. "*Matsuri* is the most important thing in Shinto and may not be neglected. In the true sense, living prayerfully and obediently under the gods' protection is *matsuri;* life itself should be identical with *matsuri.* Today the formal ceremonial aspects are called *matsuri.* For example, the peasants begin cultivation in the early spring by praying for plentiful crops, and at the end of autumn they finish the agricultural cycle by offering thanksgiving for a plentiful harvest and present the harvest to the gods. During this period, connected with these basic observances, numerous *matsuri* are performed."[1]

The notion of festival is so important that it can not be limited to the Shinto shrine but should be expanded to include popular celebrations and festivities in the home. Indeed, some Japanese scholars feel that such festivals form the heart of Japanese religion. The major festivals are celebrated throughout the country at about the same time, but their organization and performance are mainly local affairs. The *kami* venerated in these festivals usually are guardian spirits for the people living close to a particular shrine. In the official ceremonies the shrine priests invoke the presence of the *kami* and present offerings; the people pay a visit to be purified and blessed by the presence of the *kami.* Often the blessing of the *kami* is expressed in a paper "charm," which the worshiper purchases for a small sum and places on the Shinto altar *(kamidana)* in his home. Thus, the festival is an event for renewing the bond between the *kami* and the people, a temporary passing from the everyday, profane

[1]*Basic Terms of Shinto,* ("Compiled by Shinto Committee for IXth International Congress for the History of Religions") Tokyo: Jinja Honcho (The Association of Shinto Shrines), Kokugakuin University, and Institute for Japanese Culture and Classics, 1958, pp. 37 - 38.

world to the holiness of the sacred world. At the same time, a festival is an occasion for cooperative work and communal festivities in both the family and village (or section of a larger city).

This document describes the colorful customs in the home connected with two of the most important annual festivals, New Year's and Bon. J. F. Embree was one of the first Westerners to carry out field work in Japanese villages and to describe the customs as they appeared in the cycle of a year. His descriptions are not systematic, because they attempt to record what happened in one village as he lived in it. These excerpts provide interesting details taken from a pre - World War II village. Even then, Embree noticed the tendency for national holidays based on the Western calendar to dominate the traditional local festivals observed by the lunar calendar.

Reprinted by permission of the publisher from John F. Embree, *Suye Mura: A Japanese Village* (Chicago: The University of Chicago Press, 1939). Copyright © 1939 by the University of Chicago.

The Yearly Festival Calendar

The village holidays are, for the most part, reckoned by the lunar calendar. This lunar calendrical system of rural Japan is practically identical with that of rural China. . . .

It is notable that the fifteenth of each month, the time when the moon is full, is almost always the day of some deity or celebration. Other favorite days for festivals are the first (dark of the moon), eighth (first quarter), and twenty-third (third quarter). There are very few holidays that do not fall on one or another of these days. The day before a celebration is *goya* (eve); the day itself, *matsuri*. . . .

All the major festivals such as New Year's, Girls' Day, Boys' Day, and Bon are characterized by visits among relatives, banquets, and gay drinking parties. Lesser festivals are marked by smaller drinking parties. Often a group of close neighbors, after visiting some local shrine or after paying respects and making offerings to the deity of the day, sit together in front of the god and exchange drinks, and sometimes, of a moonlight night, sing and dance.

The yearly festivals were more generally observed in the old days than they are today. Increased work demanded by the money wheat crop and other side work encouraged by the prefectural government have tended to reduce these celebrations. Various economy programs and especially the new economic reconstruction all deplore excess "vain" expenses and encourage people to do work and more work. Also, as already noted, the towns have

tended to commercialize certain of the yearly festivals so that villagers go to the towns to enjoy the fair and the crowds, neglecting the local celebrations.

There is another series of holidays, the national festivals. These are marked by village shrine celebrations attended, as a rule, only by village officials. The rest of the villagers continue work as usual on such days. If they live along the prefectural road, they put out the national flag. The calendar indicates the national holidays with crossed flags. People off the road do not bother much about the flag, although the headman is constantly urging everyone to buy and display one. These national holidays are celebrated by the new calendar. While the new calendar and its holidays are easy to adopt in cities where the seasons are less important, it is much more difficult for a farmer to observe holidays which come when he is busy in the fields....

First Month

The lunar new year comes just at the end of winter (February by new calendar). Leafless plum trees are in bloom, and spring will soon arrive.

The new year by new calendar is a national holiday and is marked by a shrine celebration, but not much else. The third and fifth of January are also national holidays. About a month later, when the lunar new year comes, almost a week's holiday is taken by villagers. At this time relatives call on one another, take gifts, and receive feasts. In the old days one called from house to house, taking a gift to each one; but today, for economy's sake, all relatives gather in one house. One year the family goes to a party of the wife's relatives, next year the family goes to a party of the husband's relatives. The relatives take turns giving a party.

The day before New Year's, *mochi*[1] have been pounded by the family. Three large round *mochi*, called mirror *mochi*, are put before the *butsudan* and three in the *tokonoma*. Other little ones are given to Daikoku,[2] perhaps one to a neighboring Jizo.[3] They will be left until the thirteenth or fourteenth, when fresh *mochi* will be pounded for Small New Year's. The old mirror *mochi* will then be eaten.

New brides of the past year visit their homes at this time, all debts have been paid or settled for the coming year, and the servants receive their annual salary at the end of the year. New servants have been contracted for and old ones dismissed. At this time the servants are given new clothes. A manservant receives material for *kimono*, footgear, a belt, a pair of shorts, and a towel; while a maidservant receives material for *kimono* (including the lining) and underskirt, footgear, and an *obi* (*kimono* belt). They are also given a little

[1]*Mochi*, a kind of cake or dumpling made from pounding steamed glutinous rice [ed.]
[2]Daikoku, Japanese name for the Indian deity Mahakala, which in Japanese folk religion is a deity of the kitchen and associated with rice fields. [ed.]
[3]Jizo, Buddhism's patron saint of the dead, in Japan believed to be the helper of dead children. [ed.]

pocket money. This is one of their big holidays, and they usually go home for a day or two.

Everyone visits shrines and temples. New greens are put at graves and *gohei* by waterways. Most people also visit the village Shinto shrine to pay New Year's respects. People of the mountain *buraku* visit Kitadake shrine in Youra.

On New Year's morning the wooden shutters of the house are not opened at the usual early hour; indeed, some are left shut all day. In the morning the family eats special red rice and a special soup prepared with taro[4] the night before. A minimum of actual cooking is done on New Year's Day. The calling on relatives begins in the afternoon. Everyone looks festive, and everyone is sporting new clothes and new *geta*.[5]

School is in session only one hour. It is only in rural regions that this is done as the towns do not observe lunar new year.

New Year's calls and festivities last from three to seven days. On the seventh day *nanakusazoni* (or *zushi*), a soup of seven herbs, is made for supper. Only a few villagers still observe this custom, some saying that they are too busy, others that it is too much bother. Nanakusa Day is the first of the five big traditional Japanese celebrations referred to as *sekku*. The others are the boys' festival, the girls' festival, *tanabata,* and Chrysanthemum Day. This latter is not observed in Suye.

On the eighth the Yakushi *do*[6] in Imamura holds a celebration. Tea and beans are served by a *kumi* of *buraku* women.[7]

On the morning of the fourteenth, *mochi* are again pounded for the celebration of Small New Year's (*koshogatsu*). Three small dumplings on a stick called *kushidango* are put in the *tokonoma*.[8] In the afternoon children make up beaters of rice straw bound with rope and go about beating the ground. They are supposedly beating moles. Such beating is said to get rid of moles from the fields. Only children do it, and the belief is not taken very seriously. In the evening the family gathers about the fire pit to make special dolls called *shunnamejo* and toys of various kinds. A stick of acacia wood (*kokanoki*) three or four inches long and about three-fourths of an inch in diameter is taken. The bark is cut off on one end and a face painted on. Paper is cut into *kimono* and put on. A sharp piece of bamboo is stuck into the bottom—and a doll is made. They are usually made in couples and will be placed on sacks of rice before the *tokonoma* or in the storehouse where rice is kept. The next day they are removed and placed before the Jinushi.[9] Jumping monkeys, millet heads, and other toys are made and also put there. The

[4]Taro, a root grown for food. [ed.]
[5]*Geta,* wooden clogs worn on the feet. [ed.]
[6]Yakushi *do,* a small Buddhist hall. [ed.]
[7]*Kumi* of *buraku* women, a group of village women. [ed.]
[8]*Tokonoma,* an alcove, found in most Japanese houses. [ed.]
[9]Jinushi, the household *kami.* [ed.]

dolls insure plenty of helpers at rice-transplanting time four months later, the millet heads, a good crop.

The father usually does the knife work, while children cut out the dresses and mark them with ink spots to indicate family seals. Mole-beating and *shunnamejo* are local Kuma customs.

Also local is the custom of cutting *mochi* into special shapes on this day. They are cut into small square or oblong pieces to represent grains of rice, or into twisted long pieces for ears of millet or into small round ones for money (*oban-koban*—ancient coins). All these are put on branches of *yanagi* (willow) and *yenoki* (Chinese nettle) because these two trees are used on festive occasions and because in the old days *mochi* and coins used to grow on these trees. The branches of *mochi* are to assure a good crop and good income through the new year. The branches are offered at the *kamidana* and the *butsudan*, which is cleaned out and freshly decorated with flowers. A branch is put in the toilet to ask the toilet-god (Benjo-no-Kamisama) to protect one from bladder trouble, one in the kitchen, one at the stable's entrance, one at the house entrance and often one at the bath, and one at the Jinushi. Outside the house branches are taken to the local *do*, to any near-by Jizo, and to the well-god. A branch is taken to the family graveyard. After being removed, the *butsudan* branch is put away and saved until the first thunderstorm in spring, when it is burned.

The first of the month marks the end of the old year, and all old obligations are cleared before that day. From the first to the seventh, festivities and parties occur in abundance, there being a constant round of visits to relatives and eating *mochi*. The fifteenth marks the close of New Year's festivities, and, with the making of *shunnamejo* and wooden millet heads and *mochi* branches, thoughts are turned to the coming work on rice, transplanting, and resulting wealth. . . .

The thirteenth to the fifteenth [of the seventh month] is Bon, a big holiday, comparable to New Year's. At this time the ancestral souls are said to come back, to reside in the *butsudan*. They come on the night of the thirteenth and leave on the night of the sixteenth. Any house where a death has occurred during the past year receives visitors. All *buraku* people and all relatives call. They bring gifts of money or lanterns, also rice, *shochu*,[10] candles and incense sticks, and boxes of cake sold for the occasion at the local cakeshop. Bunches of noodles (*somen*), eaten all through the Bon period, are frequently given instead of candles. The guests are given feast food in return, but no fish, as this is in the nature of a funeral memorial. The *somen* replaces fish. In some *buraku* all neighbors do not call, but instead each house contributes five sen to the *nushidori*,[11] and he calls and gives money to the family who is celebrating First Bon (*hatsubon*), i.e., who have had a death in the

---

[10]*Shochu*, a cheap alcoholic drink. [ed.]
[11]*Nushidori*, head of a *buraku*, the smallest social and economic unit. [ed.]

past year. This simplified Bon calling is a result of the economy movement which is interfering with so many of the established customs.

Graves are cleaned up some days before to prepare for the spirits' return. On the thirteenth water in water containers and flowers in bamboo vases are put at the graves, and incense is burned. Any member of the household may do this, often accompanied by children. If a First Bon, relatives and *buraku* people often offer flowers at the grave of the recently dead. A mixture of rice and chopped eggplant or cucumber is also offered at graves and holy stones by some. (It is interesting to note that the first eggplant of the season is offered to the water-god and is also used at Zen temple on the occasion of *segaki kuyo*.[12])

Besides doing this, flowers and leaves of *sh'kibi* are presented to Kwannon[13] (Yakushi in Imamura) and Tenjin. Many also put flowers by Jizo, by wells and streams, and by Sarutahiko[14] stones. Jizo not celebrated on Jizo Day are given more flowers than those celebrated. All this is the same as at New Year's.

The house is also cleaned up, the *butsudan* decorated with flowers and lanterns, and offerings of fall fruit and watermelon are made. *Mochi* are also offered. Some people cook rice in a special cooking pot called *shojin nabe*, from which rice is offered morning and evening to Hotoke-sama.[15] At noon rice is offered from the family meal.

Today, people do not bow to the ghosts as they come in, but they see them off with candles and little pine torches on the sixteenth. Candles are placed at the entrance of the path to the house where the ghosts are bidden goodbye. Often a group of neighbors will have a little drinking party together after seeing off the souls.

In Taragi and Hitoyoshi straw boats about five feet long are made and sent down river loaded with offerings on the sixteenth to accompany the souls on their return. This is not done in Suye.

Bon is a day, like New Year's, for relatives to visit one another; and, as at New Year's, servants receive a two- or three-day holiday and gifts of clothing. Formerly big parties were given, but no longer, due to economy. Bon festivities are further curtailed by the fact that silk cocoons are ready to sell at this season.

A generation ago there were special Bon dances but not now.

---

[12]*Segaki kuyo,* a memorial mass. [ed.]
[13]Kwannon, a Buddhist deity. [ed.]
[14]Sarutahiko, a Shinto deity. [ed.]
[15]Hotoke-sama, a term for both Buddha and spirits of the dead. [ed.]

35

aspects of annual festivals

In addition to New Year's and Bon, there are a number of other annual festivals, the most conspicuous of which are the spring and fall celebrations, marking the seasonal junctures that are most important to an agricultural economy. Since prehistoric times rice has been a major crop, and festivals have been associated particularly with the transplanting and harvesting of rice, with some special rites, such as those for driving away insects. Today, even in the heart of large cities, Shinto shrines still tend to hold spring and fall festivals; indeed, some city festivals, such as the elaborate Gion Festival, have become national tourist attractions.

A picturesque scene of village Japan is the group of boisterous youths shouldering a shrine palanquin (*mikoshi*) and carrying it in procession through the shrine parish. In this fashion the presence of the *kami* is spread through the parish, and the protection of the *kami* is assured. Older traditional forms of indicating the presence of *kami* were various ways of setting up live trees, particularly when the head of a household was an official for the annual festival: a tree set up before his house indicated both his temporary office and the fact that he was engaged in a pattern of abstinence during the year. The abstinence varied with the region and festival, but the general principle was that he should remain free from any defiling substance or activity.

The annual harvest festival in Shinto involves the tasting of the sake (rice wine) made from the new rice crop; its importance can be appreciated when we realize that the imperial enthronement ceremonies are patterned after the harvest festival. It is also worth noting that sake is almost indispensable at festivals, both as a sacred offering and as an aid to social conviviality. All the details Tokihiko Oto mentions contribute to the total picture of religious life expressed in Japanese festivals.

Reprinted by permission of the publisher from Tokihiko Oto, *Folklore in Japanese Life and Customs* (Tokyo: Kokusai Bunka Shinkokai [Japan Cultural Society], 1963).

Religious Rituals and Festivals

As for the annual festivals of Shinto shrines throughout the country, those which are held in spring and in autumn predominate in number. At the spring festival people pray for a good crop and a peaceful life protected

from evils throughout the year. Consequently, it is in general an occasion of less excitement and animation than the autumn festival, which is on the contrary, a gay occasion to express joy and gratitude to the deity for the harvest. The summer festival which comes between these two great seasonal festivals first occurred and flourished in the city. It is held for the purpose of keeping away epidemics, flood-disaster, harm from insects, and other evil accidents of summertime. Gion-matsuri in Kyoto is a typical summer festival. It gave great influence in its style to the shrine festivals over the country. The principal ceremony of a shrine festival is essentially performed during the night, whereas the summer festival is notably a daytime ceremony, which attracts many lookerson. There is a procession with *mikoshi* (a portable shrine) and *dashi* (ornamented cars) carried through the streets and with dances called *furyu*.

The dates of shrine festivals, although generally fixed, are often changed according to the circumstances of shrines and villages. The middle days of a month are most frequently appointed festival days, then the days of the first quarter and the last quarter of the moon, that is, the seventh or eighth day and the twenty-third or fourth day are the next occasions to be feted. Some festivals are held on the days of certain zodiacal or other signs of the old calendar, and there are also ceremonies performed according to the ebb and flow of the tide, the date of which is hard to fix in the solar calendar. Some great shrine festivals come every fourth or seventh year.

There were various ways to welcome a deity at the festival. The most popular way was to set up a tree, a living tree, or a tree pole. This tree symbolized a deity's *yorishiro*, the thing on which the deity was to descend. The pine trees set up at the entrance of a house on New Year's days nowadays and sacred trees standing in the shrine precincts are the vestiges of this custom. Therefore, the essential thing in the Japanese Shinto ritual was a consecrated tree and not a shrine building. Beside a tree, a stone or an earth-mound was consecrated as an altar for a religious ceremony.

Gohei, a white paper strip attached to a stick, which is a sacred object specifically used in Shinto rituals, also symbolizes a *yorishiro*. *Gohei* was called in archaic language *mitegura*, which means a divine seat in a man's hand. There are many varieties in form and size of *gohei*. Before the use of paper was popularized, a stick with its top end cut in thin strips, called *kezuri-kake*, was employed in the place of the *gohei*.

The principal object of holding a rite for a deity is to make the attendants spiritually united with the deity by eating and drinking the same food and beverage together. Nowadays we place on the altar raw vegetables and fish for offerings to the deity, but the original form was to present food prepared in the same way as a man's meal. The indispensable offering to the deity is sacred rice-wine, *sake*. This is necessary even for a rite of the simplest form. For instance, when some people pray to the mountain deity, they offer *sake* in a simple container called *orikake-daru*, a short bamboo stick bent into the form of an arch. It was the custom for the festival of the *uji-gami*

(clan-deity) that the *uji-ko* (literally clan-children) brewed wine from rice grown in the consecrated rice-field belonging to the shrine. However, since the law of wine-brewing was put into effect, making sacred *sake* at the shrine was prohibited.

Food offerings of the festival were usually prepared by men who had passed a certain period of abstinence. The food was made without using the same fire as that used by other people. There are instances when they started a purified fire for cooking sacred food by using flint or by the still more archaic method of handling a stick in a hole through a board. A cooked rice offering is customarily filled high in a cup. An important ceremony concerning food offerings is that which is called *naorai*. It is the ceremony of tasting the offered food in the presence of the deity. Formerly it was performed before the altar according to the principle of dining with the deity, but now, the offerings are taken away from the altar and eaten by the priests and *uji-ko*[1] in another room, except in a few cases in which the original manner is strictly observed.

To perform a rite for a deity one should purify himself through abstinence. Religious abstinence is expressed in Japanese by the word *monoimi* or *shojin*. Sometimes a man or men abstain in a retreat called *shojin-ya* or *komori-do*. *O-komori*, which literally means shutting oneself up, is a conspicuous feature of Japanese religious abstinence. People who take part in a festival are obliged to practice abstinence to some extent according to their duties. Ordinary *uji-ko* generally start abstaining a day, at most a week, before the festival day, while the men who are in charge of special services in the ritual often have to practice abstinence for a month before the festival. There is even an example such as the *toya*, the head man in charge of ritual services, who is forbidden to visit a house where death or a birth has taken place and he must purify himself with salt water every day during his one-year term of service. He must restrain himself still more strictly when the festival day approaches to within a month or a week.

There are various taboos people have to observe before the festival. *Koe-shojin* is the taboo against touching *koe*, fertilizer. Ashes are also not to be touched. To see blood and to do needlework are sometimes prohibited. Abstinence from sexual intercourse is generally observed, and food taboos are also widespread. Some strong smelling vegetables such as *negi*, a species of onion, are avoided. . . .

It seems that the festivals of shrines are always carried out by Shinto priests; however, there are, in fact, many cases in which the regular rituals of shrines are conducted not by professional priests but only by lay *uji-ko*. It is inferred that in ancient times, when it was a custom for the head man of an *uji* (clan) to preside over the rituals for his *uji-gami*,[2] the oldest man of an *uji* hereditarily succeeded to the priviledge of control over the religious

[1] *Uji-ko*, parishioners of a Shinto Shrine. [ed.]
[2] *Uji-gami*, patron deity for a group of Shinto parishioners. [ed.]

matters of the *uji*. Even after the Meiji Restoration there remained the same practice in which the head man of the lineage possessed a prerogative concerning the rituals of the whole lineage.

Toya-matsuri is a festival performed by the chosen members of *uji-ko* by a rotation system. The head man who takes his turn in the ritual services is called *toya* or *tonin*, and, as in most cases his term of duty is one year, he is also called *nenban-kannushi* (priest on duty for a year) or *ichinen-kannushi* (one-year Shinto priest). The word *toya*, which originally meant a head man, is now also read as a man who takes his turn. The method of choosing the *toya* from the *uji-ko* varies by localities.

SELECTED READINGS

For works on various aspects of the theme of local festivals and individual cults in Japanese religion, see first the citations for each selection; some additional works are:

Buchanan, Daniel C. "Inari: Its Origin, Development, and Nature." *Transactions of the Asiatic Society of Japan*, Second Series, 12 (1935): 1-191.

Casal, U. A. *The Five Sacred Festivals of Ancient Japan: Their Symbolism and Historical Development.* Tokyo: Sophia University and Charles E. Tuttle Co., 1967.

Earhart, H. Byron. "The Celebration of *Haru-yama* (Spring Mountain): An Example of Folk Religious Practices in Contemporary Japan." *Asian Folklore Studies* 27 (1968): 1-18.

Visser, Marinus Willem de. *The Bodhisattva Ti-tsang (Jizo) in China and Japan.* Berlin: Oesterheld, 1914.

part thirteen

penetration of religion into everyday life

In traditional Japan, religion tended to be highly involved in everyday life and was somehow related to most occupations. From prehistoric times, religion was directly associated with the home, fertility, and agriculture. The intimate relationship between farming and religion in recent times was seen in Part 12, but fishing is another major economic activity blessed by religion. Shrines and temples along the seacoast hold special festivals to protect sailors and to pray for large catches, sometimes using decorated boats in the harbor as part of the celebration.

Religious observances were important in the traditional household, as seen in the regular offerings placed on the *kamidana* (Shinto altar) and before the *butsudan* (Buddhist altar). Traditionally, special Shinto rites of blessing were invoked when building a house, in breaking ground, and in erecting the framework. In the farm household, home and occupation were not clearly separated, and religion easily entered both spheres. To take two examples strange to modern Westerners, there was a divinity or patron saint for the toilet and one for the stable.

Another way in which religion penetrated everyday life was by providing "rites of passage" for the crucial junctures in life, such as birth, marriage, and death. In this fashion religious life was delicately interwoven with every step of an individual's life span. At the same time, religion was inseparable from the seasonal and corporate activities of the social group as a whole. In short, religious life in traditional Japan was practically inseparable from individual, social, and occupational activities.

As traditional Japan increasingly feels the pressures of modernity, these old customs are disappearing. However, religion still enters daily life in such practices as flower arranging and the tea ceremony. These practices are much more sophisticated than some of the rustic customs described in this chapter, but they share common notions, such as the sacredness of nature.

religious life in prehistoric japan

The evidence for religious life in early Japan must be reconstructed from archaeological discoveries. In this selection, J. E. Kidder sums up the religious significance of the archaeological finds from various areas of early Japan. Conspicuous among this evidence are the symbols relating to sexuality and fertility. Stone figurines represent the sacredness of fertility as the power of woman, and stone phalli attest to the generative power of the male. As the last paragraph of the selection points out, these figurines and phalli sometimes formed family altars, apparently invoking religious powers for protection and offspring.

It is difficult to reconstruct the daily life of the early Japanese, but burials present solid evidence of concern for the dead, a persistent theme in Japanese religion. (See also Part 10 and selection 11.) It is clear that the people held some notion of an afterlife and that the dead were venerated. Probably other rites of passage were also observed, but they have left no permanent records.

Another interesting find from prehistoric Japan is some stone circles, with an upright pillar surrounded by horizontal stones arranged like spokes on a wagon wheel. Lack of further evidence hinders our understanding of the stone circles, but they probably indicate an early cult venerating the sun and thus providing a basis for the mythology surrounding the Sun Goddess (Amaterasu). (See selection 2 for the mythological setting of Amaterasu.)

Reprinted by permission of the publisher from *Japan before Buddhism* by J. E. Kidder, Jr., Praeger Publishers, Inc., and Thames & Hudson Ltd. Revised edition, 1966.

Archaeological Evidence for Prehistoric Religion

The artifacts of the Middle Jomon period are replete with symbols that connote fertility. Not until after this time do the figurines become quite specifically female, but large stone clubs of phallic form, stone phalli, standing pillars in dwellings and other objects, more disguised but similarly symbolic, attest to the emphasis placed upon the magical powers of the male organ. It may be that in the Middle Jomon a desire for greater permanence in the symbols resulted in the making of these in stone that had before that

time been fashioned in soft materials, or it may have been due to the arrival of new ideas among the mountain-dwelling societies whose receptivity responded instinctively and expressed these ideas symbolically. It is, of course, even difficult to demonstrate that these symbols were engendered in the mountain regions, but one centre of production is on the west side where sophistication replaced realism, and it certainly does appear that their diffusion spread from the Tosan both east and west and later into the Tohoku. . . .

The methods of burial were not fully standardized, nor does difference in time seem to be a factor in the variation of procedures. About half were carried out in a flexed position in the majority of which heads were oriented towards the south-east; others may be extended, and pointed in all directions of the compass. Of the former, the great percentage were laid on their backs, legs drawn up, but some were deposited on one side fully flexed. Others lie face down, knees near the chest; or extended on the back, side or face. At the Yoshigo shell-mound one of the skeletons was surrounded by a black organic substance interpreted as a burial mat that must have enveloped the corpse, and two skeletons at Ubayama, and similarly at Tsugumo and Ataka, lay by burnt earth and charcoal remains made by a fire perhaps sacrificial in nature. The bones themselves were unmarked by the fire. Traces of red ochre, particularly on skulls and chest-bones, are to be seen on quite a number of skeletons primarily in North Japan and most frequently on children. This may mean that a secondary burial system was in practice by some groups. Other isolated occurrences are of interest: at the Satohama shell-mound, Miyagi, an elderly man and child were buried in an embrace, both in flexed position, and at Yoshigo bones of an adult and child were found together in a clay jar. Flat circular stones were occasionally placed on the chest of the deceased for protection. . . .

The question of burials arises again in connection with the stone circles of North Japan. Recent efforts have been instrumental in bringing a number to light and elucidating facts on known circles. The count now stands at thirty or more in Tohoku and Hokkaido, and the reported destruction of many even during the lifetime of local residents must mean that this is only a fraction of the original number. The ones that can be dated by associated pottery correspond chiefly to Late Jomon, the most ambitious period in circle construction, and others appear to fit in the Latest period. Many cannot be dated at all satisfactorily because of the absence of related finds, but on the basis of a general similarity it is believed that most either belong to the Neolithic period or represent a perpetuation of Jomon ideas.

The great majority of these circles, especially in Hokkaido, consist of stones that are rarely more than 3 feet in height standing in a circle, most often natural and uncut. [See figure 9.] The diameter of these circles varies considerably; some are more oval, but when so, the orientation too is variable. Komai's study has tended to show that some were cemeteries in which small

stones were frequently laid in great quantities within the outline of menhirs. Human remains, however, have not been found, but this is not surprising considering the extreme humidity of the soil. Others provide no indications of their use or significance, but in a particular group that will be discussed below, there is much likelihood that early manifestations of stone and sun worship are represented. . . .

The *Kojiki* and *Nihon Shoki*, the most ancient records of the Japanese people, put into writing in the eighth century, imply that veneration of the Sun Goddess is of extreme antiquity, and whilst this influence was largely of partisan inspiration, it does seem likely that some solar worship was practised before the Yamato people, the authors of these stories, organized themselves or entered the country. In fact, its origins probably date to the second millennium BC. And again, the worship of spirits of stones, particularly stones of unusual and suggestive shape, is also a very ancient custom not to be disassociated from these Oyu formations. One is reminded of the Izanagi and Izanami myth. These two gods were most responsible for the creation of the island country; they begat the Eight Islands, and propagated them with gods, though only after a first defective offspring. By way of inception, on

Figure 9. Sun-dial arrangement of stones of the Nonakado circle, Akita Prefecture; height of standing stone 38 inches. Reprinted by permission of the publisher from *Japan Before Buddhism*, by J. E. Kidder, Jr., Praeger Publishers, Inc. and Thames & Hudson Ltd. Revised edition, 1966.

an island near present-day Osaka, because of its central location, a Pillar of Heaven was set up; the wedding ritual included circling this pillar, done incorrectly the first time, but later amended so that the results were fruitful. One of the offspring of this pair was the Sun Goddess whose descendants landed in South Japan and eventually made their way to the Yamato Plain, the Osaka-Nara area today. Although the solar myth itself has little philosophical profundity to it, the ideas concerning its origins and subsequent history finally became sharp enough to reach a recorded stage by the eighth century, but the implications concerning its belief are for a long and very ancient tradition.

In addition, with regard to the link between stone worship and phallicism, standing stone clubs of Middle Jomon times have already been mentioned. Of the same period are standing pillars in a group of houses at Yosukeone, Nagano. In the north-west corner of the pit-dwellings was built a stone platform on which stood a slender upright stone; arrayed on the platform and around it were such objects as stone clubs, clay figurines and broken pottery. Quite obviously the platforms and pillars mark the family altar or shrine which brings together concepts of stone worship and protection for the processes of and the benefits derived from procreation.

37

Beliefs surrounding birth, marriage, and death

This selection, like selection 34, is taken from J. F. Embree's description of life in a pre - World War II village. As in Embree's previous excerpt, we notice the clear social implications of religious celebrations and the religious aspects of social events. Marriage was primarily a social arrangement between two families, and the only essential ritual was the formal exchange of sake between bride and groom. As is noted in selection 35, sake is inseparable from many celebrations, and it is crucial to marriage. Formerly the marriage ceremony was in the home, but now couples tend to be married in a Shinto shrine or in a professional reception hall. The exchange of a ritual gift, the *noshi,* seals the marriage between the two families.

Many beliefs and practices are associated with birth, all of which work for the protection of mother and child by driving away evil forces. Some of Embree's observations are local peculiarities; others are practiced throughout Japan. The "Goddess of Mercy," Kwannon (or Kannon), was always seen as a protector of pregnant women and small children, and the child was always dedicated to the local *kami*, the *ujigami*. The specific offerings and practices at the time of childbirth vary greatly from region to region and from countryside to city.

The religious treatment of the dead is now handled primarily by Buddhism, but we saw in the previous selection that religious concern for the dead dates back to pre-Buddhist and prehistoric times. Some of the vague beliefs concerning death and afterlife are recorded here. Not mentioned is the fact that villagers usually have voluntary associations to aid one another on the occasion of a death. When there is a death in any family belonging to the association (called *ko*), all contribute to the cost, labor, and ceremony of the funeral. (See selection 11 for details.)

Reprinted by permission of the publisher from John F. Embree, *Suye Mura: A Japanese Village* (Chicago: The University of Chicago Press, 1939). Copyright © 1939 by the University of Chicago.

Marriage

At the groom's house similar preparations have gone on all day, and the guests are received at the gate by the groom's relatives. The house is spick and span. The same pattern is followed—tea, presentation of bride's gifts, banquet.

However, before this begins, while guests are seated in the *zashiki*,[1] the bride and groom are taken into a separate room (or behind a screen in the same room) and the *san-san-ku-do* ceremony is performed under the direction of the go-between. This is the marriage ceremony of the "three-three-nine times" drink. Two children pour out the *sake* in three cups one on top of the other. First the groom has a drink out of the smallest cup, then the bride, then the same is done with the second and the third cup. Drinks are also exchanged between the bride and the groom's father; and there are also exchanges with the *nakaudo*[2] and his wife. A serving girl brings in some dried seaweed and cuttlefish of which a small amount is handed to each to be wrapped up in a tiny piece of paper and put away.

After the *san-san-ku-do* the *noshi* is brought into the banquet hall on a

---

[1] *Zashiki*, the room for receiving guests. [ed.]
[2] *Nakaudo*, the go-between who made formal arrangements for the marriage. [ed.]

tray. The *noshi* is a small strip of dried fish in a red and white paper folded in a special pattern. This *noshi* is a more elaborate form of a similar paper also called *noshi* which is attached to all formal gifts, including wedding gifts. It is presented to the groom's father, and the go-between announces that "the *noshi* has been received." No one seems to know just what this symbolizes, but apparently it indicates that the gift of the bride has been received. Like many other parts of the wedding ceremony, this is not indigenous to Kuma[3] so that not only has the meaning disappeared but radical variations occur. For instance, according to some, *noshi* are exchanged between bride and groom, and sometimes the groom presents a *noshi* to the bride's family in which case the go-between announces that "the *noshi* has been presented." After this the bride's *tsunokakushi*[4] is removed, and the formal ceremony is over. . . .

At marriage the *butsudan* is opened so that the ancestors may know of the happy event. On some occasions the *san-san-ku-do* marriage ceremony is actually performed in front of the *butsudan*. . . . No priests are involved in the wedding ceremony. . . .

Birth

Birth beliefs are primarily Shinto but contain many Buddhist elements. As already noted, a pregnant woman considers herself under the protection of Kwannon. The soul of the child is supposed to come from the *kami*, native gods of Japan, more especially the *uji-gami*, patron god of the *mura*,[5] but when and how is not very definite. At the time of the naming ceremony, offerings are made to the *kamidana* and in the *tokonoma*[6] of *shochu*[7] and cakes. However, this naming ceremony is rather a mixture of Shinto and Buddhist features. The *shochu* and cakes offered at the *tokonoma* are Shinto. The name is sometimes pasted by the *tokonoma*, too, but the tasseled rosary is Buddhist and the name paper is more often placed by the *butsudan*.

The afterbirth is wrapped up in paper. At sunset the father of the child takes it away and buries it in the yard or near the family graves, after which he steps over the spot to insure the child's obedience. If some animal, as for instance a dog, should run over the spot before the father steps on it, the child will fear that animal. Sometimes the afterbirth is thrown into or buried under the toilet.

The umbilical cord, when it comes off within a week or ten days, is carefully wrapped with a bit of the child's hair and put away in a safe place with the child's name written on it.

[3]Kuma, a county in Kumamoto Prefecture, within the island of Kyushu. [ed.]
[4]*Tsunokakushi*, a white piece of silk, part of the traditional wedding headdress. [ed.]
[5]*Mura*, village. [ed.]
[6]*Tokonoma*, alcove. [ed.]
[7]*Shochu*, a cheap alcoholic drink. [ed.]

The name of a child is sometimes given or changed according to the advice of a *kitoshi*.[8] Thus, one boy's name is Toru, but, as he was born in a bad year, the *kitoshi* advised that he be called the name of some animal. Sheep (*hitsuji*) was chosen, and so the child is called Hitsuji or Hischan in everyday life, though the village office records him as Toru. After five years of age he will be safe and can be called by his given name.

The child's soul is, at first, not very stable, so he is kept at home until the visit to the *ujigami* shrine of the village or the *buraku*.[9] Before this, if he crosses water, the water-god may take his soul. Should it be absolutely necessary to take a child across before the proper time, some salt must be offered to the god. There is some connection between this taboo and the animals' (horses and cows) naming ceremonies. All calves and colts have a naming ceremony (*kamitate*) on the third day after birth. The name is chosen in the same manner as that of babies, written out and pasted by the *butsudan*, but before this is done there is a ceremony called *kawa watasu* (crossing the river). Some water is spilt in the yard, and the cow and the calf are made to cross the pool. Some people explain this as being equivalent to the first crossing of a river by a baby; others, however, think that this symbolizes the bath which a child is given on its naming day. . . .

Death

At funerals the Buddhist priest comes into his own. His chief sources of income are funerals and memorial services.

At death the man's soul does not immediately leave the house but hovers about until the funeral. After burial it starts its journey to heaven or hell, depending on its virtues in life and the prayers of its living relatives. The soul of a purely Shinto believer (only the Shinto priest in Suye) does not go to the paradise of Amida but hovers indefinitely about the village shrine.

When one dies, the soul goes either to heaven or to hell. Heaven is in the west, and there dwells Amida. Those who believe in Amida and are good during their lifetime, i.e., charitable, go there. The regular belief is that souls become gathered into Buddha's lap on death and become Buddhas. One's death and becoming Buddha is called *nehan* (nirvana).

Some younger people (twenty to forty years of age) believe that there is no heaven and hell except in one's self. That is, if one is sincere and does good acts, one has a heaven in one's self.

The belief in *nehan* as a loss of self and desires is not known in the village; belief in reincarnation is also lacking. There are, however, a few popular beliefs, referred to as superstitions: that if one is very scared of snakes, one was once a frog, and that, if one looks very much like some grandparent who has died, one is referred to as that person reborn. This latter is considered to be not literal but in a manner of speaking.

[8]*Kitoshi,* a popular diviner or fortune teller. [ed.]
[9]*Buraku,* ward.

Most of the ideas of heaven and hell come from the priests' talks and are not very much thought about by the people except when they get old. Certain of the funeral preparations are done in order to facilitate the dead man's progress in heaven, for instance, the *rokudo* Jizo,[10] the board stand with six (or three in most *buraku*) candles. These candles are to be offered to each of the six Jizo who guard six different stages through which a man must pass on his way up. The three *mon*[11] (now represented by one or two *sen*[12]) are to pay the man who poles the boat across the river on the way to heaven. Most of these things are done as a matter of custom, and many people cannot explain why they are done. This applies to the rice placed before a corpse and later thrown into the grave to be eaten in afterlife when all souls gather at Zenkoji, a temple in Nagano. Folded white papers are worn in the hair of female mourners and behind the ears of male mourners during the procession to the grave, where they are thrown in. Another bowl of rice with various funeral foods is placed on a tray in front of the coffin. A piece of paper with a hole in the center is pasted to the rice bowl, for the evil spirits to escape through.

One characteristic attitude is that, according to one's belief in life, so will one's soul be disposed of at death—if Shin sect, one goes to Amida's heaven; if Zen sect, to some other type of heaven; if Shinto, to the village shrine.

Each *buraku* has certain burial customs peculiar to itself. Despite the fact that most people of the village are all of the one Shinshu sect, any variation in burial custom is conventionally ascribed to the dead man's being "of a different sect." There is no feeling that one method of burial is worse or better than another.

38

Religious life in a rural village

One of the best illustrations of the presence of religion in the midst of everyday life is the description of life in a specific village. Ichiro Hori provides this illustration from his field work in Satoyamabe-mura, balancing his descriptive account with some wider generalizations. He uses the notions of "little tradition" and "great tradition" to describe the

[10]Rokudo Jizo, six statues of Jizo (one for each of the six parts of hell). [ed.]
[11]*Mon*, a coin no longer in use in the 1930s. [ed.]
[12]*Sen*, one hundredth of a yen, a coin not in use in contemporary Japan. [ed.]

interaction between local and universal traditions. Eventually, local customs such as ancient Japanese practices and universal traditions such as Buddhism became so interrelated that they are now experienced by the people as inseparable. (For other treatments of religious syncretism see Part 8.)

In this village of 682 families, there is an amazing array of religious phenomena, all integrated into a total system. In the main Shinto shrine itself are found belief in an ancestral *kami,* concern for spirits of the dead, relationship to a major Buddhist temple, and veneration of a famous emperor. The villagers not only participate in the life of this shrine but also belong to a Buddhist temple and participate in the rites of their extended family.

The other religious phenomena of the village read like an encyclopedia of Japanese religion. There are stone phalli for fertility, stones for the guardian deity of horses, and many other monuments. The many stones may be seen as the heritage of the village as a whole, but special religious associations *(ko)* are also numerous. The syncretistic Koshin-ko (which is the topic of selection 14) is prominent, but so are Buddhist, Shinto, and popular associations. In addition, each family has its own set of religious practices within the home. Satoyamabe-mura may not be exhaustive of the entire Japanese tradition, and it does not reflect modern urban Japan, but it does contain a cross section of the many interwoven religious elements which characterized daily life in traditional Japan.

Reprinted by permission of the author and publisher from Ichiro Hori, *Folk Religion in Japan: Continuity and Change,* edited by Joseph M. Kitagawa and Alan Miller (Chicago: The University of Chicago Press, 1968). Copyright © 1968 by the University of Chicago.

Social Structure and Folk Religion

I believe that the essence of Japanese folk religion lies in the interaction of two belief systems: a little tradition, which is based on blood or close community ties; and a great tradition, introduced from without, which is adopted by individual or group choice. The belief patterns found everywhere in Japanese rural society are complex, multilayered, and syncretistic. These patterns are based both on the existence of native religion centering in the worship of ancestors and on the various kinds of religion brought from outside by missionaries or believers who belong to the great traditions or to the more advanced little traditions.

Little tradition here refers to the native or folk religions, including the advanced Shinto, which was shaped by ancient Japanese geographic and cultural circumstances; great tradition refers to Confucianism, religious Taoism, and Buddhism — highly developed religious and philosophical importations. These two systems became intertwined after centuries, and Japanese folk religion developed as an integral whole out of the interaction of many separate elements. . . .

Folk Beliefs in Japanese Rural Society: The Case of Satoyamabe-mura

The relationship between folk beliefs and everyday life in an average rural community can be illustrated from my field research in Satoyamabe-mura, Nagano prefecture.[1] This village consists of 682 families divided into thirteen *o-aza* (large sub-village units) and thirty-three *ko-aza* (sub-village sections). The central Shinto shrine of this village, which all villagers have the duty and right to serve, is called Susuki-no-miya (literally, "Pampas-grass shrine"), in reference to the tradition of the origin of the local kami, who is supposed to have journeyed down the nearby river from a neighboring mountain on a pampas-grass leaf. The Susuki-no-miya now enshrines two kami: Takeminakata-no-kami, the ancestral kami of famous ancient feudal lords and the religiously powerful Suwa family who had presided over the neighboring district of Suwagun, and who were known as the Jin-shi (kami's family) until the end of the Ashikaga shogunate (A.D. 1338–1573); and Gozu-tenno, who was originally believed to be a kami of epidemics but later became known as a guardian against epidemics. The latter is a type of *goryo-shin*.[2] . . .

In addition, there is a Buddhist-style miniature shrine and a Buddhist bodhisattva's statue (Bato-kannon, in Japanese; Hayagriva, in Sanskrit) in the inner shrine. This is a remnant of the commingling of Shinto and Buddhism in the medieval period, and indicates that this shrine has been influenced by beliefs from the Zenko-ji temple in Nagano, one of the most flourishing Buddhist temples, belonging to both the Tendai and Jodo sects. There is also a small branch shrine which enshrines Prince Shotoku, a crown prince of the sixth century who played a decisive role in the introduction of Buddhism into Japan. He is especially honored by the Buddhist Shin sect as well as by carpenters and other craftsmen.

Thus, at least four religious elements are found in this shrine: belief in an ancestral kami of a politically powerful and religious family (a developed little tradition); belief in *goryo-shin* (super-community, but belonging to a little tradition); belief in Zenko-ji temple (great tradition); and belief in Prince Shotoku (great and little traditions).

The main Buddhist temple in Satoyamabe-mura is Tosen-ji. It belongs to the Shingon sect and was originally built to serve the main Shinto shrine

---

[1]Nagano prefecture is in central Honshu, the main Japanese island. [ed.]
[2]*Goryo-shin*, unfriendly spirits of the dead. [ed.]

(Susuki-no-miya). A large number of families have religious celebrations at this temple during the annual Bon festival, at the anniversary rites for ancestors, and during funeral rites.

Beyond these two central religious affiliations, each family and each person in the village has relationships with many other religious belief systems, the most important of which center in the *iwai-den* or *iwai-jin*, which house the tutelary kami of the extended family. Twenty-eight kinds of Shinto and Buddhist deities are enshrined in ninety-one of these *iwai-den*. Among them the Inari shrine contains the largest number, comprising 46 per cent of the total. . . .

Attention should also be given to the other religious phenomena in this village, such as the many stone shrines, stupas, phalli, monuments, memorial statues, charms, and taboo symbols. There are now about 144 small shrines and stone symbols, among which are forty-two Nembutsu stupas and Amida figures, twenty Koshin stupas, a number of offering stupas for the Lotus Sutra (formally, *Saddharmapundarika-sutra* in Sanskrit), memorial stupas for pilgrimages, Bato-kannon statues (Buddhist guardian deity of horses), Nijusan-ya stupas (for worship on the twenty-third night's moon after the new moon), statues of Doso-jin (kami of the road and travel and of sex), statues of Kodama-gami (kami of silk and the silkworm), and others. Moreover, there are many religious associations (*ko*) in this village.

> Koshin-ko.—*Koshin belief is an amalgamation of Shinto, religious Taoism, and Buddhism. Koshin is believed to have many and various functions in the village. He is, for instance, the agricultural kami, the protector against misfortune, the kami of soil, the kami of craftsmanship and so forth, and one* buraku *has two or three associations for service to this kami. In Fujii* buraku *there are four such* Koshin-ko, *one association each being organized by the eight Hanaoka families, the fourteen Futatsugi families, the four Fujii families, and the fourteen consisting of Akagi, Nehagi, Sakashita, Yamoto families. These associations often overlap with the* iwai-den *system or combine two or three* iwai-den. *The members of each association must meet six times yearly at the duty house* (toya) *and, after a small festival, discuss the economic and cooperative matters of the community and the common problems of daily public life. Often the old persons talk about the folk traditions, legends, and history of the village. They feast together and, following the old customary Koshin belief, sit up throughout the night.*
>
> Nembutsu-ko.—*This is composed of the believers in Amida Butsu (Amitabha Buddha). Their main function in the community is to serve the spirits of the dead and sometimes to help during funeral rites. This association often combines with the Koshin-ko and is sometimes called* Koshin-nembutsu-ko.
>
> Ise-ko.—*Members are believers in the mythical ancestral goddess of the imperial family which has been enshrined at Ise shrine. Each member of this association must pay monthly dues. One or two delegates, who are decided upon by lot, worship at the Ise Shrine in Mie prefecture once a year. They distribute the charms and the calendars published by this shrine to each member. This association includes almost all members of the village. Almost the same function is performed by* Akiba-ko.
>
> Akiba-ko.—*This is the association of believers in Akiba-sama, the protector against fire.*

Nijusan-ya-ko.—*This association for the worship of the 23rd night's moon after the new moon is a volunteer group of women who meet once a lunar month at the village shrine or the duty house. They remain together throughout the night in order to worship the moon which appears at the next dawn. Nijusanyasama is believed to be the guardian of easy childbirth and good fortune.*

Kannon-ko.—*This is an association of believers in Bato-kannon, the Buddhist deity of the horse. The members are primarily horse drivers and owners of horses and cattle.*

Other *ko associations are* Yama-no-kami-ko *(an association of believers in the mountain deity) and* Kinoene-ko *(an association of believers in Daikoku, a kami of good luck and good harvest, the festival of which is held each Kinoene Day (Elder Rat Day).*

In addition to these complicated religious observances, each family has its own Shinto and Buddhist altars in the living room which serve the spirits of the family ancestors and where the kami are prayed to for good health and good harvest. In the kitchen there are usually altars of Daikoku-sama and Ebisu-sama, both of which are generally believed to be kami of good harvest and good luck. Moreover, there are many Shinto, Onmyo-do (way of Yin-yang), and Buddhist charms and amulets on the pillars and walls, distributed by wandering preachers from some of the larger shrines and temples. The villagers also believe there are many kami—of the well, the fireplace, the privy, the gate, and so forth—in each house.

39

social and aesthetic expression of religion: the art of tea

Because tea is the national beverage of Japan, it shares some of the features of coffee drinking in the West: it is a common drink of refreshment taken with meals or in a period of relaxation, often in social company. But the ceremonial concern for tea in Japan goes so far beyond this mundane level that it has become a "cult," or "art," as Suzuki describes it. Indeed, the process of preparing and serving tea is so elaborate that there are recognized schools and "masters" in the art. Many people, especially young ladies, take lessons in the tea ceremony as a means of spiritual training and to gain poise.

Daisetz Suzuki is concerned not with the social or manual aspects of serving tea but with its philosophical and religious meaning in Zen. The total atmosphere for the tea ceremony is one of simplicity and harmony with nature; the tea hut and the person alike are stripped of artificial obstacles. By eliminating the unnecessary from the surroundings and from the actions of the tea ceremony, one is able to participate in the rhythm of nature. As a Western interpreter has put it, "Rustic utensils and surroundings were brought into harmony to remind him of the Buddhahood in a clod of earth, and the withdrawn repose of the cottage and its garden turned his mind to the permanent behind the ephemeral—to the intersection of time and eternity."[1]

The last part of this selection is a translation of a statement on the art of tea by the Zen master Takuan (1573 - 1645). The art of tea has been practiced in Japan for centuries, and long ago it was realized that this art can be turned all too easily into mere sociability or vain pride. To avoid these pitfalls, Takuan (1573 - 1645) described the simple setting and tools for the proper appreciation of the art of tea. Noteworthy is the concern for the little things, the mood of the seasons, the sound of the boiling kettle. In this context worries are set aside and the mind is refreshed. When we view the tea ceremony, it is difficult to decide whether religion has penetrated an everyday activity or whether this mundane activity has been elevated to the position of a cult.

Reprinted by permission of the publisher from *Zen and Japanese Culture,* by Daisetz T. Suzuki, Bollingen Series LXIV (copyright © 1959 by Princeton University Press): pp. 271-272, 276-278.

Zen and the Art of Tea

What is common to Zen and the art of tea is the constant attempt both make at simplification. The elimination of the unnecessary is achieved by Zen in its intuitive grasp of final reality; by the art of tea, in the way of living typified by serving tea in the tearoooom. The art of tea is the aestheticism of primitive simplicity. Its ideal, to come closer to Nature, is realized by sheltering oneself under a thatched roof in a room which is hardly ten feet square but which must be artistically constructed and furnished. Zen also aims at stripping off all the artificial wrappings humanity has devised, supposedly for its own solemnization. Zen first of all combats the intellect; for, in spite

[1]Edward G. Seidensticker, in Yasunari Kawabata, *Thousand Cranes,* trans. Edward G. Seidensticker (New York: Berkley Publishing Corporation, 1965), p. v. In this novel Kawabata, Japanese winner of the Nobel prize for literature, has woven a fascinating tale into the context and mood of the tea ceremony.

of its practical usefulness, the intellect goes against our effort to delve into the depths of being. Philosophy may propose all kinds of questions for intellectual solution, but it never claims to give us the spiritual satisfaction which must be accessible to every one of us, however intellectually undeveloped he may be. Philosophy is accessible only to those who are intellectually equipped, and thus it cannot be a discipline of universal appreciation. Zen—or, more broadly speaking, religion—is to cast off all one thinks he possesses, even life, and to get back to the ultimate state of being, the "Original Abode," one's own father or mother. This can be done by every one of us, for we are what we are because of it or him or her, and without it or him or her we are nothing. This is to be called the last stage of simplification, since things cannot be reduced to any simpler terms. The art of tea symbolizes simplification, first of all, by an inconspicuous, solitary, thatched hut erected, perhaps, under an old pine tree, as if the hut were part of nature and not specially constructed by human hands. When form is thus once for all symbolized it allows itself to be artistically treated. It goes without saying that the principle of treatment is to be in perfect conformity with the original idea which prompted it, that is, the elimination of unnecessaries. . . .

Takuan on the Art of Tea (Cha-No-Yu)

The principle of *cha-no-yu* is the spirit of harmonious blending of Heaven and Earth and provides the means for establishing universal peace. People of the present time have turned it into a mere occasion for meeting friends, talking of worldly affairs, and indulging in palatable food and drink; besides, they are proud of their elegantly furnished tearooms, where, surrounded by rare objects of art, they would serve tea in a most accomplished manner, and deride those who are not so skillful as themselves. This is, however, far from being the original intention of *cha-no-yu*.

Let us then construct a small room in a bamboo grove or under trees, arrange streams and rocks and plant trees and bushes, while [inside the room] let us pile up charcoal, set a kettle, arrange flowers, and arrange in order the necessary tea utensils. And let all this be carried out in accordance with the idea that in this room we can enjoy the streams and rocks as we do the rivers and mountains in Nature, and appreciate the various moods and sentiments suggested by the snow, the moon, and the trees and flowers, as they go through the transformation of seasons, appearing and disappearing, blooming and withering. As visitors are greeted here with due reverence, we listen quietly to the boiling water in the kettle, which sounds like a breeze passing through the pine needles, and become oblivious of all worldly woes and worries; we then pour out a dipperful of water from the kettle, reminding us of the mountain stream, and thereby our mental dust is wiped off. This is truly a world of recluses, saints on earth.

The principle of propriety is reverence, which in practical life functions as harmonious relationship. This is the statement made by Confucius when

he defines the use of propriety, and is also the mental attitude one should cultivate as *cha-no-yu*. For instance, when a man is associated with persons of high social rank his conduct is simple and natural, and there is no cringing self-depreciation on his part. When he sits in the company of people socially below him he retains a respectful attitude toward them, being entirely free from the feeling of self-importance. This is due to the presence of something pervading the entire tearoom, which results in the harmonious relationship of all who come here. However long the association, there is always the persisting sense of reverence. The spirit of the smiling Kasyapa and the nodding Tseng-tzu must be said to be moving here; this spirit, in words, is the mysterious Suchness that is beyond all comprehension.

For this reason, the principle animating the tearoom, from its first construction down to the choice of the tea utensils, the technique of service, the cooking of food, wearing apparel, etc., is to be sought in the avoidance of complicated ritual and mere ostentation. The implements may be old, but the mind can be invigorated therewith so that it is ever fresh and ready to respond to the changing seasons and the varying views resulting therefrom; it never curries favor, it is never covetous, never inclined to extravagance, but always watchful and considerate for others. The owner of such a mind is naturally gentle-mannered and always sincere—this is *cha-no-yu*.

The way of *cha-no-yu*, therefore, is to appreciate the spirit of a naturally harmonious blending of Heaven and Earth, to see the pervading presence of the five elements (*wu-hsing*) by one's fireside, where the mountains, rivers, rocks, and trees are found as they are in Nature, to draw the refreshing water from the well of Nature, to taste with one's own mouth the flavor supplied by Nature. How grand this enjoyment of the harmonious blending of Heaven and Earth!

SELECTED READINGS

For works on various aspects of the theme of penetration of religion into everyday life, see first the citations for each selection; some additional works are:

Hirayama, Toshijiro. "Seasonal Rituals Connected with Rice Culture." In *Studies in Japanese Folklore,* edited by Richard M. Dorson, pp. 57-75. Bloomington: Indiana University Press, 1963.

Segawa, Kiyoko. "Menstrual Taboos Imposed upon Women." In *Studies in Japanese Folklore,* pp. 239-50.

Sakurada, Katsunori. "The Ebisu-gami in Fishing Villages." In *Studies in Japanese Folklore,* pp. 122-32.

Wakamori, Taro. "Initiation Rites and Young Men's Organizations." In *Studies in Japanese Folklore,* pp. 291-304. (See also other articles in this volume.)

part fourteen

natural bond between religion and state

A combination of factors in Japanese history has resulted in a peculiarly intimate bond between religion and the state, and this bond forms a persistent theme in the religious life of the Japanese people. The Japanese have long possessed a sense of national identity and common destiny, as an island country with a unique tradition in ancient times and a continuing sociopolitical unity today. The mythology of antiquity lays the foundation for the notion of Japan as a divinely created country led by the imperial line in descent from the Sun Goddess. With this ancient heritage as a foundation, it is not surprising that the overwhelming majority of religious institutions in Japanese history have assumed a position of subservience to the state, or have at least supported the Japanese nation.

This theme runs throughout Japanese history, yet it undergoes various changes. For example, the idea of religion serving the state in Shotoku's Constitution, excerpted below, is not the same as the ideological support for modern nationalism in *Cardinal Principles of the National Entity*, the last selection in Part 14. The use—or, one might say, the abuse—of a tradition does not always bring out the essential values of a tradition. To take an example from Western history, the use of Christianity as motivation for the medieval Crusades does not mean that the essence of Christianity is the crusading spirit. Japanese religion by nature tends to support the cultural and political order of which it is a part. This was assumed in traditional Japan, and was planned in modern Japan. For example, the Imperial Rescript on Education used religious or semireligious loyalty to emperor and state to unify the people into a modern nation-state. But most Japanese feel that the *Cardinal Principles of the National Entity*, whose use in the educational system helped inculcate the unswerving patriotism expressed in Japan's wars with China and Russia and later in World War II, was an abuse of the Japanese notion.

40

shotoku's constitution: Religion and state in ancient japan

One of the earliest Japanese documents expressing the intimate relationship between state and religion is the so-called Seventeen Article Constitution of Prince Shotoku. According to tradition, Prince Shotoku wrote this document in the early seventh century, and although his authorship may never be proven, the Japanese estimation of Prince Shotoku is very high: he is revered as one of the great early statesmen in Japanese history and as a founding father of Japanese Buddhism. (See selection 7 for the elevation of Prince Shotoku to semidivine status.) This so-called constitution is more a rationale for political action than an actual constitution, but the first three items show the special role of religion in this rationale.

The author presupposes the universal reverence for *kami* and weaves this into support for Confucian and Buddhist values as a means of reinforcing the state. The first article of the Constitution, quoted below, emphasizes the Confucian virtue of social harmony, which is the basis for political stability. The second article pays homage to Buddhism as the way in which men will be preserved from evil. The third article combines the Japanese idea of the divinity of the emperor with Chinese cosmic notions of the harmony necessary between Heaven and Earth. In later times, the particular formulation of the state-religion relationship varied, but religion usually supported the state, while the state patronized religion.

Reprinted by permission of the publisher from W. G. Aston, translator, *Nihongi: Chronicles of Japan from the Earliest Times to A.D. 697* (London: George Allen & Unwin Ltd., 1956).

Shotoku's Constitution

I. Harmony is to be valued, and an avoidance of wanton opposition to be honoured. All men are influenced by class-feelings, and there are few who are intelligent. Hence there are some who disobey their lords and fathers, or who maintain feuds with the neighbouring villages. But when those above are harmonious and those below are friendly, and there is concord in the discussion of business, right views of things spontaneously gain acceptance. Then what is there which cannot be accomplished!

II. Sincerely reverence the three treasures. The three treasures, viz. Buddha, the Law and the Priesthood, are the final refuge of the four generated beings, and are the supreme objects of faith in all countries. What man in what age can fail to reverence this law? Few men are utterly bad. They may be taught to follow it. But if they do not betake them to the three treasures, wherewithal shall their crookedness be made straight?

III. When you receive the Imperial commands, fail not scrupulously to obey them. The lord is Heaven, the vassal is Earth. Heaven overspreads, and Earth upbears. When this is so, the four seasons follow their due course, and the powers of Nature obtain their efficacy. If the Earth attempted to overspread, Heaven would simply fall in ruin. Therefore is it that when the lord speaks, the vassal listens; when the superior acts, the inferior yields compliance. Consequently when you receive the Imperial commands, fail not to carry them out scrupulously. Let there be a want of care in this matter, and ruin is the natural consequence.

41

the imperial rescript on education: religious support for modern nationalism

This selection has greater historical significance than its brief length suggests, for it summed up the nationalistic fervor that stemmed from the Meiji Restoration, and it served as the training guide for absolute commitment to the state until 1945. Powerful symbols such as the emperor and hierarchical patterns of loyalty were invoked to support this educational program. A nationwide school system was developed in the Meiji period (1868 - 1912), and the imperial rescript and a portrait of the emperor were hung in every school. Pupils were required to bow before them much as American pupils pledge allegiance to the flag. Religious undertones may be seen even in the American practice, but the religious character of the Japanese ceremony is more direct. The emperor, often known as a "manifest *kami*," was venerated as a descendant of the *kami*, the living symbol of their spiritual tradition as well as their ethnic and national unity. In short, veneration of the emperor was used to train the people to hold absolute loyalty toward the state.

The content of the rescript, although formally stated, is rather simple: the source of education is the realization that Japan is a sacred empire

handed down by the imperial line and to which all are loyal and obedient. The emperor is the visible symbol of the state to which all must (out of sense of obligation) give themselves totally: "Should emergency arise, offer yourselves courageously to the State" in order to protect the imperial throne. Respect for the constitution is mentioned, but the Japanese constitution was handed down from authorities above, not demanded by a grass-roots movement of the people. However, this document succeeded—not because it invoked a new principle but because it reflected and elaborated a central aspect of Japanese tradition. In this sense, the Rescript on Education did not create the notion of loyalty to the Emperor, but it did embody this tradition. At present, one lively discussion among Japanese intellectuals is how Japan can retain her distinctiveness as a national tradition and yet participate in international affairs.

Reprinted by permission of the publisher from Dairoku Kikuchi, *Japanese Education* (London: John Murray Publishers, 1909).

Imperial Rescript on Education

Know ye, Our subjects:

Our Imperial Ancestors have founded Our Empire on a basis broad and everlasting, and have deeply and firmly implanted virtue; Our subjects ever united in loyalty and filial piety have from generation to generation illustrated the beauty thereof. This is the glory of the fundamental character of Our Empire, and herein also lies the source of Our education. Ye, Our subjects, be filial to your parents, affectionate to your brothers and sisters; as husbands and wives be harmonious, as friends true; bear yourselves in modesty and moderation; extend your benevolence to all; pursue learning and cultivate arts, and thereby develop intellectual faculties and perfect moral powers; furthermore, advance public good and promote common interests; always respect the Constitution and observe the laws; should emergency arise, offer yourselves courageously to the State; and thus guard and maintain the prosperity of Our Imperial Throne coeval with heaven and earth. So shall ye not only be Our good and faithful subjects, but render illustrious the best traditions of your forefathers.

The Way here set forth is indeed the teaching bequeathed by Our Imperial Ancestors, to be observed alike by Their Descendants and the subjects, infallible for all ages and true in all places. It is Our wish to lay it to heart in all reverence, in common with you, Our subjects, that we may all attain the same virtue.

The 30th day of the 10th month of the 23rd year of Meiji.
(The 30th of October, 1890).

(Imperial Sign Manual. Imperial Seal).

42

ReLIGION as IÐEOLOGY

The international scene changed significantly from the time of the Imperial Rescript on Education in 1890 to the time of the 1937 publication of *Kokutai no Hongi*, or *Cardinal Principles of the National Entity of Japan*. In less than fifty years, Japan passed beyond the threat of colonial intervention on her own soil and herself became a kind of colonial power. Japan was successful militarily in two wars, the Sino-Japanese War of 1894 - 95 and the Russo-Japanese War of 1904 - 05, and she profited financially from World War I. Japan controlled Formosa (Taiwan) and Korea as well as parts of continental China, and nationalism and militarism were inflated by this success.

Whereas the Rescript on Education was aimed at unifying the people within a newly formed nation-state, the government's *Cardinal Principles of the National Entity* was intended to gain unqualified support for the military goals of a state which constituted a world power. Excerpts from the latter document reveal a consistent twofold argument. First, the *problems* of Japan are caused by neglect of the native tradition and adoption of Western values. Western thought is contrary to Japanese soil because it does not realize the unique heritage of Japan, and it encourages an individualism which destroys Japanese social ethics. Second, the *solution* to the problems of Japan is rejection of Western thought and recovery of the ancient Japanese heritage, for Japan is a sacred land founded by the *kami* and ruled by the emperor, and every citizen will express filial piety to his parents and absolute loyalty to the emperor. This loyalty, especially for the warrior, means giving his life for his country.

In short, this document of unqualified patriotism, not unlike documents from other countries, calls for support of political and military activities, whatever they might be. Most Japanese agree that this was a use of the native tradition to support an unfortunate war (for the same reason, many Japanese are against the use of Japan as a base for United States military operations). In addition, many Japanese feel that religion and war are incompatible, and they actively support peace movements. The *Kokutai no Hongi* was prohibited by the Allied occupation forces in the so-called "Directive for the Disestablishment of State Shinto" of late 1945, and it is no longer used in Japanese education. (This directive is cited in full in selection 5; for mention of *Kokutai no Hongi*, see provision I.i. of selection 5.)

Cardinal Principles of the National Entity of Japan

The various ideological and social evils of present-day Japan are the fruits of ignoring the fundamentals and of running into the trivial, of lack in sound judgment, and of failure to digest things thoroughly; and this is due to the fact that since the days of Meiji so many aspects of European and American culture, systems, and learning, have been imported, and that, too rapidly. As a matter of fact, foreign ideologies imported into our country are in the main the ideologies of enlightenment that have come down since the eighteenth century, or their extensions. The views of the world and of life that form the basis of these ideologies are a rationalism and a positivism, lacking in historical views, which on the one hand lay the highest value on, and assert the liberty and equality of, individuals, and on the other hand lay value on a world by nature abstract, transcending nations and races. Consequently, importance is laid upon human beings and their gatherings, who have become isolated from historical entireties, abstract and independent of each other. It is political, social, moral, and pedagogical theories based on such views of the world and of life, that have on the one hand made contributions to the various reforms seen in our country, and on the other have had deep and wide influence on our nation's primary ideology and culture. . . .

Paradoxical and extreme conceptions, such as socialism, anarchism, and communism, are all based in the final analyses on individualism which is the root of modern Occidental ideologies, and are no more than varied forms of their expressions. In the Occident, too, where individualism forms the basis of their ideas, they have, when it comes to communism, been unable to adopt it; so that now they are about to do away with their traditional individualism, which has led to the rise of totalitarianism and nationalism and incidentally to the upspringing of Fascism and Nazism. That is, it can be said that both in the Occident and in our country the deadlock of individualism has led alike to a season of ideological and social confusion and crisis. We shall leave aside for a while the question of finding a way out of the present deadlock, for, as far as it concerns our country, we must return to the standpoint peculiar to our country, clarify our immortal national entity, sweep aside everything in the way of adulation, bring into being our original condition, and at the same time rid ourselves of bigotry, and strive all the more to take in and sublimate Occidental culture; for we should give to basic things their proper place, giving due weight to minor things, and should build up a sagacious and

worthy Japan. This means that the present conflict seen in our people's ideas, the unrest in their modes of life, the confused state of civilization, can be put right only by a thorough investigation by us of the intrinsic nature of Occidental ideologies and by grasping the true meaning of our national entity. Then, too, this should be done not only for the sake of our nation but for the sake of the entire human race which is struggling to find a way out of the deadlock with which individualism is faced. Herein lies our grave cosmopolitan mission. It is for this reason that we have compiled the *Cardinal Principles of the National Entity of Japan*, to trace clearly the genesis of the nation's foundation, to define its great spirit, to set forth clearly at the same time the features the national entity has manifested in history, and to provide the present generation with an elucidation of the matter, and thus to awaken the people's consciousness and their efforts....

Our country is established with the Emperor, who is a descendant of Amaterasu Ohmikami, as her center, and our ancestors as well as we ourselves constantly behold in the Emperor the fountainhead of her life and activities. For this reason, to serve the Emperor and to receive the Emperor's great august Will as one's own is the rationale of making our historical "life" live in the present; and on this is based the morality of the people.

Loyalty means to reverence the Emperor as [our] pivot and to follow him implicitly. By implicit obedience is meant casting ourselves aside and serving the Emperor intently. To walk this Way of loyalty is the sole Way in which we subjects may "live," and the fountainhead of all energy. Hence, offering our lives for the sake of the Emperor does not mean so-called self-sacrifice, but the casting aside of our little selves to live under his august grace and the enhancing of the genuine life of the people of a State. The relationship between the Emperor and the subjects is not an artificial relationship [which means] bowing down to authority, nor a relationship such as [exists] between master and servant as is seen in feudal morals.... The ideology which interprets the relationship between the Emperor and his subjects as being a reciprocal relationship such as merely [involves] obedience to authority or rights and duties, rests on individualistic ideologies, and is a rationalistic way of thinking that looks on everything as being in equal personal relationships. An individual is an existence belonging to a State and her history which form the basis of his origin, and is fundamentally one body with it....

In our country, the two Augustnesses, Izanagi no Mikoto and Izanami no Mikoto, are ancestral deities of nature and the deities, and the Emperor is the divine offspring of the Imperial Ancestor who was born of the two Augustnesses. The Imperial Ancestor and the Emperor are in the relationship of parent and child, and the relationship between the Emperor and his subjects is, in its righteousness, that of sovereign and subject and, in its sympathies, that of father and child. This relationship is an "essential" relationship that is far more fundamental than the rational, obligatory relationships, and herein are the grounds that give birth to the Way of loyalty. From the point

of individualistic personal relationships, the relationship between sovereign and subject in our country may [perhaps] be looked upon as that between non-personalities. However, this is nothing but an error arising from treating the individual as supreme, from the notion that has individual thoughts for its nucleus, and from abstract consciousness. Our relationship between sovereign and subject is by no means a shallow, lateral relationship such as [means] the correlation between ruler and citizen, but is a relationship springing from a basis transcending this correlation, and is that of self-effacement and a return to [the]"one," in which this basis is not lost. This is a thing that can never be understood from an individualistic way of thinking. In our country, this great Way has seen a natural development since the founding of the nation, and the most basic thing that has manifested itself as regards the subjects is in short this Way of loyalty. Herein exists the profound meaning and lofty value of loyalty. Of late years, through the influence of the Occidental individualistic ideology, a way of thinking which has for its basis the individual has become lively. Consequently, this and the true aim of our Way of loyalty which is "essentially" different from it are not necessarily [mutually] consistent. That is, those in our country who at the present time expound loyalty and patriotism are apt to lose [sight of] its true significance, being influenced by Occidental individualism and rationalism. We must sweep aside the corruption of the spirit and the clouding of knowledge that arises from setting up one's "self" and from being taken up with one's "self" and return to a pure and clear state of mind that belongs intrinsically to us as subjects, and thereby fathom the great principle of loyalty....

In our country filial piety is a Way of the highest importance. Filial piety originates with one's family as its basis, and in its larger sense has the nation for its foundation. Filial piety directly has for its object one's parents, but in its relationship toward the Emperor finds a place within loyalty.

The basis of the nation's livelihood is, as in the Occident, neither the individual nor husband and wife. It is the home....

The life of a family in our country is not confined to the present life of a household of parents and children, but beginning with the distant ancestors, is carried on eternally by the descendants. The present life of a family is a link between the past and the future, and while it carries over and develops the objectives of the ancestors, it hands them over to its descendants. Herein also lies the reason why since of old a family name has been esteemed in our country. A family name is an honor to a household built up by one's ancestors, so that to stain this may be looked upon not only as a personal disgrace but as a disgrace to a family that has come down in one line linking the past, present, and future. Accordingly, the announcing of one's real name by a knight who has gone out to the battlefield was in the nature of an oath to fight bravely by speaking of one's ancestors and their achievements, so as not to cast a slur on the name of an esteemed family....

Bushido may be cited as showing an outstanding characteristic of our national morality. In the world of warriors one sees inherited the totalitarian structure and spirit of the ancient clans peculiar to our nation. Hence, though the teachings of Confucianism and Buddhism have been followed, these have been transcended. That is to say, though a sense of indebtedness binds master and servant, this has developed into a spirit of self-effacement and of meeting death with a perfect calmness. In this, it was not that death was made light of so much as that man tempered himself to death and in a true sense regarded it with esteem. In effect, man tried to fulfill true life by way of death. This means that rather than lose the whole by being taken up with and setting up oneself, one puts self to death in order to give full play to the whole by fulfilling the whole. Life and death are basically one, and the monistic truth is found where life and death are transcended. Through this is life, and through this is death. However, to treat life and death as two opposites and to hate death and to seek life is to be taken up with one's own interests, and is a thing of which warriors are ashamed. To fulfill the Way of loyalty, counting life and death as one, is *Bushido*. . . .

We have inquired into the fundamental principles of our national entity and the ways in which it has been manifested in our national history. What kind of resolve and attitude should we subjects of the Japanese Empire now take toward the various problems of the day? It seems to us that our first duty is the task of creating a new Japanese culture by sublimating and assimilating foreign cultures which are at the source of the various problems in keeping with the fundamental principles of our national entity.

Every type of foreign ideology that has been imported into our country may have been quite natural in China, India, Europe, or America, in that it has sprung from their racial or historical characteristics; but in our country, which has a unique national entity, it is necessary as a preliminary step to put these types to rigid judgment and scrutiny so as to see if they are suitable to our national traits. That is to say, the creation of a new culture which has characteristics peculiar to our nation can be looked forward to only through this consciousness and the sublimation and assimilation of foreign cultures that accompanies it. . . .

To put it in a nutshell, while the strong points of Occidental learning and concepts lie in their analytical and intellectual qualities, the characteristics of Oriental learning and concepts lie in their intuitive and ascetic qualities. These are natural tendencies that arise through racial and historical differences; and when we compare them with our national spirit, concepts, or mode of living, we cannot help recognizing further great and fundamental differences. Our nation has in the past imported, assimilated, and sublimated Chinese and Indian ideologies, and has therewith supported the Imperial Way, making possible the establishment of an original culture based on her national entity. Following the Meiji Restoration Occidental cultures poured in with a rush, and contributed immensely toward our national prosperity;

but their individualistic qualities brought about various difficulties in all the phases of the lives of our people, causing their thoughts to fluctuate. However, now is the time for us to sublimate and assimilate these Occidental ideologies in keeping with our national entity, to set up a vast new Japanese culture, and, by taking advantage of these things, to bring about a great national development.

SELECTED READINGS

For works on various aspects of the theme of the natural bond between religion and state in Japan, see first the citations for each selection; some additional works are:

Brown, Delmer M. *Nationalism in Japan: An Introductory Historical Analysis.* Berkeley: University of California Press, 1955.

Hall, Robert K. *Shushin: The Ethics of a Defeated Nation.* New York: Columbia University Press, 1949.

Holtom, Daniel C. *Modern Japan and Shinto Nationalism: A Study of Present-Day Trends in Japanese Religions.* Rev. ed. New York: Paragon Reprint Corp., 1963.

Kanamori, Tokujiro, et al. *Religion and State in Japan: A Discussion of Religion and State in Relation to the Constitution.* Bulletin No. 7. Tokyo: International Institute for the Study of Religions, 1959.

Miller, Alan L. "Ritsuryo Japan: The State as Liturgical Community." *History of Religions* 11 (1971): 98-124.

part fifteen

the dilemma of organized religion in modern japan

Every religious tradition undergoes minor changes with the passage of time, but Japanese religion today faces a dilemma which is more serious. What is at stake is whether Shinto and Buddhism, the major organized religions in Japan, will continue to hold the attention of a majority of the population. The dilemma is complicated because it arises not only out of factors internal to the two religions but also out of external factors such as a shift from a predominantly agricultural socioeconomic orientation to urban-industrial life patterns.

Although the reasons are complex, it seems safe to conclude that internal factors in Buddhism and Shinto helped bring about a tendency toward formalism and a loss of vitality in their respective traditions. Buddhism's attachment to feudal values and the institutions of the Tokugawa period and Shinto's tie with narrowly nationalistic values and programs after the Tokugawa period were especially responsible for the lack of vitality in the postwar period. And the reformers within each tradition have been unable to renovate the traditions as a whole.

Religious life continues, however, and one major avenue for religious expression is the many New Religions discussed in the next part. However, another indication of the state of religious life in the modern period is the rather widespread disinterest in organized religion. Increasingly, particularly in the cities, people have no Shinto altar (kamidana) in their homes or make very few offerings; and if there are more Buddhist altars (butsudan), they are kept more out of respect for the ancestors than out of sympathy with Buddhism. A minority opinion of modern Japan, as represented in the novel The Pornographers, is disdain or sacrilegious scorn for all organized religion.

fORMALISM IN BUDDHISM

Although Buddhism in Japan was the repository of profound philosophy and the developer of dynamic sects, its dominant characteristic from Tokugawa times to the present has been formalism and lack of vitality. In this selection Zenryu Tsukamoto (a famous Buddhist scholar) uses the term *formalized Buddhism* to describe this situation, and he is openly critical of the manner in which the situation arose. Singled out for criticism are the subservience of Buddhist temples to feudal lords and the neglect of Buddhism's religious mission to serve the political rulers. The result was that funeral masses became the main religious function of Buddhism, a "formality" that could be carried out whether or not priests and people found religious fulfillment in Buddhism.

The extreme conservatism of Buddhist sects and family religion worked together to support feudal values even after the end of the feudal age simply because they had been part of the status quo. The result was that Buddhism in the modern age is still waiting for reform.

Buddhism's weakness in the modern nationalistic period meant that it was powerless to oppose militarism and imperialism, and Buddhism's early support of state and emperor was extended in the 1930s and early 1940s into positive, unqualified support of World War II. Tsukamoto outlines the details of Buddhist support for the war, concluding with the severe indictment that "it is not to the honor of the Japanese Buddhist order that no Buddhists sacrificed themselves to an antiwar movement during the long aggressive war in China." His indictment even casts light on the contemporary scene, since he characterizes much of Buddhism today as feudal and "reactionary."

Reprinted from Zenryu Tsukamoto, "Japanese and Chinese Buddhism in the Twentieth Century," *Journal of World History*, Volume VI-3, 1960. Reproduced with permission of UNESCO.

Japanese Buddhism in the Twentieth Century

... Not only the Church of Chinese Buddhism but also of Japanese Buddhism were formalized and lost their vitality in the course of the nineteenth century; they no longer held sway in their guidance of society. The political leaders of these two countries, impressed by the advances of Euro-

pean and American countries in the wake of Western Civilization, lost interest in "old Buddhism," despised it, thought it useless, and suppressed and persecuted it. Yet, religion in general resuscitated its original spirit throughout this suppression and persecution, took the chance to recover from the previous decline, and undergoes at present a revolutionary progress.

The modern Buddhist world in China and Japan, on account of government suppression and persecution, accomplished a transformation and managed reforms which were not evident in other Buddhist Asiatic countries. Let us first make a perusory survey of twentieth century Japanese Buddhism.

Many schools of Japanese Buddhism had served the feudalistic lords during the feudal age (Tokugawa; use of the word feudal is quite loose, since the system was in reality absolutism, absolute power in the hands of the *shogun*), which lasted for two hundred and sixty years or more previous to the Meiji period. These schools secured their position and prosperity by cooperating with the feudal lords in their maintenance of the feudal social order; at the same time they fixed their position in the feudal system. The Tokugawa family lords obliged all the people to belong to some temple, called *danka,* in their efforts to suppress Christianity. This meant that all Japanese families, under the leadership of a family head, were, at least nominally, Buddhist believers. Every temple became a branch temple of the *honzan,* or head temple of the school. The abbot of the head temple of every school supervised the high priests of the branch temples and, in turn, was subordinate to the lord or *shogun.* The high priest of every temple not only performed the ancestor rituals and funerals required by those families in his *danka* but also acted as a sort of inspector-guardian of the peace, reporting to the feudal lord both those who professed belief in heretical teachings and those who planned treacherous action against the social system. Thus, the Tokugawa lords made the temple clergy cooperate in maintaining the feudal society, employing the priests literally as inspectors of the people through the *danka* system. Politically forced to be "believers," there were surely some among them who were sincere believers, but the function of the Buddhist temple in the Tokugawa age was confined to the performance of rituals for the dead. Even the rituals for the dead of the *danka* families were magical in nature, completely incomprehensible to the Japanese people, because they were read in the Chinese style of pronunciation. Eventually, the life of the priests became so stable that the priests themselves became lazy, lost interest in their mission as priests and in their study of Buddhist Truth. Under the stability of this feudal system, Japanese human reason was impotent, and Buddhism became what I term "formalized Buddhism."

Meanwhile, the lords of the Tokugawa family hailed Confucianism, in particular the school of Chu Hsi, as the guide for government, and ordered the political underlings to study Chu Hsi and to propagate his teaching as an example for both politics and morals. The Chu Hsi school, as already well known, protested vigorously against Buddhism, more so than other schools,

and they insisted that Buddhism was not only useless but also harmful to a real social life guided by Confucian principles. The Tokugawa intelligentsia, generally called *shitaifu,* who were thoroughly educated in Confucianism, gradually became separated from all Buddhist affairs and despised the Buddhist religion. Even the monks themselves neglected their religious mission, which should be an endeavor to solve the problems of current social life and personal suffering. Instead they indulged in fixed dogmatic study of the doctrines respective to their school, recited the sutras for the deceased, and left aside entirely the religious problems connected with the actual society.

Just as the lords in their castles governed the people by a stratified feudal system, the abbot of each Buddhist school governed the clergy by a hierarchical system. The schools clung to traditional dogma and merely endeavored to maintain and follow the tradition. It was only natural that this "formalized Buddhism," the Buddhist order fixed in its *status quo,* lost all vitality and was unable to meet the rapid social changes which were to occur during the nineteenth century. Professional priests who only preached resignation to the people of the lower classes could only serve one purpose, the maintenance of the *status quo.* The force of Europe and America, which made its assault in the late nineteenth century, awakened the human reason of the Japanese which had been imprisoned and lay dormant inside the walls of this feudal system. The Meiji Emperor system succeeded in establishing itself in 1868, when the *shogun* and lords were defeated by the centralized power of the *samurai* of the lower classes. The leaders of the Meiji era endorsed Shinto as the state religion in order to give a strong backing to the Emperor system, and they separated the Shinto gods from the Buddhist temples where they had for so long a time coexisted with the Buddhist deities. Buddhist priests were obliged to believe in Shinto, and the rulers both despised and denigrated Buddhism. . . .

Although the numbers of educated people in Buddhist orders were small at this time, they tried, in spite of much suffering, to make suggestions for reform of the old system of the orders. They also mapped out plans to fight against not only the new Shinto assertion but also the new system of the Christian missionaries. . . .

Under these circumstances the scientific study of Buddhism which was prevalent in Europe, especially philological and historical studies, was introduced to Japan, and gave a revolutionary light to the Buddhist world in Japan. . . .

The philological and historical free study of Buddhism in Japan advanced with remarkable results; yet, in spite of this advancement, the feudalistic system of the Buddhist schools and their dogmatic study did not make any headway. Each school, which had continued for so long a time under the relation of *honzan* and branch, and under the *danka* system, was naturally

shaken by the introduction of democratic thoughts during the Meiji Restoration, and all the schools were eventually ruled by the Conference of Buddhist Priests in imitation of the Diet system. Just as the process of democratization was never completed under the divinization and strengthening of the Emperor, the Buddhist schools remained in the same way an association in imitation of the Emperor-system state, and even exerted themselves to maintain a feudal order rather than tend towards modernization. . . .

In the course of Japan's rapid modernization since the Meiji Restoration these new Buddhist Movements, that had organized the Buddhist priests and laity who were aware of the value of human reason, enthusiastically inspired the Japanese Buddhist Church. However, to the disadvantage of the Church as a whole, these Movements functioned outside the various Buddhist schools, which were composed of temples and priests still entrenched in the conventional propagation of the faith; on the contrary, the various schools did not welcome these Movements and were rather inclined to sneer at them.

The Meiji Restoration had been successful with the slogan "protect the Imperial family and attack our foreign enemies." The "attack our foreign enemies" gradually changed into the opening of the Japanese nation; and Japan not only introduced the nationalism of European countries but also proceeded to establish a Race State in which the Emperor occupied the center. Japanese Buddhism, ever since Buddhism's introduction into Japan, had always had an intimate relation with the Emperor system (*tenno* system), aided the Imperial family, was aided in turn by them, and developed largely along these lines. The Buddhist orders, that had been previously harassed by the new political leaders who were protecting the Emperor system, had now become enthusiastic cooperators with the *tenno* system, in sharp contrast to the servitor status under the *shogun* of the Tokugawa period. The leaders of the Buddhist orders outwardly tried to revive the force of their own schools, and inwardly tried to strengthen and maintain the feudalistic system. . . .

Although no reformation suitable to modern life took place, new education, social services, publications, etc., as commemorative works accelerated an adaptation to modern society. . . .

The family system, in which rituals for ancestors are important functions, still exists in Japanese society and tends to maintain the feudal system, even in the cities. The farmer society, where peasants, lovers of the soil, industrious workers without cares about their poverty-stricken simple lives, have continually supported the Japanese state, has also clung to rampant feudalistic customs. . . . The priests preached "resignation" as a Buddhist doctrine, a doctrine of the distorted Buddhism inherited from the Tokugawa period. No attempt was made to preach about modern life, or that the future will result from the present deeds of life and society, nor was any attempt made to preach any doctrine of awakening or advancement. Passive

and distorted theories of Buddhism were the talk of the day: no dissatisfaction with the present actual situation (which is a result of past deeds), let us simply work hard and be content with things as they are.

We do not deny that Buddhism offered spiritual food and enriched the spiritual life of the farming people and many others who form the base of Japan. On the other hand, we cannot help but acknowledge that Buddhism acted as an opium in delaying the awakening of the masses, strongly conservative that they may be in character, and served to maintain the feudal system rather than advance the modernization of Japan.

After the Sino-Japanese War (1894), the war with Russia, and participation in World War I, Japanese militarism and the Emperor system were strengthened, and the Buddhist Church began to cooperate closely with the Emperor system. For example, in 1916 the *Bukkyo gokokudan* (Buddhist Association for the protection of the State), an organ of all Buddhist schools, declared that their aim was to encourage and weld the spirit of nationalism, to protect the Imperial family and State, and to do their utmost to save the world and benefit the people. They thus exhibited themselves as the Buddhism of the Imperial State. In 1937 Japanese imperialism reached a peak by aggression in China: the Japanese government called this aggressive war a sacred war aiming at the punishment of anti-Japan Chinese or coprotection against communism. Along with this plan of aggressive war by the Japanese government, the "Buddhist Movement of the Imperial Way" became very strong within the Buddhist Church. Many slogans, such as "serve the State through Buddhism" *(bukkyo hokoku)* and "make prosperous the force of the State" *(kokuisenyo),* were loudly proclaimed; prayers for the health and long life of the soldiers were made. Sympathy for the army, ceremonies for the dead soldiers, and other religious functions in support of the aggressive war were carried on in great display; these religious functions did not stem from any doctrine of any of the schools, but were performed purely in line with the government policy of war. . . .

At the beginning of Japanese participation in World War II (1941) cooperation between Church and State was reinforced, and all Buddhist churches, including Tendai, Shingon and Jodo, transformed their order into a society for the protection of the State, both literally and figuratively, and renewed their vows of allegiance to the Emperor and the State. Slogans, such as "help and support the Great Policy" *(taisei yoku-san)* and "act as loyal subjects" *(shindo jissen),* were pasted on the walls of Buddhist temples. Rites for the protection of the State and welfare of the soldiers were performed; the fighting spirit was encouraged, and the defeats of the United States and Great Britain were hailed before the altar. The Buddhist Association which had been only an organization of the Buddhist schools was now replaced by the Great Japan Buddhist Association, an instrument for propagating the war policy. Orders from the government were transmitted through this Great Japan Buddhist Association to the Buddhist schools. According to these

orders the abbot (chief priest) himself of every school travelled and preached in all parts of Japan, aroused loyalty as Emperor's subjects from his audiences, and reiterated belief in certain victory. Organized groups of preachers continuously performed such functions with catch-word phrases like "complete the sacred war" and "help and support the Emperor." In the midst of these active campaigns the priests were unable to locate any such principles in their own doctrine, so they sought such principles on the outside.

Whether Japanese Buddhists should cooperate in an aggressive war or not was never discussed among the Buddhist orders. To be a follower of the Emperor's sacred will was regarded as the greatest honor. It is strange that some Buddhist movements in defiance of the Emperor's orders did not appear among the Buddhist schools; the Buddhist schools instead took the standpoint of cooperation between Buddhism and the "law of the Emperor," even emphasized more the law of the Emperor than the law of the Buddha. No principle which negated the policy of the Emperor was to be found in Japanese Buddhist doctrine, so no one criticized the "help and support the Great Policy" and the "act as loyal subjects". In fact, to criticize was to be ostracized from one's own Buddhist school. Yet two attitudes could be found: i) complete submission to military orders and the Emperor's orders as the greatest of honors, and ii) although complying with the Emperor's law, a considerably sceptic and passive attitude towards the orders of the Emperor. . . .

It is not to the honor of the Japanese Buddhist order that no Buddhists sacrificed themselves to an anti-war movement during the long aggressive war in China. Is it even true Buddhist doctrine that yesterday we performed rites for the protection of the State and today perform rites for peace? After the war the new democratic constitution of Japan forbid the Buddhist order to retain the "law of the ruler" (obo), on which the order had depended for more than a thousand years. However, now in order to bolster the Buddhist order there are some movements to revive the "law of the ruler"; moreover, the feudal system which still prevails on certain levels of Japanese society offers many opportunities to the advantage of these reactionary endeavors within the Buddhist order.

Japanese Buddhist followers themselves share the responsibility and decide whether or not they will realize the dignity of the individual self or merely exist under the dignity of an Emperor who is only one person in the world. The vicissitudes of Japanese Buddhism in the latter half of the twentieth century will depend directly on this question.

44

formalism in shinto

Two of the important ideals leading up to the Meiji Restoration were the restoration of the emperor as the head of state and the restoration of Shinto as the religious support of the state. However, after the Restoration, Japanese leaders discovered that these ideals were difficult to actualize: it was even difficult to specify the nature of the ideal, and implementation of the ideal was complicated by the presence of conflicting models. This selection notes especially the problems of establishing a clear policy for the role of religion in relation to the state.

At first, there was a tendency to continue the ban on Christianity and to deemphasize or persecute Buddhism. Establishment of the Department of Shinto in 1868 was an expression of the early Meiji enthusiasm for the centrality of Shinto in the state; this paralleled the state order for Shinto priests to purify themselves from Buddhist practices. Another highly significant state act was the removal of shrines from control by traditional Shinto "sects" and the placement of them all under the control of the Department of Shinto. This trend toward unification of worship and government was the official policy until 1945.

On the other hand, the government had initiated several abortive attempts to make Shinto a state religion but finally saw no alternative but to make Shinto a "nonreligious" part of the state. There had been no clear plans for Shinto as a state religion, and both Buddhism—which had revived under persecution—and Christianity had resisted the move (Western countries demanded the lifting of the ban on Christianity). These pressures practically forced the state to grant freedom of religion, but to preserve Shinto's favored status as the norm of Japanese self-identity, it was officially incorporated into the state.

Buddhism lost much of its vitality in the Tokugawa period (1600-1867), when it was made an arm of the government, and under different circumstances Shinto lost much of its vitality after the Meiji Restoration (1868), when it was made part of the national ideology. On the local level, particularly in the rural shrines, Shinto maintained its contact with the people and preserved its religious heritage of local festivals and annual celebrations. On the national level, however, the institutional life of Shinto was controlled by and for the government, and the religious life and identity of Shinto became overshadowed by political concerns. This diminished vitality and sense of identity as a religious tradition were further weakened when Shinto faced disestablishment in 1945 (see selection 5) and was forced to reconstitute itself as a religion outside the state on an equal basis with other religions.

Reprinted by permission of the publisher from Ichiro Hori and Yoshio Toda, "Shinto," in *Japanese Religion in the Meiji Era* (Tokyo: The Toyo Bunko [Oriental Library], 1956).

Shinto in the Meiji Era

Shinto during the first years of the Meiji era permeated the whole society, not simply as a religion, but as the central principle of national life: its politics, state religion, ethics, and education. Shinto gradually lost most of its influence. First ritual, then politics, then finally the idea of a state religion itself disappeared. During the middle years of Meiji, government policy toward religion changed and two distinct types of Shinto emerged as a result. One, Sect Shinto, consisted of a number of folk religions which were generally Shinto in nature. The other, State Shinto, was nothing more than an ethical cult based on ancestor worship. This essay deals mainly with the second type. The interpretation of Shinto as a cult was intimately associated with the upsurge of nationalism which began in 1897. Thereafter, the government, while paying lip service to religious freedom as guaranteed by the Constitution of 1889, accorded State Shinto special protection as the national cult. Reforms at the end of World War II resolved this contradiction.

In retrospect, many of the post-Restoration government policies appear ill-advised. The attempt to make Shinto into the national religion was one of them. Another was the abandonment of certain wise policies which the Tokugawa had instituted during its last days.

But the Restoration Shintoists were not able to recognize that these were shortcomings. Their only aim was to return the Emperor to direct rule. The only way to accomplish this was to overthrow the existing government. They had no concrete plans for what they would do once they had fulfilled their aim. . . .

. . . They were unable to substitute another theory of government for Confucianism and Buddhism.

Reverence for the Emperor was the strongest ideal of the Restoration. The most important single element contributing to this ideal was the Shinto theory of the National School. Because of the part the scholars of the National School played in the Restoration, Shinto emerged both as the national political theory and as a popular code of ethics. Both of these, of course, were in addition to its religious elements.

From the first, Restoration Shinto was intolerant of other religions. The reason generally given for this was that neither Confucianism, Buddhism, nor Christianity was genuinely Japanese. All were "contemptible" foreign religions. The members of Restoration Shinto considered Shinto, as they idealized it, to be superior to any other religion. The *Kojiki*, Japan's oldest traditional history, described the characteristics of Shinto that they idealized. Motoori Norinaga and Hirata Atsutane rejected everything which did not

conform to the pure Shinto they found in the *Kojiki*. Among the elements they rejected were the popular religious groups which later come to be called "Sect Shinto." After the government-sponsored form of Shinto became the national cult, these sects were granted the status of separate religions. Norinaga and Atsutane called them "vulgar," even though they were manifestations of Shinto. With similar narrow-mindedness, these two men rejected all other faiths outside of Shinto.

The Restoration School continued to dominate Shinto throughout Meiji. It did not depart from the outmoded ideas of Norinaga and Atsutane. It contributed nothing towards helping the new Japan adjust to changing conditions. . . .

One chapter in the Meiji Reformation ended in 1867. On November 9, Tokugawa Keiki, the last Tokugawa Shogun, requested permission to restore the actual powers of government to the Emperor. This permission was granted on the following day. The Restoration Rescript, which officially announced the beginning of Meiji, followed within two months.

This Rescript stated that the Restoration of Imperial Rule meant a return, in fact, to the government used at the time of Jimmu Tenno, the founder of Japan and first Emperor of the Japanese people. The government planned to carry out this program practically by re-establishing the Department of Shinto as it had existed in early Japan. . . .

The actual proposal to re-establish the Department of Shinto was delivered to the court in December, 1867. . . . Many leaders of Restoration Shinto enjoyed important government positions as officials in the Department of Shinto.

On April 22, 1869, the Emperor dispatched one of his officials to venerate the grave of the Emperor Jimmu in Nara Prefecture. Three days later, the Emperor himself led a procession of court nobles and daimyo to the Hall of Ceremonies where they performed a worship service before all the gods of the Shinto pantheon and swore allegiance to the Charter Oath, a general statement of the new government's aims. The Emperor then interpreted the Charter Oath and expressed his desire to continue the Imperial tradition of concern for the people's welfare. By these actions, the Emperor Meiji personally demonstrated the meaning of the unity between worship and government.

Three days later, Shinto priests who had been at the same time Buddhist priests were ordered to let their hair grow long as proof that they had renounced their affiliation with Buddhism. The following day, all of the Shinto priests came directly under the control of the Department of Shinto. This ended the system whereby shrines had been licensed by one of the two large sects, the Yoshida and the Shirakawa, or had had to depend directly on court nobles for favors. The Yoshida and the Shirakawa sects, though they had arisen as a result of theological differences, had become financially and politically powerful, so powerful that they dominated most of Shinto. Shrines

not connected with them had been obliged to go directly to the nobility to find other means of financial assistance. This order by the Department of Shinto brought all shrines directly under government control.

In June, 1871, the government took the first step in making Shinto the national religion by issuing the following proclamation:

> The function of shrines is to provide a place of worship for all the people of Japan. They are not the sole property of any individual or family. Some shrines still obtain priests in accordance with ancient procedures, but in most cases the daimyo who originally established the shrine has continued to appoint its priests. Often where ownership of the land has changed several times, the connection with the daimyo who established the shrines has ceased, and they have become laws unto themselves. Even in small villages, the priests have made the succession of the priesthood hereditary and use the shrine revenues for their own income; they consider themselves independent. Priests have become a class apart; this is exactly opposed to unifying worship and government, and has many harmful effects. . . . From now on, the government will appoint the priests for all shrines, from the very largest at Ise to the very smallest throughout the country. . . .

Meiji religious policy had tried to substitute Shinto for other religions. This Shinto contained many of the elements necessary to an advanced religion. Its theology included a faith in the end of the world as well as salvation from sin and repentance by means of sacred charms and ceremonies of lustration. On these points Shinto could not avoid conflict with Buddhism and Christianity. When the government tried to force this faith upon the people, therefore, it violated their freedom. This attempt at coercion resulted from confusion over the functions of government and religion. Therefore, the leaders of the other religions naturally attacked this policy. The self-confident champions of democratic rights, represented among those who had received a European education, joined these religious leaders. Their demand for religious freedom received its stimulus from Europe.

Not all those who demanded religious freedom were reflecting Western thinking, however. Many Japanese, particularly Buddhists, based a claim for religious freedom on their Japanese tradition. One priest of the Shin Sect, Fukuda Gyokai, said:

> I have known nothing but the traditional Buddhist chant of *nembutsu*. Now that I am in my seventies, I cannot suddenly change, no matter what the government orders, to tell you that worship of the Shinto gods and patriotism are enough, and that you need give no concern to the future life. Since there has not as yet been an Imperial Rescript urging you to stop saying *nembutsu* and to stop thinking about nirvana, I must urge you to continue your prayers, to encourage them in others, and to go to paradise together. I can do nothing more than to implore you to strengthen your will, to remember the prayers which have been handed down to you, and to decide that you must attain nirvana. . . .

The desire for religious freedom gradually increased in spite of government attempts to make Shinto the national religion. Article 28 of the Constitution of 1889, promulgated on February 11, 1889, said:

Japanese subjects shall, within limits not prejudicial to peace and order and not antagonistic to their duties as subjects, enjoy freedom of religious belief....

Shinto at the beginning of Meiji was more than a body of religious thought or a group of religious ceremonies. It was the basis of a revolution which overthrew the old society. After the Restoration, it became the complex guiding principle in the new Japanese society. It brought together government, ceremonies, and education. But the Restoration made it imperative that Japan do more than return to the past. It had to modernize speedily. The slogan, "cultural enlightenment," which followed a few years after the Restoration, indicated this need.

Two divergent tendencies in the Meiji Restoration determined the course of future Japanese history. First, the Restoration resurrected the ancient and pure folk-vitality of Shinto, and second, it applied the old customs to conditions of the modern world. The first led to suppressing ways of thought other than Shinto, an attitude which came out of Shinto's basic character. Just as a spring when released jumps to more than normal length, so anything which is oppressed clamors for freedom. The Western theories of religious freedom and separation of religion from government encouraged the Japanese instinct to clamor for freedom. Cultural enlightenment and intercourse with foreign countries resulted in the importation of these theories and their use as a basis for individualism. The conservatism of Shinto and the progressiveness of the Western ideas inevitably clashed.

45

Religious life in postwar japan

The two previous selections are interpretations of the historical processes by which Shinto and Buddhism gave way to formalism. This selection describes the effects of this formalism in the attitudes and behavior of people living in one ward (Shitayama-cho) of Tokyo in the 1950s. The excerpts on religion are taken from a large book reporting the extensive interviews and surveys conducted in this ward.

Traditionally, the regional shrine is directly responsible for the spiritual welfare of its parishioners *(ujiko)*, and the parishioners are vitally concerned with this spiritual home. In the following excerpt, Dore shows

how this ideal falls short in postwar Shitayama-cho. Support for the shrine is complicated by the fact that the Allied occupation (SCAP) established the law that religious affairs must be strictly separated from public affairs such as the ward association. (For the order disestablishing Shinto, see selection 5.) It is more difficult to gain voluntary contributions for rebuilding the burnt-out shrine, and people donate without enthusiasm, out of a sense of social duty. About half the households in this ward have a *kamidana* (Shinto altar), but the sense of religious dependence on both the household *kamidana* and the ward shrine is rather weak.

Buddhism seems to fare better in this survey, since a rather high percentage of established families maintain the *butsudan,* the Buddhist memorial altar. And Dore himself concludes "that conformity to traditional religious practices centering round the *butsudan* and the *ihai* (memorial tablets) is much greater than conformity to those centering round Shinto shrines and the *kamidana*." However, mere numbers and traditional conformity are ambiguous—on one hand, they point to a continued veneration for family ancestors; on the other hand, they provide the foil for the joke that Buddhist priests are nothing but undertakers. This is borne out by the fact that the overwhelming majority of visits to Buddhist temples by ward residents were in connection with memorial masses.

In critically assessing the religious situation in postwar Japan, it would be a mistake to expect the same kind of religious behavior that is held to be the ideal in the West—a conscious decision or exclusive affiliation to one religious group and regular attendance at periodic worship services. By contrast, Japanese religion has always operated within an implicit religious world view embracing several traditions. To the extent that this world view is meaningful for the Japanese people, it continues in the spirit of the earlier religious heritage. What the survey points out, however, is that the traditional world view itself is being questioned, as reflected in the expressions of the people. Both Shinto and Buddhist shrines and temples survive, along with their customary formalities; however, it is apparent that great changes are occurring in the minds of the people, changes which seriously question the vitality and viability of these two traditions.

Reprinted from R. P. Dore, *City Life in Japan: A Study of a Tokyo Ward,*
1958; originally published by the University of California Press; reprinted
by permission of The Regents of the University of California and Routledge
& Kegan Paul Ltd.

Religion in a Ward of Tokyo

The ward as such was officially concerned with the *uji-gami*, the Soga
shrine to whose parish it belonged. Shitayama-cho had been included in its
parish because it formed part of an estate stretching towards the shrine. The
latter was twenty minutes' walk away, and unlike three closer shrines did
not lie on the natural lines of communication out of the ward. For this reason
relations between the shrine and the ward have always been somewhat less
intimate than is usual for the district. Nevertheless, like the other twenty-two
wards which made up the parish of the Soga shrine, Shitayama-cho contributed to the shrine's upkeep; its residents, by virtue of their residence, were
all 'children of the god-family' of the shrine; and the ward as a whole participated in the shrine's annual festival.

Before the war the shrine was managed by a council consisting of representatives (*ujiko-soodai*) appointed by the ward association of each of the
twenty-three wards in the parish. Contributions for the shrine were collected
and the shrine's *fuda* (amuletic paper or wooden tablets bearing the name
of the *kami* of the shrine) were distributed through these representatives, the
ward association, and the neighbour groups, all the subtle pressures which
the use of these channels offered being utilized to secure a full collection of
contributions. Information concerning the activities of the shrine was conveyed through these representatives to the ward association, from the ward
association to each neighbourhood unit, and thence, by circulating notice-
board to each household.

In obedience to S.C.A.P. directive, this system of shrine administration
and upkeep was abolished. In its place, a new body was formed called the
'Worshippers' Association' (*Suukeikai*). It is a small body of prominent men
in each of the twenty-three wards who are, as the priest of the local shrine
put it, 'sort of' representatives of the wards. Not all the twenty-three wards
had revived their ward association since the war, but where such an association existed, the priest had approached its leaders and asked them to appoint
a member of the Worshippers' Association. Where there was no ward association the priest had directly contacted prominent men (*yuuryo-kusha*) and
asked them to join. There was now no longer a fixed number of these 'un-
official' representatives per ward. Advantage had been taken of the flexibility
of the new organization to recruit as many wealthy men as possible. Thus, as
well as preserving the substance of the old, some advantage was derived from
the form of the new.

Some idea of the way in which this informal organization operates may be given by describing how contributions were collected for the rebuilding of the Soga shrine. The shrine was burned down during the war, and in 1951 the broad steps, flanked by an imposing concrete balustrade and the guardian 'Chinese lions' led only to a small wooden temporary altar which stood forlornly in the middle of a broad concrete base. Plans to rebuild the shrine had long been complete, but with rising costs the original estimate of 2 million yen (£2,000) had increased to 3 million yen and in mid-1951 only one million had been subscribed. For fifty yards along either side of the approach to the shrine a slatted wooden framework about ten feet high had been erected. It was divided into twenty-three sections and over each section was written the name of one of the wards which were part of the parish of the shrine under the old dispensation. For every contribution received a wooden board was hung in the appropriate section and on it written the name of the donor and the amount.

In mid-1951 some sections were well-filled—mostly those devoted to wards very close to the shrine. The Shitayama-cho section bore only one board recording a donation of 30,000 yen. . . .

Another official of the Ward Association, Kataoka, was also a member of the Worshippers' Association and by contrast conscientious, if not enthusiastic. Kataoka, with his obvious delight in occupying positions of authority and his committee-man skill, was nevertheless barred from higher positions of authority by his limited means combined with a tendency to arouse resentment by a slightly overbearing and pompous manner. Nevertheless he was doing his best, by taking an active part in the Worshippers' Association, the P.T.A., the C.P.T.C.A., and the Ward Association, to develop his connections against the day when his means should make a wider scale of activities possible.

At a meeting of the officials of the ward association, Kataoka reported the decisions of a recent meeting of the Worshippers' Association. So far only a third of the money had been collected, and there was a noticeable absence of contributions from Shitayama-cho. Each ward had been allocated a target on the basis of the number of households contained in it. Shitayama-cho's target was 90,000 yen or 300 yen (6s.) per household. The discussion ran somewhat as follows:

Okazaki: 'Have we really got to pay up?'
Kataoka: 'Well, I don't know. That's our apportionment, and when so many of the other wards have contributed we can hardly hold our heads up if we don't (katami ga semai).'
Nakazawa: 'Sakura [the ward president] has given us a good start anyway. [Hear, Hear!'s.] But it's no good going round asking other people to contribute until T is settled. [The T of p. 32; the richest man in the ward] Once we get him to pay out we can go to S [a hotelier] and K [a fairly affluent wholesaler]. Then we can start generally.'
Okazaki: 'How is it best to collect the money, though?'

Izumi: 'I don't see what's wrong with K going round and collecting it as *ujiko-soodai.*' [Representative of the children of the god-family, i.e. the title of the ward association representative under the old system.]

Kataoka (apparently embarrassed, perhaps by the writer's presence) : 'Well, there aren't any *ujiko-soodai* any longer. There's only a Worshippers' Association. Of course there's talk that there will soon be a new law to make it possible again, but I don't know.'

Sakura: 'Yes, I think it's best to keep the ward association out of it for the time being at any rate. It would be best for someone from the shrine to come down collecting. One of us officials could go round introducing him, of course. I shouldn't think anyone would grumble about that. If the worst comes to the worst and the money doesn't come in, I suppose we shall have to take it out of ward funds a bit at a time, so much a month.'

The general feeling of the meeting seemed to be unanimous. No one felt any enthusiasm for the rebuilding of the shrine, and there was no suggestion that it was a worthy object. In most cases this was the result of a general lack of interest in any matters connected with shrines and the *kami*. In one or two cases it was the result, not of a lack of interest in all shrines but of the lack of any interest in this particular Soga shrine. One of those present, Izumi, was a member of the council of one of the shrines nearer to Shitayama-cho and a conscientious visitor for what appeared to be genuinely religious reasons.

But, though lacking in enthusiasm, all appeared to accept the duty of making contributions to the shrine. 'Have we really got to pay up?' was the nearest approach to a note of protest. No one suggested that religious faith was a private matter and should be left to individuals. It is doubtful if 'religious faith' entered anyone's head as a relevant factor in the situation; contributing to the upkeep of the local shrine has long been accepted as part of the duty of a good citizen on much the same level as paying taxes. Nor did anyone suggest that the ward as a whole should transfer its allegiance to a more convenient shrine and one to which more residents would be likely to pay spontaneous visits; only an emergency would ever justify such an unfriendly act towards the Soga shrine. In other words, long years of association had created what was called earlier a *giri*-relation[1] between the ward on the one hand and the priest and the *kami* of the local shrine on the other. To break off that relation or neglect the duties which that relation involved would be to lay the ward open to the charge of 'not knowing *giri*.'. . .

There was, indeed, little evidence of any belief in a special relationship between the people of Shitayama-cho and the *ujigami* of the Soga shrine. Fifty-three percent of households in Shitayama-cho had *kamidana*—the 'god-shelves' plain wooden boxes with ritual decoration which contain the *fuda*[2]

---

[1] *Giri* is the sense of social obligation which one person or group feels toward another person or group. [ed.]

[2] *Fuda*, paper charms or talismans. [ed.]

of the shrines for which they act as substitutes—and eighty percent of these *kamidana* did contain the *fuda* of the Soga shrine. Most parents took newly-born children for a *miya-mairi* ceremony, a registration rite at which the *ujigami* is asked to take note of the baby's arrival and extend it his future protection, but most went to one of the nearer shrines rather than the Soga shrine for the child's next ceremony at the age of three. But here, again, 'local patriotism' was the operative notion; there was no suggestion that anything was actually lost by not going to the *ujigami* supposed to be responsible for protecting her particular district.

What such protection used to mean is well described by the ethnographer Yanagita Kunio in his description of the village in which he grew up.

> It would sometimes happen in the summer evenings that children would go out to play and get lost and fail to come home. Then there would be great consternation, but generally the child would come back. The first thing the people of the village would think of then was the '*ujigami-sama*'.[3] People would say that it was the *ujigami-sama* who saw that he came back; there would even be plausible-sounding stories going round that the child had met an old man with white hair who had told him that everybody at home was anxious and that he ought to go back. There was this idea that the *ujigama-sama* was the ruler of the village, a sort of hidden protector of the villagers . . .
>
> It would be difficult for people living in Tokyo today to imagine the importance the *ujigami-sama* had for the people of my native village.

This idea is not entirely dead in Tokyo. One woman who said that she had made one visit to the Soga shrine in the past year added as an explanation: 'After all, it is thanks to the *ujigami-sama* that we are able thus to live peacefully in this district.' But this was a rare instance; the only other piece of evidence of any such belief concerning the relation between the *ujigami-sama* and the community came, not from Shitayama-cho but from a neighbouring ward. The shrine of this parish had been destroyed during a fire raid while surrounding streets had been left untouched. It was considered that the *kami* had taken all the fire bombs on to itself in order to spare the local inhabitants, its children, and it was said to be for that reason that the general level of contributions to the rebuilding fund was so high; the shrine building had been almost completed by the summer of 1951. Perhaps the Soga shrine was too far away for it to be thought to have performed the same function for Shitayama-cho.

The *ujigami*, in theory, not only provides general protection for its *ujiko*, but may also be the object of personal prayers by any one of them. However, as far as individual visits to the shrine were concerned, the Soga priest knew of only one resident of Shitayama-cho, a middle-aged widow, who came regularly to pray at the shrine on the traditional shrine-visiting days, the 1st, 15th, and 28th of each month. And of all the shrine visits which a hundred

---

[3] *Ujigami-sama,* the patron deity of local Shinto shrines. [ed.]

respondents said they remembered having made in the past year (averaging less than ten per person even including the 365 visits of one individual) only 11% were to the Soga shrine. . . .

The wife of the priest of the Soga shrine was apt to complain of the financial embarrassment which the apathy of post-war parishioners brought to her family. On one occasion she remarked wryly, that the Buddhist temples had less to complain about; 'They look after the *hotoke-sama.*' The implication that it is their stake in the *hotoke-sama* (the spirits of the dead) which keeps the temples on their feet is probably a just one. The religious rites and beliefs with which the Buddhist temples are chiefly concerned are those which centre around the worship of the spirits of the dead. They are, that is, rites in which either the family is the worshipping unit, or, at least, consciousness of membership of the family is an important constituent of the worshippers' attitudes.

The Buddhist rites in the home centre around *butsudan*, the 'Altar of the Buddhas', which may be a simple wooden box or an elaborate lacquer-and-gilt altar, six feet high and of careful and expensive workmanship. This contains the *ihai*, tablets bearing the posthumous names of former members of the family. Sometimes there are their photographs as well, and occasionally family heirlooms. One man in Shitayama-cho kept in the *butsudan* the swords which were the symbols of his family's former samurai status; another had a history of his native district. There were also genealogical scrolls, and 'registers of the past' (*kakochoo*) recording the death-days of former members of the family. (One family also kept its money in the *butsudan* under the ancestors' care.)

In addition to all these *family* symbols, some *butsudan* contain the symbols of the Buddhist faith, scroll paintings or brass images of Kannon, Amida and other Buddhas and Bodhisattvas; photographs, often of a very high quality, of famous Buddha statues in Nara or Kyooto, brought back from a sight-seeing tour; sometimes the amuletic *fuda* of some famous temple. (And, in one case, the similar *fuda* of a Shinto shrine. Another woman had a photograph of Christ—'The priest knows about it and he says it's all right.') Whereas every *butsudan* had *ihai* of the family dead, however, only a very little over a half had any of these symbols of the Buddhist faith proper.

In ordinary speech no distinction is made between the spirits of the dead and the Buddhas and Bodhisattvas of the Buddhist faith. They are both called *hotoke* (*—sama*). There is evidence, though, that the two are differently conceptualized, and it will be convenient to distinguish the two as *hotoke* and *Hotoke* respectively. A further distinction can be made among the *hotoke*, between Grandpa, Father, or brother Jiroo on the one hand, and 'the ancestors' (*senzo*)—all the *hotoke* who have been dead for so long that no surviving member of the family has personal memories of them—on the other. These will be distinguished as 'close-relative *hotoke*' and 'ancestor *hotoke*'. The distinction is reflected in the *ihai* kept in the Altar of the Buddhas. After

a certain length of time (in theory, after the fiftieth year, though there is great variation in this respect) the *hooji* rites[4] on the anniversaries of the death-days of particular ancestors cease to be held. Thereafter the individual *ihai* is removed and the ancestor is subsumed under the one general *ihai* bearing the legend, 'Ancestors of the various generations of the—family' and thus become the object only of the general rites for the ancestors at the equinoxes and at the summer Bon festival.

Not every household necessarily has a *butsudan*. The governing principle is that all dead spirits must have their *ihai* kept in some *butsudan*, preferably that of their most direct descendants, rather than that all households must have a *butsudan* at which they can worship their forebears. Where family consciousness is strong, however, younger sons who set up house away from the main family, may take duplicates of the *ihai* (generally those of parents or equally close relatives) in the main family altar. But of the 45% of younger sons in Shitayama-cho who did have altars, only a few had them for this reason. Most of them installed altars on the death of a child or a wife.

Of those families in Shitayama-cho which have been established for more than one generation (and must, therefore, have at least one direct ancestor) 80% had a *butsudan*. The remaining 20% (twenty-four families) did not have one for a variety of reasons. A few were Christians. There were also a small number of families who were 'out-and-out' Shintoists, who that is to say, follow Shinto, rather than Buddhist, funeral and ancestor rites. Shinto rites are essentially similar in nature to Buddhist rites and clearly modelled on them, but the memorial tablets are kept in an elaborated *kami-dana* (a *soreisha*) instead of in a *butsudan*.

Sometimes, again, an eldest son who has left his rural home and allowed a younger brother to succeed to the *de facto* headship of his parental family has left the ancestral tablets to be cared for by him, too. But there were other families which had no such 'excuse'. Families which were bombed out during the war and lost their *butsudan* as a consequence, have not always replaced them in their new homes. Some had simply had new *ihai* made and kept them on a temporary wooden shelf. One man gave as his reason the fact that there was a 'superstition' (his word) that if a *butsudan* was bought on any other occasion than on that of a death in the family it would be likely itself to cause someone to die. Others had no explanation to offer. 'Since we've moved here we haven't bothered to get a new *butsudan* or new *ihai* or anything,' said the owner of a small cosmetics factory, adding, 'I'm ashamed to say.'

As this implies, a certain amount of apathy there may be, but positive rejection of the duty to look after and pay respect to the ancestors' *ihai* is rarely met with. The only expression of such an attitude in over two hundred

[4] *Hooji* rites, Buddhist memorial services. [ed.]

households, was the remark of one woman that her husband 'has strong objections to people worshipping before *butsudan* and *kamidana*', and that for that reason the family's *butsudan* was being looked after by his sister in the country. This man, interestingly enough, a lawyer and one of the few professional men in the ward, was also marked out from his neighbors by the strong antipathy which he displayed towards all forms of ward community activities.

There were, however, few such instances. It is a fairly safe generalization that conformity to traditional religious practices centring round the *butsudan* and the *ihai* is much greater than conformity to those centring round Shinto shrines and the *kamidana*.

The worship of the spirits of ancestors, though in all its forms much influenced by the Buddhist religion and by Confucian ideas partly absorbed via that religion, can exist independently of Buddhist institutions. The Emperor's ancestors, to whom essentially similar rites are addressed by the Imperial family, are not *hotoke* but *kami* and they are enshrined in Shinto shrines. Ieyasu, the founder of the last house of Shogun, was also a *kami* to whom several shrines were devoted, so was an even more recent national hero, General Nogi, and, indeed, all those who died in battle are enshrined as *kami* in the Yasukuni shrine. Apart from these national associations some ordinary families, for a variety of reasons, follow Shinto burial and ancestor-worshipping practices. Nevertheless, in the vast majority of families, these rites are associated with the Buddhist religion, and it is necessary for their full performance to have some connection with a Buddhist temple.

From this family temple the priest comes to perform funeral ceremonies and the rites held in front of the family *butsudan* on the anniversaries of ancestors' death-days. Alternatively, these latter ceremonies are held actually at the family temple. In some sects a part of the ashes are deposited at the family temple. In others an *ihai*, a duplicate of that in the family *butsudan*, is also left at the family temple. It is from the fees for such services that the priest derives his income. It is one of Japan's perennial jokes that a priest is a man who does business in funerals. In a somewhat merciless humorous monologue, a favourite of Tokyo music-hall audiences, one priest says to another, 'If this goes on much longer I shall have forgotten the taste of decent wine. I haven't had a funeral for weeks. I must say, though, that I admire your enterprise, going around and finding out where people are ill. Here, what about a quick one, just a sort of advance celebration like?'

The business, if not highly paid, at least guarantees a living. At some of the Tokyo temples with a large number of parishioners it is quite efficiently organized with an advance booking system and waiting rooms in which the latest magazines are provided for families waiting their turn for an anniversary ceremony.

Most Buddhist temples are almost exclusively concerned with death and the family cult, and few people in Shitayama-cho ever go to a temple for any other reason. Thus, when a family migrates from the country to Tokyo it

normally only seeks a new family temple nearby when a death in the family makes it necessary. Many families in Shitayama-cho gave as their 'family temple' that of their parents in a distant part of the country. Ninety-four people out of a hundred acknowledged that they had such a family temple. (Of the others, two were Christians, two Shinto, and two just said they had nothing to do with that sort of thing.) Of these, however, sixteen did not know the name of their temple and seven did not know which of the many Buddhist sects it belonged to. In theory, a loyalty to a sect persists through the generations, so that a migrating branch family will pick a family temple of the same sect as that of the main family, but so blurred are sectarian distinctions and so irrelevant are they to the actual purpose of family temples as a part of the family cult, that several cases were found in Shitayama-cho where the sect had been changed for reasons of convenience.

Of these ninety-four people, fifty-three said that they had visited their family temple in the previous year. They estimated that they had made 241 visits between them. Of these 206 were in connection with anniversary ceremonies. The other thirty-five visits, shared by nine people, were on the occasions of temple services (four people), casual visits 'when I happened to be passing' (four people) and 'a sight-seeing visit as guide to some business acquaintances up from the provinces'.

46

secularism: from ritual to pornography in a modern novel

Dore's research in the previous selection indicated that a few people were indifferent to organized religion and at least one man, according to his wife, " 'has strong objections to people worshipping before *but-sudan* and *kamidana*.' " Such people seem to be in the minority, however, and this should be kept in mind while reading this selection. This excerpt from a translated Japanese novel does not attempt to present the typical picture of life in Japan; rather, it focuses on the unusual and extreme case of the life of several pornographers. This is *not typical,* but novels often present a creative, inside view of a culture, a view not easily attained by a sociological survey.

This novel, which takes place in postwar Osaka, is filled with characters who have not the slightest attachment to Japan's traditional religious life. Osaka is the financial center of Japan, and in the first episode these pornographers are busy making money from their trade, which at the moment involves the production and distribution of "blue movies." For the moment, Subuyan is the leader of the group. Having cast aside all the stereotyped plots and scenes, they hit upon the brilliant idea of shooting their pornographic film in a Shinto shrine. This brief sketch is full of ironies, the most dramatic of which is the interruption of filming by the appearance of a devout old lady. Cocky, the assistant Shinto priest who is part of the shady film company and who has suggested the shrine film, almost automatically intones the ancient benediction. This fictional account captures one of the poignant dichotomies of modern Japan: innocent devotion to traditional values by some, particularly the old, offset by complete disregard for traditional values by others, especially the young.

The second episode describes the events surrounding the wake for Subuyan's common-law wife, Oharu. The four pornographers have no use for a Buddhist priest and the usual religious memorial service, but as the evening wears on and they discuss the horrors of death, they feel the need to somehow commemorate this death. A suggestion is made: "So instead of a sutra, let's show a pornographic film." For these men, there are no sacred models to appeal to, so they invoke the only symbolic system they know. Replacement of a sutra by a pornographic film is a complete reversal of traditional religious life. The fictional episode mirrors an increasing sense of estrangement from traditional values and a quest for meaning without the aid of organized religion.

The Pornographers

The shrine where the film was to be made was dedicated to the Emperor Ojin and stood in a grove of trees, just across the lotus pond from Cocky's shed.

In Subuyan's youth his father would take him to the Shrine of Kusonoki for the traditional prayers in the early morning of every New Year's Day, just after the temple bells had sounded. So now, his scruples still not quieted, he stood with his palms pressed together reverently before doing anything else. But what could he pray for? There seemed to be no common ground between the world of Ojin and that of pornographic films. Cocky, in the

meantime, fully at home, had gone into the inner shrine and was bustling about as he noisily chanted one of his favorite blessings.

"Here's a light plug over here. We're lucky. Nowadays even the Sacred Candle is electric," he said, brushing away the dust as he set the stage in order.

Banteki[1] presented a memorably exotic sight. As if the Shinto priest's robes were not enough by themselves, an electric cord dangled from beneath the pleated skirt. This was a remote-control device; for Banteki, with a true artist's passion, insisted on doing the camera work himself.

According to the plot, a schoolgirl was to come to pray for something or other; and the priest, after smoothly enticing her into the inner shrine and chanting a prayer over her, vigorously goes at her. The girl's role would be played by the model who had caught that unhappy infection while starring in the first movie. This would be her second appearance.

"Well, how about it? Let's get going," said Banteki, who, camouflaged with glasses and mustache, proceeded forthwith to plunge boldly into the action, wholly undaunted by the glaring lights. Subuyan too gradually felt his spirits rising; and he hustled about, now urging this camera angle, now that. Still, in the midst of all this—was it the white stripes at the neck of the middy blouse or was it the pleated skirt that provoked the association?—he found himself all at once superimposing the image of Keiko[2] upon that of the figure pinned squirming to the mat; and he felt himself suddenly choke up at the sight of bared legs and general disarray.

But then at the height of the action, the hollow sound of the shrine bell suddenly obtruded itself, to the horror of all participants. A devout old lady had come to offer worship at the outer shrine. Subuyan pressed his forefinger to his lips, softly hissing for silence; Banteki and the woman froze at an extremely awkward juncture; and Cocky, presumably with the intention of reassuring the old lady outside, began to give forth with the benediction, which was his forte: "Lo, in ages past, ye gods who descended to our mountain peaks, august Sumemutsu, sovereign Kamuromi, thou who shaped the world . . ." And the old lady, her innocent faith wholly unscathed, pulled the bell cord once more and, after its hollow toll had subsided, turned and went the way she had come.

"Hey, let's work that in!" said Banteki, whose genius it was to capitalize even upon misfortune. A worshipper, in other words, would come just at the crucial moment, and the camera would cut back and forth between the figure wrapped in tranquil prayer and the scene of wild lust being enacted just a door's width away.

"Just get out there and pray, that's all," ordered Banteki as he and Subuyan thrust Cocky through the door. And so the camera caught Cocky piously tolling the bell with the lights turned up a bit to give the impression of sunset.

[1]Banteki, a photographer who was one of the group of pornographers. [ed.]
[2]Keiko, the daughter of Subuyan's common-law wife. [ed.]

This film was called *The Bulging Pillar,* and it was to achieve the reputation of a genre classic. . . .

Later Subuyan's wife, Oharu, dies, and Subuyan is aided by his fellow pornographers in arranging the wake for Oharu.

"How about a priest? Was she registered at any temple?" Cocky asked.

But Oharu had been a woman who instead of worrying much about the afterlife had flung herself whole-heartedly into this one. After she and Subuyan had become more intimate, she even had gone so far as to put away the altar with the traditional picture of her dead husband in front of it. Nor was Keiko any more concerned about religion. But finally, since it was something that was always done, Subuyan decided to call in the seedy priest from the broken-down neighborhood temple to chant a sutra or two.

As the night wore on, Keiko, still weary from watching beside her mother's deathbed, began to nod sleepily. The alert Banteki noticed this, and she was sent to bed on the second floor. Now the four men were left to themselves, and, as might be expected, the prevailing tone of the wake became less reserved.

"Well, whatever you want to say, if somebody dies and gets laid out like this, they're pretty fortunate," said Subuyan. "My mom died from the fire bombs. It was just like she had been in a pressure cooker or something. They wrapped her up in a mat and threw her on a truck with a bunch of other dead bodies. Right there on the banks of the Yodo, they piled them all up, poured gas over them, and whoom!—up they went, and that was that."

Subuyan had struck a rich vein. Everyone had something to contribute.

"Ah, that was terrible, wasn't it? People burning to death. Their bodies would shrivel up like a ball, so that they'd end up just like a baby inside its mother."

"Did you ever see any who got caught in the wind blast from the bombs? The air would go shooting into them from every hole, and they'd blow up like a rubber ball and die."

"It was kind of nice, the way they'd die in slit trenches. Their faces would always be pale."

"A lot of them died, all right. After a raid it was like a sort of exhibition of ways to die. They'd be there, their bodies all twisted, the upper and lower parts together, and some of them weren't quite dead. All twisted and looking right at their own knees—I wonder what a guy would think?"

"I saw this kid laying there, holding on to his ankles, and his feet were torn off."

"The thing I won't forget was this schoolyard where they brought all the bodies. They'd be covered with mats with only their heads sticking out. It would always rain after the fire raids and these burned-black bodies would soak it up and swell up like monsters. Sometimes the skin was burned so

much it would crack, and there you could see the flesh beneath, all red."

"You know, when I think of it, this is the first time I've seen anybody dead since the air raids," said Subuyan.

"What are you talking about? Didn't we bury your baby?" remonstrated Cocky.

"Oh yeah. That was a human being, too, I guess."

"Some get buried at sea. Some get burned up. Some have nice wakes like this. But they're all human beings."

"Once you die, that's the end."

"Say, Banteki, did you bring any films along?"

"Films? This is no time for business, Subuyan!"

"Who said anything about business? This is Oharu's wake, isn't it? And she was my wife. The wife of Subuyan the pornographer. So instead of a sutra, let's show a pornographic film."

"Hey, now you're talking. Here, I'll help," said Cocky, as he and Hack sprang to their feet, brimming with enthusiasm, and pushed the altar aside.

They hung the screen above Oharu's coffin and extinguished the holy candles. After a short pause the beam from the projector pierced the darkness, and one of the early masterpieces, *The Bulging Pillar*, flashed on the screen.

"Subuyan, this'll be a lot better than a sutra."

"Hey, Subuyan, how about being the *benshi*?"[3]

"Good enough," answered Subuyan, standing up. "Here we see a young virgin who has come to offer a prayer to God. What does she ask? 'Oh, dear God, won't you please send me a handsome boy to love me?' " But as Subuyan carried out his role, in his heart he was thinking of something quite different. Oharu, you went for it, too, didn't you, Oharu? Even right from the beginning. I was just thinking now that it was you that started things off between us. You woke me up. You had a stomach cramp, you said, and I could feel your breasts pressing against my back. Of course I was eager enough. Why wouldn't I be? You were in your prime then, and there was plenty of reason for me to be eager. I guess I'll never hold you again.

The altar was put back in its proper place, and everyone had a pleased, contented look.

SELECTED READINGS

For works on various aspects of the dilemma of organized religion in modern Japan, see first the citations for each selection; some additional works are:

Basabe, Fernano M.,; Shin, Anzai; and Lanzaco, Federico. *Religious Attitudes of Japanese Men: A Sociological Survey*. Tokyo: Sophia University and Charles E. Tuttle Co., 1968.

[3]*Benshi*, narrator. [ed.]

Basabe, Fernando M.; Shin, Anzai; and Nebreda, Alphonso M. *Japanese Youth Confronts Religion: A Sociological Survey.* Tokyo: Sophia University and Charles E. Tuttle Co., 1967.

Creemers, Wilhelmus H. M. *Shrine Shinto after World War II.* Leiden: E. J. Brill, 1968.

Kitagawa, Joseph M. *Religion in Japanese History.* New York: Columbia University Press, 1966.

Kiyota, Minoru. "Buddhism in Postwar Japan: A Critical Survey." *Monumenta Nipponica* 24, Nos. 1-2 (1969): 113-36.

pARt sixteen

the new Religions

Organized religions in the modern period are generally characterized by formalism and lack of vitality, but in contrast stand a large number of new religious movements. These so-called New Religions are the antithesis of the old, organized religions, demonstrating both extensive growth in membership and enthusiastic participation. A new religious movement inevitably holds several advantages over established traditions, such as the burst of enthusiasm that fills the first few generations of followers and the fact that new religious movements are not restrained by the dead weight of the prior institutions of an established tradition but instead create new socioreligious organizations (often incorporating earlier religious themes). These advantages may easily turn into disadvantages. If the founding enthusiasm is insufficient and the new socioreligious forms are unstable, the New Religion may well collapse, as has happened in many cases. And if the New Religion becomes highly institutionalized, it in turn becomes an "established tradition" and inherits all the problems of maintaining a tradition, often at the expense of enthusiastic participation.

An initial stimulus for such movements is the inspiration of popular leaders, who establish their own scriptures and liturgies. The movements are kept alive by emphasis on lay leadership and lay participation in all aspects of the movement. In short, if today the organized religions represent formalism, the New Religions represent renewal in the Japanese tradition. Of the hundreds, perhaps thousands, of New Religions that have arisen since the early 1800s, several dozen have gained large memberships and have developed comprehensive organizations.

Tenrikyo is one of the earliest of the new religious movements, and it formed a kind of precedent which was important in the formation of subsequent movements. Konko Kyo, another significant nineteenth century movement, was described in selection 16. Soka Gakkai differs considerably from these two movements, not only by virtue of its twentieth century origin but also due to its contrasting nature and organization.

Soka Gakkai developed more around the sacred power of the Lotus Sutra than around a charismatic personality; it also displays a "rational," highly efficient sect organization. On the whole, the New Religions represent a remarkable diversity which cannot be indicated by two or three examples; these brief descriptions provide only a glimpse of the religious life within these movements.

47

tenrikyo: the inspiration of a living-god

This selection provides insight into a foundress's original inspiration and the institutional formation of a religious movement around this charismatic leader. The opening quotation of the selection is the voice of God, who has entered the body of Mrs. Miki Nakayama and has claimed her as his "living Temple." The document then fills in the background for this remarkable revelation, centering around the rites of exorcism to drive out the evil spirits causing sickness in the foundress's son. Such rites of exorcism, with the medium experiencing temporary possession, were not uncommon in nineteenth century Japan (see selections 18 and 33); what is unusual in this case is the fact that the God did not leave the medium's body at the end of the rite; this constituted the divine revelation which founded Tenrikyo.

From this time, Miki, as she is commonly known, was seen as a divine figure. Her fame as a religious resource spread first because of her ability to give women easy childbirth, and gradually missionaries propagated faith in Miki and the divinity revealed to her. Because Miki had the status of a living-*kami,* everything she said or did had divine significance. In addition to the sacred scripture, *Ofudesaki,* she also created the Tenrikyo religious service, with a hymn called *Mikagura-uta* and ritual gestures to act out the hymn.

Miki's message can be summed up briefly as follows: since creation, God the Parent has wanted people to live a joyous life, but they are lost in greed and selfishness, thus covering up their true divine nature. Religious awakening occurs when each of us realizes, like Miki, that we are the creation of the gods, that our bodies are "loaned" to us. This helps us overcome the greed and selfishness which makes us miserable

and at the same time leads us to the "joyous life" of religious celebration (in Tenrikyo rituals) and service to others.

Tenrikyo, like Konko Kyo, was one of the thirteen officially recognized branches of Sect Shinto. The official system of Sect Shinto was abolished after World War II, and the proclamation of religious freedom enabled Tenrikyo to lead a more independent career. Tenrikyo seems to have served as a prototype for other New Religions because it laid down a precedent: it was the first such movement to succeed in developing from a charismatic leadership to a full-scale organized religion. (See figure 10 for an aerial view of Tenri headquarters.)

Reprinted by permission of the publisher from *A Short History of Tenrikyo* (Tenri, Japan: Tenrikyo Kyokai Honbu, 1967, fourth edition).

The Life of the Foundress

"I am the Creator, the true and real God. I have the preordination for this Residence. At this time I have appeared in this world in person to save all mankind. I ask you to let Me have your Miki as My living Temple."

Quite unprepared for such a revelation, her husband Zenbei was much surprised to hear it, and so were all those present, his family, relatives, and the exorcist Ichibei who was at prayer. Needless to say, they had never heard of such a god as 'the true and real God,' so that they could not give a ready consent to the demand to offer Miki as the Temple God. While at a loss what to do, Zenbei remembered a series of quite strange happenings which occurred one after another during the last year. It started on October 26, 1837, when the eldest son Shuji, who was then seventeen years old, was sowing barley as usual in the field with his mother. Meanwhile, he suddenly began to suffer from a severe pain in the left leg, so severe that he wished to return and barely managed to get home. . . . Of course, Shuji, who was the dearest son to his parents, was at once put under medical treatment, but it did not seem to have any effect upon him. Being advised to send for an exorcist and to have him pray, they sent a servant to the exorcist Ichibei in Nagataki village and asked him to exorcise the pain of Shuji. Then miraculously the pain left him, but the next day it began to attack him again. Again they sent a servant to Ichibei to have him exorcise Shuji and then the pain stopped again. But on the next day it was the same again. On the third day the pain left him at last, and he was well for about twenty days, when again his leg began to ache severely. Now Zenbei went in person to Ichibei in Nagataki village, and was given the advice to hold a ritual of exorcism called *yosekaji*

Figure 10. An aerial view of Oyasato (Tenri Headquarters), in the city of Tenri, Nara Prefecture. Reprinted by permission of the publisher from *A Short History of Tenrikyo* (Tenri, Japan: Tenrikyo Kyokai Honbu, 1967, fourth edition).

at home. So coming back, Zenbei, calling in Ichibei and Soyo[1] of the Magata village, held the ritual in the household. Ichibei offered an earnest prayer and tried to practise a curing with Soyo as the medium, who stood still, in her hands two sacred staffs from which cut-paper was hanging. Then the pain in the leg suddenly left Shuji. But in about half a year, he began to suffer from the pain once more. So he held the ritual of *yosekaji*, and he got well. However, he felt the pain again. Thus he repeated it as many as nine times a year.

Meanwhile, the ninth year of Tempo came, and it was at ten in the evening of the 23rd of October, when the three of the family began to have a severe pain respectively, Shuji in the leg, Miki in the loins, and Zenbei in the eyes. They at once sent for Ichibei, who was found to have been at the house of a family named Inuri in the same village on that day. Ichibei came and was surprised to find things quite serious. He was asked to offer incantations and prayers as soon as possible, but unfortunately he was not prepared for it. So that night he went back and early the next morning he came again to perform incantations, and sent for Soyo who was to become the medium, but she was out and nobody knew where she was. There was no other way but to have Miki stand with the sacred staffs in her hands and to offer prayers and incantations through her. Now Ichibei offered his prayers in earnest. Zenbei, reflecting back upon the outline of the happenings in that way, could not but feel that there was something behind it all.

However, they could in no way give a ready consent to the demand put under the name of the original God, so he made up his mind to reject the demand, saying that there were many children to be brought up, and that he was so busy as a village official that he could not afford to offer Miki as the Temple of God, and that if he was a god who would save people in the world, he was requested to descend elsewhere, because there were many other good places as well.

At that time Miki was forty-one years old, and Zenbei fifty-one, both of whom were in the prime of life as householders. The eldest son Suji was eighteen, the eldest daughter Masa fourteen, the third daughter Haru eight, the youngest Kokan was yet no more than two, counting in the Japanese way.

Rejected thus, the pains of Miki became even greater, and the original God would not draw back. In such a situation praying being compelled to stop, he consulted with the relatives who were staying at the house, and the relatives and friends who were called together that day, but no one would persuade him to accede to the demand.

So Zenbei came near Miki who was sitting at the ritual place, and refused compliance with the demand on the grounds that his children were all too young, and that Miki was a householder who could not be spared. At the reply, however, Miki assumed the more solemn attitude, saying rather

[1]Soyo, a woman who served as medium for Ichibei. [ed.]

soothingly and persuadingly, "It is no wonder that you fear so much, but the day will come in twenty or thirty years when you would all be convinced of the justice of My demand." But Zenbei and the others repeated the rejection, saying that they could never wait for so long as twenty or thirty years, so they wished Him to draw back at once. At the reply, Miki began to assume a wild appearance, the sacred staffs in her hands flung up, and the paper on the staffs was torn. So, putting their heads together about what they should do, they refused again and again, but the original God would not draw back. They were compelled to keep consulting day and night for three days, during which they refused repeatedly, and then the voice of the original God said, "If you should refuse, this house shall be destroyed."

At his sharp and harsh words, Zenbei and the other people were frightened into deep silence once more, while Miki who from the beginning had taken no meal, sitting upright and solemn with the sacred staffs in her hands, urged the people to accede to the demand. If it should continue like this, what would become of her? Zenbei began to be anxious about her fearing for the worst, and at the same time to feel the possibility of being convinced. For however troubled he might be, he could not but find in the words of God wishing to save the world some truth convincing enough to him.

So Zenbei made up his mind to act upon his resolution, and gave his answer with a firm determination, to offer Miki willingly as the Temple of God. It was 8 o'clock in the morning of October 26, the ninth year of Tempo.

As soon as the reply was made, Miki became pacified, and at the same time Miki Nakayama became the Temple of *Tsuki-Hi*, God the Parent. The mind of God the Parent entered the body of Miki, and She came to establish the ultimate teaching of saving the people of the world.

As we are taught in the Ofudesaki:

> "What I think now is spoken through Her mouth. Human is the mouth that speaks, but Divine is the mind that thinks within.
> Listen attentively to Me! It is because I have borrowed Her mouth, while I have lent My mind to Her,".....

The mouth of the Foundress is not different from that of an ordinary person, but the words spoken through the lips are those of God the Parent, and it is God the Parent Himself that is speaking through the mouth of the Foundress. Her outward appearance is quite similar to that of an ordinary person, but it is the mind of *Tsuki-Hi*, God the Parent that dwells in Her body. Therefore the teachings which were later given through the lips, through the pen, through action, and through wonderful salvation, are the very ones directly given by God the Parent....

The Foundress first urged the family that they should be reduced to poverty. The Foundress not only taught the family the need of being reduced to poverty, but She Herself set an example by giving away Her property which

She had brought to the family when She married, and then clothes of family members and food.

When we part with things, and wipe out our worldly desires, we shall have our mind brightened, and then the path to the life of *yokigurashi* will be opened up. But that was not all the Foundress urged, She went so far as to urge the family to take down the main house....

In this way the Foundress went through a hard time for as long as fifteen years. Fifteen years after the opening of the way of faith, that is, on February 22, in the sixth year of Kaei, Her husband Zenbei passed away, at the age of sixty-six, the Foundress was then fifty-six. Though in this deep sorrow, just as God the Parent ordains, the youngest daughter Kokan who was seventeen years old, went to Osaka to promulgate the holy name of Tenri-O-no-Mikoto to the world. Miss Kokan walked to Osaka accompanied by several attendants, and taking up their lodgings in an inn near the Dotonbori street, she promulgated the holy name of God the Parent, chanting, "*Namu,* Tenri-O-no-Mikoto" in the crowded streets beating wooden clappers. It was the first mission of our religion to the world. Soon after the main house of the Nakayama family found a buyer in a village to the north from Shoyashiki. When the house was taken down, the Foundress served to the helpers *sake* and some food, saying, "I want to set about My task of building a new world. I wish you to celebrate My enterprise with me." The helpers were all deeply impressed with Her cheerful attitude of mind, saying, "It is natural to feel sad when one takes down one's house. We have never seen or heard of such a cheery taking down of a house."....

While she was passing through such a narrow path of faithful life with bright spirit, filled with the parental affection of whole-hearted saving of mankind, She came to be famous first as the god of easy delivery, as is often said, "*obiya* (the grant of easy delivery) and *hoso* (the smallpox healing) are the opening of universal salvation." It began with the easy delivery granted to the third daughter Haru, when she had been staying with the Foundress to give birth to her first baby. Among the villagers, a woman named Yuki Shimizu was the first to be given the grant.

As the rumor of wonderful easy delivery was spread all over Yamato Province, there began to appear in the country a large number of worshippers, who crowded about Her with such devotion as to call Her a living deity of delivery....

Soon after, the Foundress taught the words and gesture of the '*tsutome*' or service for the first time;

"Sweep away all evils and save us, O, Parent, Tenri-O-no-Mikoto." It was on this occasion that the gesture was first adopted in the service. For up to that time, the service had been performed by repeating the name of God the Parent, "*Namu,* Tenri-O-no-Mikoto; *Namu,* Tenri-O-no-Mikoto," clapping the wooden clappers. '*Namu*' means *Tsuki-Hi*, the Parent.

Since then the form of service was brought to perfection, that is, in the

third year of Meiji, the Foundress taught the second and fourth sections of the Mikagura-uta, and in the eighth year of Meiji, the accompanying words and gesture of *kagura teodori* were almost completed, and then the eleven kinds of gesture were taught, and at last in the fifteenth year of Meiji, the present words of the service were completed.

48

the teachings of nichiren shoshu soka gakkai

Soka Gakkai (or Sokagakkai) first arose in the 1930s as an educational society with a religious foundation in Nichiren Buddhism. Its slow growth was cut short by government persecution during World War II, but since the early 1950s it has experienced a fantastic expansion. From its early stage, this movement has upheld absolute faith in the Lotus Sutra and Nichiren, objecting to any compromise or mixture of this faith. Soka Gakkai prefers to emphasize this connection with Nichiren Buddhism and rejects the label "New Religion" that has been applied to many recent religious movements.

The following selections are from one of the English translations published by Soka Gakkai for dissemination. It illustrates the kind of religious life found in the largest and most active New Religion: resolution of everyday problems, dynamic faith, and active missionary work. "The Objective of the Sokagakkai" is to worship the *Gohonzon,* a symbol of the Lotus Sutra, so that all people may eliminate suffering and attain happiness. Subsequent sections portray the ideal religious life as including daily worship *(gongyo),* conversion of others *(shakubuku),* and discussion meetings *(zadankai).* These discussion meetings are a powerful means of attracting and holding members, especially among the rootless people of the cities.

Every member should study the doctrine of Buddhism, but an even more climactic religious experience is the pilgrimage to the Head Temple Taisekiji. The claim that six million members (out of a population of about 100 million) would visit this temple in 1970 indicates the size of the movement. Not mentioned in these excerpts is the activity of Komeito (Clean Government party), the political arm of Soka Gakkai. From its founding in 1964, in a few years it developed into a major opposition party; therefore, Komeito is a controversial phenomenon in its own right.

Figure 11. Soka Gakkai's Sho-Hondo (Prayer Hall for World Peace), officially opened in 1972, with Mt. Fuji in the background. Reprinted by permission of Mr. Tomiya Akiyama, Chief, International Bureau, Board of Information, The Soka Gakkai.

Soka Gakkai is the New Religion that is most active in countries outside Japan, such as the United States, where it is usually known as Nichiren Shoshu.

Reprinted by permission of the publisher from *The Nichiren Shoshsu Sokagakkai* (Tokyo: The Seikyo Press, 1966). This work, now out of print, has been corrected at the request of Mr. Tomiya Akayama, Chief, Foreign Relations Bureau, Information Centre, The Sokagakkai; these official corrections are indicated in footnotes.

The Objective of the Sokagakkai

The objective of the Sokagakkai lies, first of all, in teaching the individual how to redevelop his character and enjoy a happy life, and in showing all mankind how eternal peace can be established, through the supreme Buddhism, the religion of mercy and pacifism. Through this supreme religion, a person can escape[1] from poverty and live a prosperous life, if only

[1] "Escape from" has been corrected to read "overcome." [ed.]

he works in earnest; a man troubled with domestic discord will find his home serene and happy; and a man suffering from disease will completely recover his health and be able to resume his work. Through the power of the Gohonzon, a mother worried with her delinquent son will see him reform, and a husband who is plagued with a neurotic wife can have her return to normalcy. We often hear of a man whose business is failing and who, after being converted to Nichiren Shoshu, has a brilliant idea, or makes a contact with an unexpected customer and begins to prosper again.

Most people are afflicted with various problems—either spiritual, physical or material, but everyone who believes in the Gohonzon (the object of worship in Nichiren Shoshu) can solve any problem and achieve a happy life. Men who are timid or irritable can gradually become normal before they become aware of the change in their character.

The true intention of the Daishonin[2] is to save the whole world through the attainment of each individual's happiness in life. Consequently, members of the Sokagakkai are actively trying to make, first of all, the Japanese people realize this great Buddhism as soon as possible. But there is no nationality in religion. Nichiren Daishonin made a wonderful prediction about seven hundred years ago to the effect, "As the Buddhism of Sakyamuni found its way to Japan from India by way of China, conversely, Our Buddhism will return from Japan to India by way of China."

Without a doubt, the Buddhism of the Daishonin will spread all over the East in the near future,[3] and finally throughout the whole world. World peace as well as the welfare of individual nations can be achieved only when the true religion is made the basic thought. If you take this Buddhism as the guiding principle of your daily lives, the happiness of the individual will be closely reflected in the prosperity of the society in which you live.

Each country can achieve prosperity without any harm to, or discord with, any other country. This is the spirit of Kosen-rufu (propagation of Nichiren Daishonin's teachings) and the Nichiren Shoshu Sokagakkai is positively striving to achieve this sublime purpose....

Members' Daily Activities

The Sokagakkai's objective is to make all people happy. To achieve this, the members themselves enjoy happiness through their practice of Buddhism and at the same time introduce the immense blessings of the Gohonzon to others. The Sokagakkai promotes various activities so that each individual member can deepen his faith and also help the unhappy.

Gakkai members' most fundamental activities are Gongyo, daily prayer, and Shakubuku, introducing the True Buddhism to non-believers.

[2]Daishonin, literally "great saint," a title which in this case means Nichiren. [ed.]
[3]"Over the East in the near future" has been corrected to read "over the East in the future." [ed.]

The practice of Gongyo is indispensable for all Gakkai members. Neglecting it would be the same as living without eating! At the same time, the practice of Shakubuku for agonized and troubled people is also indispensable. Thus, Gongyo and Shakubuku are the fundamental practices for believers and at the same time the source of the unfathomable blessings of the Gohonzon.

Another important Gakkai activity for general members is the *Zadankai*, discussion meetings, where they talk freely with other members and with non-believers who attend the meetings for the first time.[4] This helps the members to enrich their knowledge of the True Buddhism.

The study of Buddhism is also encouraged, as well as *Tozankai,* pilgrimage to Taisekiji,[5] which is also an important activity for members.

Members can enjoy the immense delight of having faith in Nichiren Shoshu through these various activities.

Gongyo, Daily Worship

The most important of all the activities of the Sokagakkai members is practicing Gongyo in the morning and evening. [Sokagakkai] President Ikeda spoke of the importance of Gongyo as follows:

"Suppose a man has an excellent TV set. He cannot enjoy interesting programs unless he turns it on. No matter how precious a book a man may have, he cannot gain any knowledge from it unless he opens it.

"In a like manner, you cannot gain any blessings from the Dai-Gohonzon unless you practice Gongyo. Earnest prayer to the Gohonzon is the only true source of all your acts in life, the origin of the vital life-force, the root of your study in Buddhism, and the mainspring of your blessed life."

In the early stages of faith, every member is apt to neglect Gongyo for he feels the time required is too long, or often he stops Gongyo when he has a visitor because he feels embarrassed to be seen at prayer. As every member has joined the Sokagakkai to gain happiness, he should keep his faith untiringly and never be swayed by external hindrances or difficulties which may try to disturb[6] his faith.

Shakubuku, Introduction to True Buddhism

Shakubuku literally means to correct one's evil mind and to convert it to good. It results from the delight of believing in Nichiren Daishonin's Buddhism and from the heartfelt wish for helping the unhappy through Buddhism.

[4]"Attend the meetings for the first time" has been corrected to read "attend the meetings." [ed.]
[5]"Taisekiji" has been corrected to read "Daisekiji." [ed.]
[6]"Which may try to disturb" has been corrected to read "which may disturb." [ed.]

Shakubuku is rooted in humanity, and by practicing Shakubuku, one can enjoy the great blessings of the Gohonzon. The most conspicuous blessings one can receive by practicing Shakubuku are lively spirit and vigorous life-force. Shakubuku is the source of the Gohonzon's blessings and strong vitality.

Shakubuku should be carried out for the purpose of helping people from misery and misfortune.

There are many who are not helped by politics, money or the arts. Such people, whether or not they are conscious of it, are seeking the Gohonzon to change their karma.[7] This is the revelation of the Buddhist mercy which comes from earnest practice. It is natural for believers to devote themselves to the salvation of all mankind, if they but realize the unfathomable mercy of the True Buddha.

It is desirable for members to practice Shakubuku for people who, being ignorant of the True Buddhism, are simply opposed to having faith in it. When one looks back upon the days before he was converted to Nichiren Shoshu, he will realize that he also had been more or less opposed to it. After being converted to this religion, however, he found his view of life to be false, and was awakened to the need to march forward on the highway to happiness. This fact well testifies to the necessity of Shakubuku for non-believers.

Zadankai, Discussion Meeting

Zadankai, discussion meetings, are held daily wherever the Sokagakkai members live. Meetings are held every day[8] with 20-30 members or sometimes even more than 50 attending. They talk about the True Buddhism and encourage one another so that all attendants deepen their faith. To the non-believers who attend the meeting, members try to explain fully how True Buddhism can improve human life. Naturally, the discussion meeting is filled with a cheerful atmosphere and hope for constructing a brighter future.

Discussion meetings, a traditional activity of the Sokagakkai, have been conducted since the days of first president Tsunesaburo Makiguchi. In those days, his home was the meeting place. In the days of second president Josei Toda, also, it was through discussion meetings that he embarked on the reconstruction of the Sokagakkai.

President Ikeda promoted all his Gakkai activities around the traditional *Zadankai.* He also made it a rule to read the Gosho (the collection of Nichiren Daishonin's works) for those present. Thus the foundation for the Sokagakkai's development into its present position was established by the three successive presidents with the discussion meetings as its foundation.

Some might think it easier to promote the propagation of a religion

[7]Karma, meaning here their destiny or life. [ed.]
[8]"Every day" has been corrected to read "once every other week." [ed.]

through propaganda—for example, by holding large-scale meetings rather than *Zadankai* which are attended by only a limited number of persons. In reality, however, the small discussion meetings are the best and the surest way for propagating the True Buddhism. One will clearly understand this if he considers that the fantastic advance of the Sokagakkai stemmed from the *Zadankai*.

49

the significance of the new religions in modern japan

Tenrikyo and Soka Gakkai are only two examples of the larger New Religions that have appeared within the past century or so. On the surface, movements such as Tenrikyo and Soka Gakkai may seem completely different, with their own founders and distinctive sets of doctrines and practices. However, these and other New Religions, when viewed as a whole, constitute a common phenomenon in modern Japanese religious history.

One important fact to remember when studying these movements is that so many movements appeared within such a short time span, which seems to indicate that many people became less interested in the institutional life of Shinto and Buddhism and turned to the newly established groups.

These groups are usually called *New Religions* in English, a literal translation of the Japanese term for them. However, the term *New Religions* does not mean that they represent a total break from the prior religious tradition. On the contrary, these movements, like all religious phenomena, reflect the heritage from which they emerge. The New Religions are so thoroughly Japanese in character that they exhibit all the major themes found in earlier Japanese religion. This selection traces the presence of six persistent themes of Japanese religion in these new religions, which demonstrates that the newness of the movements is found not so much in their separate elements and general themes as in the reorganization of older elements and themes. Charismatic leadership in the founding period and active lay participation in the organized

stages of the New Religions provide a new context in which the older themes can be expressed. In this historical perspective, the New Religions can be seen as attempts to renew or revitalize the older tradition. On the other hand, viewed in terms of their own dynamics, one might emphasize the innovative features of the New Religions—such as their use of mass media, greater lay participation, and greater concern for the immediate religious needs of the people. But however one balances the "old" and "new" of these movements, they are interesting case studies in which the Japanese tradition moves out of the past to meet the present and to proceed into the future.

Reprinted by permission of the author and publisher from H. Byron Earhart, "The Significance of the 'New Religions'," KBS Bulletin on Japanese Culture, 1970.

New Religions in Japan

One of the most conspicuous religious developments in recent Japanese history is the appearance and spread of "new" religious movements. Especially from the early 1800's to the present there arose many religious groups outside of the established religions of Buddhism and Shinto. Popular support was so strong that the government recognized thirteen groups as part of "sect Shinto" (Kyoha Shinto) in the late 1800's and early 1900's. But due to government control, even these groups were prevented from freely organizing until after 1945. Other groups were forced to belong to Shinto or Buddhism, or exist as non-religious associations. These new religious movements increased in numbers and strength, such that after 1945, when complete religious freedom was enacted, there arose hundreds of these "new"—but not necessarily novel—religious groups. Even at present there are a great many new religions with considerable popular support. This remarkable development has attracted widespread attention....

The New Religions in the Light of Japanese Religious History

There are at least three periods of major transformation in Japanese religious history: 1) the period of formation, from prehistory to the ninth century A.D., when all the major traditions first came into contact with each other; 2) the period of development and elaboration, from the ninth to seventeenth centuries, when these traditions became intricately interrelated; 3) the period of fossilization and renewal, from the seventeenth century to the present, when the older "established" religions became formalized and new religious movements began to arise....

When historically considered, the new religions appeared in a particular period (fossilization and renewal) of Japanese religion; but the religious nature of the new religions can be better grasped in terms of six persistent themes. Although institutionalized religion had become formalized or "fossilized," there were still many vital religious elements in the established religions and in folk religion. The new religions arose when one or more vital religious elements became the orienting point for a new socio-religious movement; sometimes the vital element burst through the bonds of established religion; sometimes the vital element coalesced out of a rather unorganized folk tradition. Most of these new religious movements began with a founder or foundress, but even this event can be seen within the framework of six persistent themes.... While each separate new religion is more or less "specialized" in terms of emphasizing one or more of the six themes, as a totality the new religions reflect the whole panorama of Japanese religious themes.

1) Man, gods, and nature. One of the most important features of the new religions is the founder (or foundress) who initiates the movement. Usually this person either receives a sacred revelation or becomes a demi-divinity or living god (*iki-gami*). Here we see the ease with which men and gods (*kami*) interchange, and recognize also the background of divine possession and shamanistic elements in Japanese religion. But there is another type of founder who is more a discoverer than a revealer of the sacred norm; this is the case with Soka Gakkai, in which the founder Makiguchi is credited with rediscovering the power of the Lotus Sutra. In many of the new religions Shinto *kami* or Buddhist divinities are selected for worship. But even more important is the general notion of living in accordance with a divine mandate. This divine mandate is quite often associated with nature as a whole, called by terms such as *dai-shizen* (great nature) or *o-mi-oya* (great honorable parent). Even in the Buddhist-derived new religions we find a notion of conformity to cosmic law, which in Japan is always somehow related to nature as a sacred entity. In general the new religions reflect this triangular interrelationship of men, gods, and nature on one plane.

2) Family (living and dead). Veneration of ancestors is one of the most indelible features of Japanese religion, and has come to be the special focus of several new religions such as Reiyu-kai. The anniversary of the birth and death of founders is widely observed in their respective groups. Even in new religions which have never emphasized veneration of ancestors, the members insist on having special means and ceremonies for the repose of the souls of ancestors. While the Japanese social structure has undergone considerable change in recent history, the family is still quite important religiously. If the home is no longer the center of religious activities that it once was, then the new religions often tend to be surrogate parents. The names of founders and divinities often express this parental atmosphere, and even the ecclesiastical structure of some groups takes on a familiar character.

3) Purification, discipline, rituals, charms. Among the new religions, some emphasize a kind of spiritual counselling, which is a more recent version of former kinds of purification. Often the founder or successor is able to assimilate the impurity and suffering of the believers, or even directly cure sickness and disability. Some form of repentance *(zange)* is institutionalized in many of these groups, and various kinds of discipline (or asceticism, *shugyo* or *gyo*) are practiced after the pattern of the founders. Even such age-old practices as reciting sutras and formulas, or engaging in *zazen*, become the discipline which enables attainment of religious fulfillment. Although each group has its own complicated terminologies and stages, the common religious background is evident. Many new religions (although often not openly emphasizing it) hand out the same charms as in every shrine and temple: protection of the household, prosperity in business, safety in travel. Every new religion has a full share of ritual activities.

4) Local festivals and individual cults. Perhaps this is the aspect of Japanese religion which has experienced the greatest transformation within the new religious movements. Although formerly some individual cults (such as the worship of Kannon and Jizo) enjoyed nation-wide distribution, they were linked neither administratively nor by believers' groups. By contrast, in contemporary new religions, the followers of a certain charismatic leader, or believers in a special sacred object (such as the Lotus Sutra) form the base of a national group of believers with an ecclesiastical hierarchy. Local festivals of shrines and temples tend to be replaced by the "festivals" of the new religions, now carried out on a nation-wide basis. At the same time, it should be noted that the new religions perpetuate much of the old rhythmic system of annual festivals, since most groups observe the all-important New Year's festival, as well as spring and fall festivals, just as the Buddhist-derived groups observe traditional Buddhist celebrations. Generally shrines and temples become less important than the central headquarters of the new religions, and pilgrimage to ancient holy spots is less frequent than pilgrimage to the new religions' headquarters.

5) Religious practice and daily life. The new religions are proud of their claim of making religion relevant to daily life, but by this they mean something different than in former times. Formerly religion was naturally related to economic life (fishing, farming, etc.) and to the different stages of life (birth, marriage, death). But nowadays the new religions relate religion to daily life by providing access to the religious power, fulfillment, and tranquility which resolves the pressures of daily (modern) life. Many such religions have institutionalized forms of counselling, confession, or blessing. These aim at purifying the person from his defilement or guilt; at the same time they remove the person's troubles or suffering *(nayami)*. Even the means of discipline or devotion, or asceticism *(shugyo)* aim at the purification and tranquility of the person in everyday life.

6) Bond between religion and nation. Ironically, in spite of the fact that the state severely controlled or suppressed religion before 1945, in extreme cases arresting the leaders and destroying their headquarters, nevertheless, all the new religions explicitly or implicitly support the Japanese nation. The new religions revere divinities *(kami)* associated with the founding of the country; also, their reverence for cosmic powers and their respect for hierarchical values naturally form a pyramid of values at whose peak is the body politic. In this aspect, as in other aspects, the various new religions represent divergent opinions as to how these ends will be attained. Some groups verge on prewar attitudes of the necessity for the state to inculcate proper ethical and "spiritual" values. On the other hand, many groups openly advocate world peace and international brotherhood. But neither extreme envisions any overthrow of political power, and both claim that theirs is the true spiritual fulfillment of the Japanese people. The famous Soka Gakkai and its political branch Komeito have tended to be conservative (seeking to elect their political candidates), rather than openly revolutionary; on the other hand, the internationally minded new religions present their tolerant attitudes from a distinctly Japanese viewpoint.

The preceding historical and analytical consideration of the new religions in the light of the totality of Japanese religion provides the context in which we can assess the significance of the new religions. For this consideration yields the key to the emergence and nature of the new religions. They emerged out of a general atmosphere of stagnation and social crisis, which the founders were able to resolve on the basis of their personal revelation and charismatic leadership. The nature of the new religions is chiefly the same as that found in prior Japanese religion, but the reshaping and expression of this content unfolds in a peculiar manner. The new religions are novel not so much in content as in their formation of new socio-religious groupings. Put quite simply, they are usually distinguished from the established religions by having specific founders and church-like intentions of dissemination. Once the new religions are comprehended in terms of their general emergence and religious nature, we can approach the question of their broader significance.

The Significance of the New Religions

Perhaps the most important single observation that should be made of the new religions is that they are authentic religious phenomena. Every religious tradition in its infancy seems to be singled out for accusations of insincerity, immorality, or duplicity, and the Japanese new religions are certainly no exception. It goes without saying that at any time and place there appear pseudo-religious movements (for non-religious purposes such as personal and political ambition), and legitimate religious traditions are

frequently used for illegitimate aims. Although some Japanese new religions probably were pseudo-religious movements, and although some may have been misused for questionable purposes, such problems are inevitable in the ambiguity of the historical process, and never limited to one time or place or religion. The Japanese new religions are authentic religious phenomena because their basic thrust is to bring people into contact with a sacred reality. All human life seeks to orient itself in time and space, arranging itself around a central sacred power of reality. It is to be expected that different cultural areas have developed and handed down different historical traditions. The Japanese religious heritage may differ from the more familiar Western religious models, but nevertheless it displays a coherent logic of its own. It seems that the authenticity of the new religions can be questioned only by questioning the authenticity of the Japanese religious tradition in general.

If anything, the new religions testify to the perseverance and adaptability of the Japanese religious tradition. The new religions are evidence which can be used to reject two "overworked generalizations: one, the Japanese people are not really a religious people; and two, modernization always makes people less religious."[1] The effects of industrialization, urbanization, and mechanization have exacted a heavy toll on the established religions, particularly because of the high degree of social mobility which disrupts the traditional ties between family, local geographical unit, and religious practice. However, the new religions have rallied to meet this challenge and have produced new forms of socio-religious organization which readily thrive in this new social climate. With risk of oversimplification, the new religions may be seen as examples of revitalization of earlier Japanese religion.

In brief, these new religious movements represent both a preservation and transformation of traditional Japanese religious values. And the real question which seems to underlie the questioning and criticism of the new religions, both in Japan and abroad, is the question of the currency of traditional religious values in a modern world.

SELECTED READINGS

For works on various aspects of the Japanese new religions, see first the citations for each selection; some additional works are:

Earhart, H. Byron. "The Interpretation of the 'New Religions' of Japan as Historical Phenomena." *Journal of the American Academy of Religion* 37, No. 3 (September 1969): 237-48.

Earhart, H. Byron. *The New Religions of Japan: A Bibliography of Western-Language Materials.* Tokyo: Monumenta Nipponica, Sophia University, 1970.

[1]Delmer M. Brown, "Japan's Century of Change: The Religious Factor," *Japan Christian Quarterly*, XXXV, No. 1 (Winter, 1969), 24 - 33.

Fujiwara, Hirotatsu. *I Denounce Soka Gakkai.* Translated by Worth C. Grant. Tokyo: Nisshin Hodo Co., 1970.

Holtom, Daniel C. *The National Faith of Japan: A Study in Modern Shinto.* New York: Paragon Reprint Corp., 1963.

Ikado, Fujio. "Trend and Problems of New Religions: Religion in Urban Society." In *The Sociology of Japanese Religion,* edited by Kiyomi Morioka and William H. Newell, pp. 101-17. Leiden: E. J. Brill, 1968.

McFarland, H. Neill. *The Rush Hour of the Gods: A Study of New Religious Movements in Japan.* New York: Macmillan Co., 1967.

Murata, Kiyoaki. *Japan's New Buddhism. An Objective Account of Soka Gakkai.* New York: Walker/Weatherhill, 1969.

Offner, Clark B., and van Straelen, Henry. *Modern Japanese Religions: With Special Emphasis upon Their Doctrines of Healing.* Tokyo: Rupert Enderle, 1963.

Straelen, Henry van. *The Religion of Divine Wisdom, Japan's Most Powerful Religious Movement.* Kyoto: Veritas Shoin, 1957.

Sugihara, Yoshie, and Plath, David W. *Sensei and His People: The Building of a Japanese Commune.* Berkeley and Los Angeles: University of California Press, 1969.

part seventeen

the history and future of japanese religion

This final chapter turns from the past and the present to the uncharted future of Japanese religion. To foresee the direction and pace of subsequent events, one must assess the weight of the past and the tendencies of the present. Scholars who make this assessment usually point out the major outlines of the tradition, the serious problems facing the tradition, and the alternative solutions to these problems.

Probably the safest generalization to draw from these readings is that the current ambiguous state of religion in Japan will continue for some time. Japan possesses a distinctive religious heritage which will no doubt extend into the future; it will undergo change but will not lose its Japanese character. The organized religions will strive to reform themselves as the New Religions try to consolidate their gains.

One problem facing Japanese religion is the changing scene in Japan. Many of these changes can be summed up in the word *modernization,* which embraces the shift from a primarily agricultural and rural country to a primarily industrial and urban nation. In this dramatic shift, social patterns have changed, and the role of religious life in the new situation is unclear. Also poorly defined is the ancient, unique heritage of Japan in the midst of her increasingly international character. Such problems as cultural relativism and modernization are universal, of course, and are not limited to Japan. What is peculiar to Japan is a distinctive world view within which the Japanese attempt to understand themselves as they approach the problems. And the problems are never completely resolved, nor does the tradition ever stop its own transformation.

50

JapaNese ReLiGioN in the modeRN woRLd

Contemporary Westerners should realize that they are neither the first nor the sole investigators of the problem of modernity and its implications for religious life. This selection is a reminder of this fact: the author of the article is Japanese, his viewpoint is Asian (Oriental), and the date of publication is 1926. We do not have to agree completely with the article to appreciate the timeliness and relevance of its arguments even today.

Masaharu Anesaki was the first holder of the chair for the study of religion in Tokyo University, the founder of the "scientific" study of religion in Japan, and a scholar who had traveled and studied throughout the world. Writing shortly after World War I, Anesaki recognized an ambiguity in the fast pace, mechanization, and "progress" of the modern world. He saw the need for every tradition to open itself to freedom and scientific inquiry. Some readers will see Anesaki's faith in science as too idealistic, too optimistic; however, Anesaki's article is idealistic in the best sense—it seeks out and holds true to the highest ideals he knew. And at the same time, he realized that faith in an infinite progress is meaningless without some goal or sense of happiness.

It is in defining the goal that traditions become important. Anesaki was fully aware in the 1920s that religion could too easily provide goals for the people by simply supplying reactionary movements. (He included Shinto in this category.) However, he knew progressive movements are not free from suspicion either. Anesaki reached out for a humanistic criterion by which to criticize every tradition: "Any civilization and every effort for progress is only valuable and worthy of human dignity so far as it contributes to a fuller realization of the unity of life." He also reminded Occidentals not to consider "civilization as their monopoly" and Orientals not to "put obstructions to its [civilization's] spread and expansion." This plea for understanding among the various cultures of the world especially is a valuable suggestion today.

Abridged from "An Oriental Evaluation of Modern Civilization" by Masaharu Anesaki, in *Recent Gains in American Civilization*, 1928, edited by Kirby Page. Reprinted by permission of Harcourt Brace Jovanovich, Inc.

Civilization and Modernity, East and West

Now let us see whether there are any signs of decay in modern civilization. The enthusiasm for progress has no limit, because every zenith reached reveals further horizons. But can human nature be indefinitely satisfied by an endless pursuit without goal? May not the story of the Flying Dutchman be applied to the present situation? Pursuit of happiness is certainly a vital incentive to life, and in the present condition of modern civilization activity has become happiness in itself. Yet happiness is an extremely fugitive figure, the more so in an age of speed. No need of enumerating jazz bands, cubist pictures, agitating demonstrations of all kinds, anything and everything exciting. Many of those signs are certainly a part of the aftermath of the Great War but there is something more and deeper-lying in the situation which was discernible even before the war and seems to last longer than this temporary disturbance. May all this not be a manifestation of the strained situation in which modern man is put, just on account of the progress achieved? Even without approving John Ruskin's contentions, every one can see evils in the mechanization of life. Man has made machines for himself but is becoming himself a tool of the machines. If this dictum be not wholly true, no one would dare deny it entirely. Beside the tool-like position in which the average workman finds himself, nearly every man and woman nowadays lives more or less under the control, often tyranny, of mechanized devices or organizations. Quite naturally the human impulse for freedom takes its revenge; the frenzy for activity and speed seems to be partially a manifestation of this spirit of revolt. . . .

For finding a pathway or rather opening a high-road out of the present strait, several opposites may be considered. We have above referred to the medieval ideal of perfection in contradistinction to the modern one of progress; similar ones could be cited, such as repose and composure, instead of activity and speed, bliss against mere utility, faith, against experimentation, authority, against freedom. Every one of these certainly has some bearing upon the present situation. What the Roman Catholic Church stands for in condemning "modernism" represents fundamentally the attitude of denouncing the tendencies of modern civilization such as free activity, the spirit of experimentation (often branded as destructive criticism), and the idea of renovation tending to revolution. The rise of the more or less mystic Christian Science in the stronghold of Puritanism; the relatively easy acceptance found in America by Yoga, Vedanta, or Couéism;[1] the seemingly re-

---

[1]Coueism, the teaching of Emile Coue (1857-1926), a French psychotherapist with a popular following. [ed.]

markable revival of ancient Shinto ideas in Japan, the most modern nation of the East; these and many other similar phenomena are certainly reactionary. The word "reactionary" in a case like this is usually used to denote a quite transient phase of set-back in the larger process of progress. But can all these reactionary movements be so lightly disposed of as nothing but ephemeral? Even if so, who can, on the other side, be sure that "progress" is not so? If Gandhi's spinning-wheel be ephemeral, may the British rule of India be everlasting—ephemeral or eternal in the sense of duration, in the sense of depth and extent, in the sense of moral and social values? When the power of instinct revolts against the control of reason, it is certainly reactionary but it can have a meaning more than ephemeral. Similarly, when an old national heritage reacts against a newly introduced culture, the reactionary force is not necessarily transient. Considering these things, what have we to discern in the movements, whether progressive or reactionary, in modern civilization? . . .

In some respects the primitive or ancient society has stronger ties than the modern. But it is evident that the former was based chiefly on natural or instinctive ties, while the legal, or "contractual," solidarity has proceeded from national to international society, and the rise of the universal religions made possible a solidarity on the basis of faith and ideals. Is it not the mission of modern civilization to bring to full light and force all these ties of social solidarity and achieve a democratic community of human brotherhood? . . .

Science starts with curiosity, steps forward by observation and experimentation, and its goal should be a full grasp of truth underlying natural occurrences and human events. These motives or steps of science are often united. . . .

Science in this sense is a way of revealing the truth of oneness of existence, otherwise expressed by Christianity in the teaching of the unique Creator and by Buddhism in the doctrine of one and the same Buddha-nature pervading all. Modern science does so well in its investigations into physical nature but is now remarkably stepping forward to the search of the mysteries of human life, both individual and social, intellectual and spiritual. Modern science has accumulated a wonderful amount of material and secured a mastery of its methods; the consummation should be a fuller realization of its ideal aim of perfecting the fullness of life through the knowledge of truth. A fullness of life in developing the best aspects of human nature in all the individuals and in all the groups of man, by giving full opportunities to the dispositions, characters, and talents, as well as to the desires, hopes, aspirations of all mankind—the attainment of the true democracy. A fullness of life in supplying means and tools of human existence and elevating all those materials to the ideal aim of the perfect life—the realization of the moral and spiritual purpose of industry.

This is a very general idea about the constructive and promising side of modern civilization which seems to be coming out in the progress of

modern civilization and particularly as the other evil sides of civilization are more and more keenly felt by thoughtful people. In this constructive prospect the mere glorification of modern civilization will have little share; thoughtful consideration will show that our civilization should not be self-contented but be modest and truth-seeking enough to see helpful and supplementary forces to be derived from all the branches of civilization and culture without distinction of ages and races. For as stated above the activity of modern civilization is not entirely contradictory to the dignified composure of medieval civilization, and similarly the progressive activity of the Occident is not an irreconcilable antithesis to the contemplative attitude of the Orient. According to our view those two are opposites united in basic principle, that is, the rich development of life aiming at the final goal of perfecting human life towards the divine.

Existence is continuous in spite of its varieties, life is one in spite of its changes, because things and beings are outcomes of one and the same source, offsprings of the unique Father, creatures sharing in the life, which fills all in all and accomplishes all through all. Any civilization and every effort for progress is only valuable and worthy of human dignity so far as it contributes to a fuller realization of the unity of life. Modern civilization, in spite of its many defects and present anomalies, is certainly a great contribution to this aim and purpose of human life. Direct the motive forces of modern civilization to this ideal aim, let the leaders of civilized societies fully realize the purpose of life. Then we could hope that modern civilization shall succeed in not destroying but fulfilling the best fruits of ancient and medieval civilizations, to no exclusion of the Oriental or any other. Then civilization would be the common heritage of the whole of mankind. For this reason Occidentals should not regard civilization as their monopoly, nor Orientals put obstructions to its spread and expansion. Therein shall vanish the pride and arrogance of the Nordic or white, the envy and indignation of the Asiatic or colored races. All must go, the vanity of mere activity and speed, as well as the pessimism of a fateful decline of the Occident.

51

the search for identity by modern japanese

Harp of Burma was published after World War II as a story for Japanese children, but it soon became popular among adults. The novel is set in Burma during and shortly after the war, when the Japanese soldiers were prisoners of war awaiting return to Japan. It is an unusual war story in that it focuses not so much on military affairs as on the morale of the soldiers.

This brief excerpt is from a discussion of the Japanese prisoners in their internment camp. With time on their hands they are reflecting on the differences between Burmese life and Japanese life. For example, is the compulsory military training of Japan better than the compulsory religious training of Burma? This in turn raises the question of the contrast between traditional Japan and modern Japan.

Debates of these surface contrasts lead to more basic issues, such as the definition of humanity, man's relationship to nature and technology, and what constitutes civilization in the modern world. In the discussion, we view the Japanese prisoners trying to hold onto their traditional roots while eliminating undesirable elements: they want to preserve their distinctive heritage, yet they want to avoid war and remain at peace with the Burmese; nature is to be valued, yet technology is inevitable; civilization is a high ideal, but it is difficult to attain in an atomic age. These debates, framed imaginatively in the context of a novel, dramatize the contemporary Japanese in their quest for identity in the modern world.

Reprinted from *Harp of Burma* by Michio Takeyama, with permission of the publisher, Charles E. Tuttle Co., Inc.

Japanese Prisoners of War in Burma

The Burmese are so religious that every man spends part of his youth as a monk, devoting himself to ascetic practices. For that reason we saw many young monks of about our own age.

What a difference! In Japan all the young men wore soldiers' uniforms, but in Burma they put on priestly robes. We often argued about this. Compulsory military training or compulsory religious training—which was better?

Which was more advanced? As a nation, as human beings, which should we choose?

It was a queer kind of argument that always ended in a stalemate. Briefly, the difference between the two ways of life seemed to be that in a country where young men wear military uniforms the youths of today will doubtless become the efficient, hard-working adults of tomorrow. If work is to be done, uniforms are necessary. On the other hand, priestly robes are meant for a life of quiet worship, not for strenuous work, least of all for war. If a man wears such garments during his youth, he will probably develop a gentle soul in harmony with nature and his fellow man, and will not be inclined to fight and overcome obstacles by his own strength.

In former times we Japanese wore clothes that were like clerical robes, but nowadays we usually wear uniform-like Western clothes. And that is only to be expected, since we have now become one of the most active and efficient nations in the world and our old peaceful, harmonious life is a thing of the past. The basic difference lies in the attitude of a people; whether, like the Burmese, to accept the world as it is, or to try to change it according to one's own designs. Everything hinges on this.

The Burmese, including those who live in cities, still do not wear Western clothes. They wear their traditional loose-fitting robes. Even statesmen active in world politics dress in their native Burmese costume, to avoid losing popularity at home. That is because the Burmese, unlike the Japanese, have remained unchanged. Instead of wishing to master everything through strength or intellect, they aim for salvation through humility and reliance on a power greater than themselves. Thus they distrust people who wear Western clothes, and whose mental attitude is different from their own.

Our argument tended to boil down to this: it depends on how people choose to live—to try to control nature by their own efforts, or yield to it and merge into a broader, deeper order of being. But which of these attitudes, of these ways of life, is better for the world and for humanity? Which should we choose?

One of the men who scorned the Burmese said: "I've never seen such a weak, lazy people. Everything they have, from electric lights to railroad trains, was manufactured for them by some foreign country. They ought to modernize, take off their *longyi*[1] and put on their pants. Even the schools here are only for dramatics or music; there aren't any business or technical schools. They say the level of education is high, but that's compared to the rest of Southeast Asia—all it amounts to are priests teaching the sutras[2] in their temple schools. At this rate the country will go to rack and ruin. No wonder it's a British colony."

Someone objected, saying that exchanging *longyi* for pants wouldn't

[1]Longyi, loose Burmese pants. [ed.]
[2]Sutras, Buddhist scriptures. [ed.]

necessarily bring happiness. "Look at Japan!" he said. "And not only Japan—the whole world is in a mess. When people get conceited and try to impose their will on everything, they're lost. Even if they have a few successes, it's worse in the long run."

"Are you saying it's all right to go on forever being uncivilized, like the Burmese?"

"Uncivilized? Sometimes I think we're not as civilized as they are."

"You're crazy. Do you mean to tell me we're not as civilized as the people of this filthy, backward place, who don't even try to work and educate themselves to stand on their own feet?"

"That's right. We have tools for civilization, but at heart we're still savages who don't know how to use them. What did we do with these tools but wage a gigantic war, and even come all the way here to invade Burma and cause terrible suffering to its people? Yet they accept it and go on living quietly and peacefully. The Burmese never seem to have committed our stupid blunder of attacking others. You say they're uneducated, but they believe in Buddhism and govern their whole lives by it. They spend part of their youth as monks, and the way of the Buddha becomes second nature to them. That's why their hearts are serene, why they live at peace. Isn't that a far nobler kind of education?"

"But what about the low standard of living? It isn't fit for a human being. In the first place, their kind of Buddhism doesn't make sense. Abandon the world. Put up with your miseries. Don't worry about whether things are getting better or worse, just concentrate on saving your soul—and salvation comes only after you leave the world and enter a new life as a monk. That's what comes of taking Buddha's words literally, I understand. You get this Hinayana Buddhism[3] in Burma. They all became monks. They're not concerned about the real world. Life on earth seems so insignificant they have no desire to invent new things, and it never occurs to them to try to improve their conditions. They still haven't developed a system that lets everybody live in freedom. Can you call that happiness? At this rate there'll never be any progress."

---

[3]Hinayana Buddhism, the monastic Buddhism common to southern Asia, in contrast to the Mahayana Buddhism dominant in Japan. [ed.]

chRistmas: a modeRn japanese festival

Americans may be surprised to find Christmas used as an example of a "modern festival" in Japan. The surprise is twofold: first, we know that fewer than one percent of the Japanese population belongs to institutional Christianity; second, Christmas is not usually seen as an example of modernity and democracy. One point that David Plath is making is that Japanese celebration of Christmas is a symbolic form borrowed from the West to express her modernity. Toward the end of this article, Plath argues that the Japanese, like other "modern" people, are no longer sure what constitutes their tradition. In this uncertain atmosphere, Christmas has been accepted along with other modern importations, such as decorated cakes.

A Westerner may object that what has been borrowed is only the external forms of Christmas—above all, the commercial trappings. But this should remind us that the commercial, musical, and familial aspects of Christmas cannot be so easily divorced from specifically religious meanings. Christmas is modern partly because it is tied up with the consumer world of department stores and seasonal sales. Christmas is democratic partly because Christmas parties allow men and women to celebrate together, something they could not do in the ordinary Japanese seasonal parties. It also seems significant that most of the Christmas lore is borrowed from America, not Europe—another symptom of America's world influence.

Plath emphasizes that traditions are not just passive agents but are active forces which help a people restate themselves, and "the American popular Christmas is one such self-restatement." It is also worth noting that the form of restatement is that of a festival—festivals have always been an important part of Japanese religious life. (For other examples of festivals see Part 12.)

Reprinted by permission of the author and publisher from David W. Plath, "The Japanese Popular Christmas: Coping with Modernity," *Journal of American Folklore*, 1963.

Christmas in Japan

Many peoples today are scanning Western cultures in search not only of ways to become modern, but also of ways to cope with living in a modern

milieu. They seek not only the institutional forms of modernity; they seek as well those symbolic forms that can make modernity a meaningful way of life. American popular culture has generated a number of such symbolic forms: one need only instance the global popularity of cowboy movies, jazz, or Disneyland. Likewise the American popular Christmas—the cult of Santa Claus, trees, reindeer, presents, and so on—which emerged under modern conditions, and which is being widely adopted outside the United States as part of the modern style. To judge from newspaper reports and from the evidence assembled by James Barnett, scarcely a nation today fails to contain at least a few citizens who celebrate the annual visit of Santa. The Japanese have been doing so, with growing enthusiasm, for nine decades; and the popular observance of Christmas has come to be a Japanese commonplace. . . .

Today Christmas is celebrated throughout the Japanese islands. In some urban shopping centers the decorations are up by mid-November; and news commentators quip about "instant Christians" who flock to the Ginza bars on Christmas Eve. In the rural areas as well there are youth-group parties and household gift-exchanges. A survey I conducted in central Nagano prefecture in 1960 found that (1) approximately half of the households in the sample, rural as well as urban, have a home Christmas celebration, and that (2) Christmas is the only holiday in a list of more than two dozen that has gained a significant number of adherents since the war.

In describing the present-day celebration I will focus upon the Anchiku region of central Nagano prefecture, with glances to the wider national scene. My materials derive from fieldwork in Anchiku in 1959–60.

Christmas Day is not a legal holiday in Japan, as it is in the United States. Work and school-work are not vacated on its account, at least not in Anchiku, although I have heard of Tokyo schools that begin their "New Year's vacation" in time for Christmas. In other words, Christmas activities take place after the day's work is done.

Interestingly enough, though, recent proposals for doubling the number of national holidays include a new holiday for December 25th. It would be known as "International Goodwill Day"—an inspiration that prompted several newspapers to wonder whether such a gesture would be regarded as international goodwill by people in Islamic and Buddhist nations. Again, Christmas usually is listed in calendars issued by Shinto and Buddhist organizations in Japan, which apparently do not interpret it as a religious threat.

Note that the date is December 25th. This is, of course, Anglo-American usage, in contrast to other usages such as the Dutch Christmas on December 5th. Christmas thus falls within the traditional Japanese year-end holiday season, and it is bracketed by the winter solstice on the one side and by New Year's Eve on the other. Historically there has been no major Japanese holiday on the 25th. . . .

Christmas comes early enough so that it does not interfere in a crippling

way with household preparations for the New Year. The only persons seriously bothered are storekeepers and their salespeople, who by mid-December are embroiled in year-end bargain sales. Christmas also comes close on the heels of the solstice observance, and most Anchiku households still honor the day, usually by preparing a dish of "solstice squash" (toji no kabocha).

In the downtown stores and streets of Tokyo or Osaka the decorative trees, Santas, angels, and candy canes are every bit as gigantic as in Chicago or San Francisco. Not only that; in Tokyo I have seen them torn down on December 26th and at once replaced by equally gigantic decorations heralding the remaining few days of the year-end sale. In Anchiku, however, decor is more restrained. Supermarkets, bakeries, department stores, and such display a small evergreen and perhaps a few paper streamers with "Merry Christmas" blazoned upon them in Roman letters and in Japanese syllabary. But street decor is limited to the year-end bargains.

The dramas and readings that are a familiar part of the American popular celebration—Dickens, Menotti, Clement Moore—are rarely heard in Japan. But the topic of Santa Claus is frequently encountered on children's radio and TV programs in December, and Christmas music is inescapable. Choral societies offer Christmas concerts. And the shopping arcades, the department stores, the commercial broadcasters, all pour out floods of recorded carols. One missionary reports that Japanese Christians carol in the streets, although I did not encounter this in Anchiku. But for many families, playing recorded carols on the phonograph is a regular part of the family Christmas gathering. To my informants, the loan-word carol (karoru) includes such ecclesiastical songs as "White Christmas," "Jingle Bells," and "Rudolph the Red-Nosed Reindeer."

Christmas cards are used, but only sparingly, by American standards. School children often exchange them. They are of course appropriate to send to one's Western friends and acquaintances, but they are felt to be rather frivolous for ordinary adult intercourse; they cannot, for example, take the place of the New Year postcards. The latter are exchanged much the same as Christmas cards are exchanged in the U.S., and most families devote a good deal of time, money, and thought to them.

The Christmas tree also has a New Year's competitor. This is the "gate-pine" (kadomatsu) seen before nearly every Anchiku house from late December until mid-January. Gate-pine decor varies over a wide range; some families put up elaborate clusters of 10-foot firs and 25-foot bamboos, others merely paste on the doorpost a sheet of paper with a pine tree printed upon it. By contrast, Christmas trees usually are set up inside, and are sparsely decorated. The tree has fared somewhat better in competition than the card, and many families set up pine decor both for Christmas and separately for New Year's (a doubly unproductive use of precious timber which becomes a handy target for the complaints of literal-minded conservationists).

Christmas parties are held both by instrumental and by expressive social groups. These parties are a syncretism with "closing-the-year parties" *(bonenkai)* long customary in December. But a *bonenkai* tends to be a man's affair, with *sake,* group singing, and displays of masculine affection. Only. professional women are allowed in the room: waitresses, geisha, entertainers. The Christmas party, on the other hand, provides a role for "proper" women. There is social dancing in place of the music of samisens, and often port wine is served rather than *sake.* Understandably enough, the Christmas party tends to be more favored than the *bonenkai* in heterosexual groups such as office staffs, or the employees of a department store, or village youth clubs, This is one reason why some Japanese see Christmas as democratic.

Democracy also is read into the exchange of Christmas gifts. In many households, Christmas gifts are distributed even though New Year's gifts *(toshidama,* literally 'year-jewel') are given to the same persons a week later. Because of the duplication, some families have elected to give only on one of the two occasions. New Year's gifts go unilaterally from the head of a household to its junior members: children of course, but also servants and apprentices if any. In many Anchiku households, Christmas presents follow the same channels. However, some families are aware of the American conception of an "exchange" of presents from every individual to every individual, and in these households gifts are given multilaterally. This kind of attention to the individual also seems democratic to some. . . .

Family Christmas foregatherings do not center around dinner, as in the American ideal, but rather upon mutual partaking of a Christmas cake. Many Anchiku housewives do indeed prepare "something different" *(kawatta mono)* for the Christmas meal, but this is just as likely to be raw fish or a rice curry as it is to be a Western dish. A few white-collar wives bake a chicken, but turkey is not available in Anchiku.

The Christmas cake also is called a "decoration cake" *(dekoreshon keki,* a loan word), emphasizing its ridges and waves of thick frosting. The cake almost always is purchased, and in the cities some bakeries prepare a supply of cakes early in December and quick-freeze them until the sales demand mounts. In the Anchiku village where I lived, a local confectioner — who prepared only Japanese-style sweets — served as agent for an urban baker, and distributed mimeographed order blanks early in December. Decorated cake is not an item in the usual American popular Christmas, although we do have our fruitcakes and cookies of various derivations. So perhaps the precedent here is European, although none of the European forms I know of seems to correspond exactly with the Japanese form.

Parents, peers, teachers, and the mass media collaborate to inform the young about Santa Claus and his visit. The stockings can not be hung by a fireplace in the typical Japanese house, so most parents place the presents by the children's pillows during the night. Some of the more literal-minded transfer Clement Moore's chimney motif to its closest Japanese counterpart,

the pipe for the bathtub stove. And the stockings are hung by the bathtub with care. (The Japanese word *entotsu* is a generic for many forms of waste-gas conveying tube that are distinguished in English as chimney, smokestack, stovepipe, and so on.)

The Japanese Santa Claus robes himself in the familiar red-and-white garment attributed to the nineteenth century American illustrator Thomas Nast. Thus arrayed, he appears in advertisements or is impersonated in the streets, either standing by Salvation Army kettles or carrying placards announcing the opening of a new pinball parlor.

In the paragraph from which I drew the motto for this report, Milton Singer epitomizes our present-day awareness of the active as well as the passive side of tradition. Traditions, he says, "are, ordinarily, the things that we take for granted, the unquestioned assumptions and the handed-down ways of our ancestors. But it has become a commonplace of modern history that even the most traditional societies are no longer sure of what it is they can take for granted. Confronted by swift currents of internal and external change, they have been compelled to restate themselves to themselves in order to discover what they have been and what it is they are to become." The American popular Christmas is one such self-restatement. Like any expressive form it defies reduction to formulae. Like any dramatic form it defies easy verbal explanation, for it deals with conditions in which (to borrow Suzanne Langer's dictum) apprehension outruns comprehension. And yet, although some of its components hold long pedigrees in Western lore, they have been creatively reassembled under modern conditions. Although some of its themes are pan-human, their configuration seems peculiarly apt in the modern milieu. One could scarcely argue otherwise in the face of massive evidence for the growing popularity of the event not only here where it was developed, but also among many peoples overseas. . . .

Overseas the spread of a popular Christmas celebration to so many peoples such as the Japanese can scarcely be explained away by once-prevalent notions of non-western imitativeness (an attribute once especially projected upon the Japanese). The popular Christmas seems to offer to many peoples one means, however small, for making sense of life in a modern milieu. And if the Japanese are somewhat more captivated by the Santa Claus cult than other non-western peoples, this would seem no more than correlate with the recognized extent of Japan's modernity.

The modern milieu differs for different peoples, and in this regard, American and Japanese justifications of the popular Christmas stress different aspects of it. Japanese tend to see its democratic tenor; Americans tend to see its implications of material well-being. (This in the context of many aspects stressed by both peoples: the happy family gathering, doing nice things for children, and so on).

SELECTED READINGS

For works on various aspects of Japanese religion in the modern world, see first the citations for each selection in this chapter and the preceding chapter; some additional works are:

Contemporary Religions in Japan. Tokyo: International Institute for the Study of Religions, 1960- . (A journal for the discussion of aspects and problems of contemporary religious life in Japan.)

Kitagawa, Joseph M. *Religion in Japanese History.* New York: Columbia University Press, 1966 (especially pp. 170-340).

Nishitani, Keiji. "The Religious Situation in Present-Day Japan." *Contemporary Religions in Japan* 1, No. 1 (March 1960): 7-24.

Plath, David W. "The Fate of Utopia: Adaptive Tactics in Four Japanese Groups." *American Anthropologist* 68, Pt. 2 (1966): 1152-62.

Union of the New Religious Organizations in Japan, Research Office, ed. "Reminiscences of Religion in Postwar Japan." *Contemporary Religions in Japan* 6, No. 2 (June 1965): 111-203. (This book-length work is continued and completed in the next five issues of the same journal.)

In Japan, as in other modern countries, literature has become one of the major modes for expressing the existential situation. Several selections in this book have been taken from literary works: Fumio Niwa, *The Buddha Tree* (selection 10), Akiyuki Nozaka, *The Pornographers* (selection 46), and Michio Takeyama, *Harp of Burma* (selection 51). Among the many other fine Japanese novels, four that might be recommended as samples of the contemporary Japanese mood are:

Abe, Kobo. *The Woman in the Dunes.* Translated by E. Dale Saunders. New York: Alfred A. Knopf, 1964.

Kawabata, Yasunari. *Thousand Cranes.* Translated by Edward G. Seidensticker. New York: Alfred A. Knopf, 1958.

Oe, Kenzaburo. *A Personal Matter.* Translated by John Nathan. New York: Grove Press: 1968.

Ishihara, Shintaro. *Season of Violence; The Punishment Room; The Yacht and the Boy.* Translated by John S. Mills, Toshie Takahama, and Ken Tremayne. Rutland, Vt.: Charles E. Tuttle Co., 1966.

DATE DUE			
JUN 1 '89	AUG 02 '93		
FEB 15 '90	NOV 23 '93		
910913	JAN 20		
	JAN		
DEC 10 '91			
MAR 03 '92	MAY 30 '94		
MAR 16 '92	NOV 21 '94		
JUN 8 '92	NOV 20 '95		
JUN 8 '92	NOV 04 '96		
JUN 1 1	APR 07 1997		
DEC 08 '92	APR 07 1999		
MAR 15 '93			
MAY 31 '93			